Blackstone's Guide to the

YOUTH JUSTICE AND CRIMINAL EVIDENCE ACT 1999

Diane Birch

and

Roger Leng

BLACKSTONE
PRESS LIMITED

Published by
Blackstone Press Limited
Aldine Place
London
W12 8AA
United Kingdom

Sales enquiries and orders
Telephone + 44-(0)-20-8740-2277
Facsimile + 44-(0)-20-8743-2292
e-mail: sales@blackstone.demon.co.uk
website: www.blackstonepress.com

ISBN 1-84174-112-4
© Diane Birch and Roger Leng, 2000

British Library Cataloguing in Publication Data
A CIP catalogue record for this book is available from the British Library

Typeset in 10/12 Times by
Montage Studios Limited, Tonbridge, Kent
Printed and bound in Great Britain by Antony Rowe Limited,
Chippenham and Reading

return it on time

Guide to the

YOUTH JUSTICE AND CRIMINAL
EVIDENCE ACT 1999

Contents

The provisions of the Act — Speaking Up For Justice — Implementation and extent

Overview — Consolidation of sentencing powers: Powers of Criminal Courts (Sentencing) Act 2000 — Background — Youth offender panels — The referral — The referral as the sole sentence of the court — The terms of the referral order — Panel meetings — The first meeting: agreeing the contract — Progress meetings — Final meeting — The consequences of discharge of a referral order — Referrals back to court for non co-operation: sch. 1, part I — Further convictions during referral: sch. 1, part II

Overview — The Act and the 'best evidence' principle — The Act and the 'cross-examination' principle — The Act and the 'limited eligibility' principle — The Act and the 'witness preference' principle — Are special measures justified? — Piloting special measures: Criminal Justice Acts 1988 and 1991 — The 1988 and 1991 Acts and live link — The 1991 Act and video recorded evidence in chief

Overview — Eligibility for special measures — Availability of special measures — Special measures directions

Preface

It would be futile to suggest that the two parts of the Youth Justice and Criminal Evidence Act 1999 are related to one another in any significant way. On the contrary, they represent two quite distinct schemes: one designed to address the sentencing of first-time young offenders, and the other to ensure a more sympathetic treatment of vulnerable and intimidated witnesses in the criminal justice process. If they have anything in common it is their complexity, but we hope that our treatment of the Act's provisions will go some way towards assisting those whose task it will be to apply them.

As might be expected in a work of this nature, the division of labour fell roughly along the lines of the Act's two parts, except that Roger Leng, in addition to providing Chapters 2 and 12 on youth justice, valiantly undertook to do battle with the complexities of the reporting restrictions described in Chapter 8. The authors, however, eschewing the statutory precedent, made frequent forays across the border in order to comment on one another's contributions and to offer consolation and occasionally inspiration when the process of disentangling the Act's more intractable provisions became almost unbearable.

We are grateful to all at Blackstone Press for their efficiency, support and (necessary) proddings, and especially to Laurence Eastham for his helpful and patient comments.

Diane Birch
Roger Leng
November 2000

Table of Cases

Table of Statutes

Table of Statutory Instruments

Chapter 1
Introduction to the Act

The Youth Justice and Criminal Evidence Act 1999 which received Royal Assent on 27 July 1999 combines two quite distinct legislative projects. In Part I, the Act carries forward the Government's ambitious plans to tackle youth crime and reform youth justice which had been set in train by the Crime and Disorder Act 1998. In Part II, the Act addresses various problems relating to vulnerable witnesses, not simply for the purpose of protecting and supporting such persons but also in the interests of maximising the evidence available in criminal courts and improving its quality. The Act was broadly supported by all sides in its passage through Parliament and has been generally well received by the legal professions and the press. Notwithstanding this broad support, some aspects of the Act proved controversial. In particular, fears have been expressed that new means for receiving evidence may undermine the oral and adversarial traditions of the criminal trial or work unfairness for defendants; and an unusual alliance of the press and the police have expressed concern that reporting restrictions to protect victims and witnesses may hamper the proper functions of the press in reporting crime and assisting investigations.

In recent years the pace of change in criminal justice has been driven by political imperatives and this has sometimes led to imperfect legislation which may cause problems for its users. This is true of the present Act, in which remarkably some provisions in the body of the Act are found to be repealed by sch. 6. Similarly problematic is sch. 5, which makes various 'pre-consolidation amendments' to provisions dealing with juvenile sentencing. Schedule 5 came into force on 1 January 2000, but is replaced and repealed by the Powers of Criminal Courts (Sentencing) Act 2000 on 25 August of the same year. It is not clear that any benefits which accrue from reforming the law eight months earlier outweigh the confusion caused by this arrangement, and it is hard to understand why the Government did not simply wait and include the desired amendments in the consolidating Act. In one respect the Government has shown consideration to the users of the Act by maintaining a web site at *http://www.homeoffice.gov.uk/yjceact/yjceact.htm* which is an excellent source of guidance on the provisions of the Act and information about implementation.

THE PROVISIONS OF THE ACT

Part I creates a new sentence of referral to a youth offender panel which will be applied to the great majority of first offenders under the age of 18. The result of the referral will be a contract agreed with the panel under which the youngster will follow a programme of behaviour designed to prevent re-offending. The Government's aim is to establish a coherent graded hierarchy of responses to juvenile offending, in which the new sentence falls between the diversionary practices of reprimand and final warning, and the more punitive sentences which may be expected to follow subsequent convictions. Referrals to youth offender panels are considered in Chapter 2.

Part II of the Act focuses mainly on the problems faced by vulnerable and intimidated witnesses when giving evidence in criminal cases. The Act's principal provisions are designed to ensure that more witnesses are competent to testify (ss. 53 to 57), that a wider range of methods of giving evidence ('special measures') will be available to vulnerable and intimidated witnesses (ss. 16 to 33), and that the opportunity for the defence to adduce sexual history evidence (ss. 41 to 43) and for the defendant to cross-examine witnesses in person (ss. 34 to 40) will be significantly curtailed.

Chapters 3 to 5 of this Guide deal with special measures. Chapter 3 traces the reasons for the move towards special measures, looks at the framework for handling cases involving child witnesses which has provided the template for the 1999 Act, and considers the case for reform in the light of recent research findings. Chapter 4 describes the witnesses who are eligible for special measures, and the making and content of 'special measures directions'. Chapter 5 details the conditions on which each of the 1999 Act's eight special measures may be accessed. Chapter 6 deals with the new restrictions on cross-examination by the accused in person and Chapter 7 is concerned with the use of evidence concerning the sexual history of a complainant. Chapter 8 considers a new scheme of reporting restrictions (found in ss. 44 to 52) for the purpose of protecting child and vulnerable adult witnesses and to encourage their cooperation during investigation and trial. Chapter 9 deals with the issue of competence.

None of this set of measures represents an entirely new way of thinking with regard to the balance to be struck in the protection of vulnerable witnesses. The terms on which children have hitherto been permitted to give unsworn evidence have developed in recent years from a presumption against competence except on proof of a sufficient degree of intelligence and understanding (Children and Young Persons Act 1933, s. 38) to a presumption in favour of receiving the evidence unless the child appears incapable of giving intelligible testimony (Criminal Justice Act 1988, s. 33A(2A), inserted by the Criminal Justice and Public Order Act 1994). The 1999 Act extends the benefits of this strategy to other witnesses of limited understanding who have, hitherto, been debarred from giving evidence altogether if they are unable to do so on oath.

The special measures to assist witnesses to give their best evidence have also been piloted with child witnesses. A raft of reforms mostly to be found in the Criminal

Justice Acts 1988 and 1991 gave children access to live television links to reduce the stress of giving evidence in the courtroom in certain cases, and also permitted the pre-recording of evidence in chief. Until the 1999 Act, however, there was no statutory power to pre-record the cross-examination of a child, although the possibility of such a measure was considered and rejected when the 1991 reforms were passed. The introduction of pre-recorded cross-examination, and the extension of the protective measures to other witnesses, reflect a view that the 1988 and 1991 reforms have bedded down well, and that there are significant advantages to be gained from extending them. Pre-recorded cross-examination and the eventual extension of special measures to witnesses other than children were recommended by the *Report of the Advisory Group on Video Evidence* (Home Office, 1989), a Group chaired by Judge Pigot, which was responsible for many of the original child witness reforms.

The provisions with regard to sexual history evidence are also rooted in existing tradition. Section 2 of the Sexual Offences (Amendment) Act 1976 restricts admissibility to evidence which is so important to the defence case that it would be unfair to exclude it. The 1999 Act introduces a different framework for achieving the same end. The new framework removes most of the judicial discretion so characteristic of s. 2, and extends the rule limiting the input of such evidence to a wider range of sexual offences.

The new regime for preventing the defendant from cross-examining certain witnesses in person is also based on an earlier provision, which was introduced by the Criminal Justice Act 1991 to protect child witnesses from intimidation. All of the new provisions for vulnerable witnesses thus build, to varying extents, on established foundations.

Also contained in Part II and its associated schedules are a variety of measures which are not driven by the need to protect vulnerable or intimidated witnesses or the need to encourage witnesses to come forward. The competence and compellability of spouse witnesses, and the competence of the accused, are dealt with largely to ensure coherence with the new rules on competence for vulnerable adults, but the opportunity has also been taken to make some related reforms. The new law on competence and compellability is discussed in Chapter 9.

The rulings of the European Court of Human Rights in *Murray* v *UK* (1996) 22 EHRR 29 and *Saunders* v *UK* (1996) 23 EHRR 313 have led to the enactment of s. 58 and s. 59 respectively (see Chapter 10). The former prevents the drawing of adverse inferences from pre-trial silence at a police station where the suspect has not been allowed an opportunity to consult with a solicitor, and the latter gives effect to sch. 3 so as to repeal a collection of powers under which evidence could be obtained under compulsion. Last but by no means least, s. 60 repeals the Police and Criminal Evidence Act 1984, s. 69, which made evidence from computer records inadmissible unless a variety of safeguards was met. Such evidence can now be received on the same terms as other mechanically-produced evidence (Chapter 11).

Chapter 12 deals with some very minor amendments to courts' powers to sentence juveniles which were made in anticipation of the full-scale consolidation of sentencing powers in the Powers of Criminal Courts (Sentencing) Act 2000.

SPEAKING UP FOR JUSTICE

The main body of measures in Part II of the 1999 Act were proposed in June 1998 by *Speaking Up For Justice*, the Report of the Home Office Interdepartmental Working Group on the Treatment of Vulnerable or Intimidated Witnesses in the Criminal Justice System. The terms of reference of the Group, which was set up by the Home Secretary to take forward a Government manifesto commitment that included providing greater protection 'for victims in rape and serious sexual offence trials' included encouraging vulnerable witnesses to give evidence, and 'enabling them to give best evidence in court'. The Group was also required to have regard to the interests of justice, so that in developing the particular proposals which are contained in Part II of the Act the rights of the defendant to a fair trial are balanced against the 'needs of the witness not to be traumatised or intimidated by the criminal justice process' (*Speaking Up For Justice*, para. 1.14). The fair trial guarantees of the European Convention on Human Rights were also in the forefront of the Group's thinking, and the Bill bore throughout its progress through Parliament the brocard announcing that it was regarded by the Home Secretary as Convention-compliant. Whether it is, particularly with regard to the provisions precluding reliance on sexual history evidence (Chapter 7) and excluding the accused, whatever his age or vulnerability, from access to the special measures provided for other witnesses (Chapter 4) remains to be seen.

IMPLEMENTATION AND EXTENT

Generally, provisions in the Act will come into force on days to be appointed by order of the Home Secretary (s. 68(3)). A handful of provisions came into force immediately on Royal Assent (s. 68(4)). These are s. 6(4), which gives the Secretary of State power to issue regulations concerning the membership of youth offender panels; various rule-making powers in Chapters I to IV of Part II and in ss. 58(5) and 61(2); s. 40(1), which makes provision for funding representation for cross-examination in sexual cases; and the general provisions dealing with interpretation, the making of regulations and orders, supplementary provisions and applicability to Northern Ireland (ss. 62 to 66 and 68).

At the time of writing there have been four commencement orders. SI 1999 No. 3427 brought into force (on 1 January 2000) the youth justice pre-consolidation amendments in sch. 5 (discussed in Chapter 12) and also certain repeals of provisions of the 1999 Act itself which are listed in sch. 6. SI 2000 No. 1034 brought into force (on 14 April 2000) s. 59, which restricts the use in evidence of answers obtained under compulsion, and s. 60, which deals with evidence from computer records, and also related consequential amendments and repeals in schs. 4 and 6. SI 2000 No. 1587 implements (on 26 June 2000) Part I of the Act which deals with referrals to youth offender panels, for the purpose of beginning the pilot projects of this new sentence. SI 2000 No. 2091 brings into force (on 4 September 2000) ss. 34, 35 and 38–40, which represent the bulk of the measures on preventing the defendant from cross-examining certain witnesses in person. Section 36, which affords the court a discretion to prevent such cross-examination in cases not covered by the two proceeding sections, has yet to be brought into force.

The Act generally extends to England and Wales (s. 68(5)) except that reporting restrictions under Chapter IV of Part II also take effect in Northern Ireland and Scotland (s. 68(6)) as do provisions relating to order-making powers and the restrictions on the evidential use of answers obtained under compulsion under s. 59 (s. 68(6)(c)). Provisions corresponding to Part II of the Act have been passed in relation to Northern Ireland by the Criminal Evidence (Northern Ireland) Order 1999 (SI 1999 No. 2789). Part II of the Order deals with special measures for vulnerable or intimidated witnesses, Part III deals with the protection of witnesses from cross-examination by the accused in person, Part IV with evidence of sexual history and Part V with the competence of witnesses.

Chapter 2
Youth Offender Panels

OVERVIEW

Part I of the Act creates a new sentence of referral to a youth offender panel. This will be the presumptive sentence for the great majority of offenders receiving their first conviction. The purpose of referral will be to agree a 'contract' with the Panel under which the young offender will agree to follow a programme of behaviour, the principal aim of which will be the prevention of re-offending. The contract will run from agreement, for a period, specified in the referral by the court, of between three and six months. Schedule 1 makes provision for referral back to court for re-sentencing where a contract cannot be agreed or is not being carried out. The schedule also makes provision for terminating a contract where the young offender is reconvicted during the currency of the contract. Part I and sch. 1 were brought into force on 26 June 2000 (SI 2000 No. 1587). However, the referral order will not be generally available until suitable arrangements are made throughout the country. In the meantime referral orders will be piloted in selected areas for at least 18 months from June 2000, with a view to national implementation in early 2002/3.

CONSOLIDATION OF SENTENCING POWERS: POWERS OF CRIMINAL COURTS (SENTENCING) ACT 2000

In recent times sentencing powers have been scattered throughout a large number of statutes, many much amended, and some dating back 70 years or more. For some years the Government has been working on a project to consolidate sentencing powers in a single instrument. This has been reflected in schedules containing 'pre-consolidation amendments' attached to both the Crime (Sentences) Act 1997 and the Crime and Disorder Act 1998 and also to the present Act (see Chapter 12). The consolidation project is now completed with the passing of the Powers of Criminal Courts (Sentencing) Act 2000 (the PCC(S)A 2000) on 25 May 2000; the Act comes into force on 25 August 2000. The effect of this will be to repeal Part I of and sch. 1 to the 1999 Act, and to re-enact precisely similar provisions in Part III and sch. 1 to the PCC(S)A 2000. Thus, henceforth the relevant legal source of these provisions will be the PCC(S)A 2000. In the text which follows both statutes will be referred to: the relevant provision of the 1999 Act will be placed first, followed by reference to the corresponding provision of the PCC(S)A 2000. The same practice is adopted in relation to other provisions which are now incorporated into the PCC(S)A 2000. It should be noted that sch. 1 is in the same terms under both the 1999 Act and the 2000 Act (except where otherwise indicated). Accordingly, references to paragraphs of sch. 1 apply to either statute.

BACKGROUND

The new sentence of referral to a youth offender panel (YOP) can be traced to the White Paper *No More Excuses* (Cm 3809, 1997) which argued that young offenders (and their parents) must take responsibility for their offending, with a corresponding emphasis in sentencing on the prevention of further offending. Those proposals were in part inspired by *Misspent Youth — Young People and Crime* (1996), an Audit Commission report on juvenile justice which had expressed concern about the minimal involvement of the offender in the juvenile justice process. The proposals were also influenced by recently published research which identified a failure to address youth offending constructively at an early juncture as a cause of later criminality (J. Graham & B. Bowling, *Young People and Crime*, Home Office Research Study No. 145, 1995).

The first round of measures to reform youth justice based on the White Paper were enacted in the Crime and Disorder Act 1998. The reforms were built upon three foundation stones: the prescription of the prevention of offending by children and young persons as the over-arching aim of the youth justice system (s. 37); the establishment of a national Youth Justice Board to advise the Home Secretary on the running and development of the youth justice system (s. 41); and the creation of inter-agency youth offending teams to co-ordinate and provide youth justice services in their locality (s. 39). Particular measures included: the imposition of a more structured procedure for diverting young offenders from court by the creation of a system of reprimands and warnings to replace the pre-existing discretionary practice of cautioning (ss. 65 and 66); a bundle of measures to tackle the causes of youth crime including parenting orders, child safety orders, child curfew orders and powers for the police to round up truants (ss. 8 to 16); and new sentences including action plan orders (CDA 1998, ss. 69 and 70; PCC(S)A 2000, ss. 69 to 72), reparation orders (CDA 1998, ss. 67 and 68; PCC(S)A 2000, ss. 73 to 75) and drug treatment and testing orders (CDA 1998, ss. 89 to 95; PCC(S)A 2000, ss. 52 to 58), all of which were designed explicitly to tackle the causes of offending rather than simply to punish (see generally R. Leng, R. Taylor and M. Wasik, *Blackstone's Guide to the Crime and Disorder Act 1998*).

In theory the new sentence builds upon the structures created by the 1998 Act and carries forward some of its key policies. In practice, local youth offending teams began operating throughout the country as late as April 2000 and at the time of writing the provisions for reprimands and warnings and new youth justice orders are still being piloted, with a view to national implementation during the year leading up to April 2001.

The sentence of referral to a youth offender panel will initially be restricted to first convictions. On the basis of the research referred to above, the first conviction is identified as a key stage in the young offender's criminal career at which vigorous positive intervention may be fruitful in terms of turning the youngster away from crime.

YOUTH OFFENDER PANELS

It is the responsibility of the local youth offending team (YOT) for an area to establish a youth offender panel for each offender who is referred to such a panel (s. 6; PCC(S)A 2000, s. 21). For the avoidance of doubt, a corresponding amendment is made to the Crime and Disorder Act 1998, s. 38(4) by adding the implementation of referral orders to the list of youth justice services which it is the duty of the YOT to deliver (sch. 4, para. 28; PCC(S)A 2000, sch. 9, para. 197). YOTs are locally based inter-agency bodies, set up under the Crime and Disorder Act 1998, s. 39, with responsibility for co-ordinating the delivery of various youth justice services. A literal reading of s. 6 (s. 21) would suggest that the YOT should constitute a fresh panel for each referral. In practice it seems likely that YOTs will constitute a number of panels with responsibility for different categories of offender, perhaps according to age or locality.

Each panel must consist of at least one person appointed by the YOT from among its members and two others who are not members of the team (s. 6(3); PCC(S)A 2000, s. 21(3)). The Home Secretary has a power to issue guidance from time to time relating to the constitution of panels and how they should conduct their proceedings and discharge their functions (s. 6(2); s. 21(2)). At the time of writing, a draft of *The Referral Order: Guidance to Youth Offending Teams* has been issued by the Home Office with the intention that a final version would be issued, updated in the light of experience under the pilot scheme, prior to national implementation. As well as such guidance, the Home Secretary has a power to make regulations for the purpose of prescribing the qualifications to be held by members of panels or the criteria for appointing such members (s. 6(4); s. 21(4)).

The panel established for a particular young offender will not be a permanent body but will be constituted as required for meetings. Day-to-day administration in relation to referral orders and youth offender contracts made thereunder will be the responsibility of the youth offending team (s. 14(1); PCC(S)A 2000, s. 29(1)). These responsibilities will include the provision of administrative staff, accommodation and other necessary facilities for the panel. During the period in which a youth offender contract is effective it will be the responsibility of the YOT to supervise the young offender's compliance with the contract, and it shall be the duty of the member of the YOT who is appointed to a particular panel to keep records of the offender's compliance or non-compliance with the contract (s. 14(2)(b); PCC(S)A 2000, s. 29(2)(b)). It is also the responsibility of the YOT to arrange the necessary first and final meetings under ss. 8 and 12 (ss. 23 and 27), and any further progress meetings requested by the panel under s. 11 (s. 26).

THE REFERRAL

YOTs will need to do a considerable amount of preparation, in terms of recruiting and training panel members and establishing programmes for young offenders to follow, before referrals can be implemented. Accordingly, the sentence of referral will not be available until the relevant court has been notified by the Home Secretary that arrangements to implement referral orders are available locally (s. 1(2)(b), (3)(b) and (4); PCC(S)A 2000, s. 16(2)(b), (3)(b) and (5)).

Referrals may be made by either the youth court or magistrates' court in relation to a person under the age of 18 at the time when the referral is made. This means that an offender over the age of 18 may be subject to a referral order which was made prior to his eighteenth birthday but which runs beyond it. A referral will also be available in some cases in which a person under 18 is convicted in the Crown Court. The normal presumption is that these cases should be remitted to the youth court for sentence (Children and Young Persons Act 1933, s. 56; PCC(S)A 2000, s. 8); where this is done the offender may be sentenced as if tried in the youth court. Where an offender appeals against a sentence imposed in a magistrates' court or youth court, the Crown Court hearing the appeal exercises the same sentencing powers as the lower court (Supreme Court Act 1984, s. 48(4)) and therefore may impose a referral as a substitute for the sentence appealed against.

Restrictions on the power to refer

The power to make a referral is subject to three main restrictions:

(a) that the offence is not one for which the sentence is fixed by law (and neither is any 'associated offence');
(b) that the court is not proposing to impose a custodial sentence or hospital order for the offence in question or any 'associated offence'; and
(c) that the court is not proposing to impose an absolute discharge for the offence under consideration (s. 1(1)).

An 'associated offence' is one for which the young offender will be sentenced at the same time as for the offence in question (s. 15(2)). Essentially the same provision applies under the PCC(S)A 2000, s. 16(1), but the term 'connected offence' replaces 'associated offence'; 'connected offence' is defined by s. 16(4). Both 'associated' and 'connected' offences include the situation where the offender has been convicted on an earlier occasion, or by a different court, and that matter has been remitted to the present court for sentence.

The effect of these restrictions is to exclude murder (for which the sentence is fixed by law for youth offenders) and other serious crimes meriting custodial sentences, as well as trivial offences suitable for absolute discharge. Where the restrictions do not apply, referral may be either compulsory or discretionary.

Compulsory referral

The conditions for compulsory referral are that:

(a)   the offender has pleaded guilty to the relevant offence and to any associated (connected) offence;
(b)   the offender has no previous UK convictions (not including any offence being treated as an associated (connected) offence); and
(c)   the offender has never been bound over in England, Wales or Northern Ireland to keep the peace or be of good behaviour (s. 2(1); PCC(S)A 2000, s. 17(1)).

For this purpose, and contrary to the normal rule, a conviction followed by a conditional discharge is to be treated as a full conviction (s. 2(5); PCC(S)A 2000, s. 17(5)), although this will not be the case in relation to an absolute discharge.

Where the conditions for compulsory referral are fulfilled, the court may not defer sentence but may, if appropriate, remit the young offender to the youth court, or another youth court for sentence (s. 4(7)(a) and (b); PCC(S)A 2000, s. 19(7)(a)). The court may also adjourn for inquiries under the Magistrates' Courts Act 1980, s. 10(3) or make various orders under the Mental Health Act 1983 (s. 4(7)(c) and (e); s. 19(7)(b) and (c)).

[As printed, s. 4(7)(d) appeared to make available the power to commit a young offender to the Crown Court for sentence (with a view to a custodial sentence beyond six months) where the conditions for compulsory referral was fulfilled. This was clearly an error since compulsory referral applies only where the court is not contemplating a custodial sentence. Accordingly, s. 4(7)(d) is repealed by virtue of s. 67(3) and sch. 6.]

Discretionary referral

The conditions under which the court has a discretion to refer the offender are that:

(a)   the offender is being dealt with by the court for more than one offence;
(b)   he has pleaded guilty to at least one offence and not guilty to at least one;
(c)   he has no previous UK convictions (to include convictions followed by conditional discharge); and
(d)   he has never been bound over in England, Wales or Northern Ireland to keep the peace or be of good behaviour (s. 2(2); PCC(S)A 2000, s. 17(2)).

Under both sets of conditions referral is limited to first convictions and to those offenders who show some remorse by pleading guilty to at least one offence. This reflects the sentencing principle that a guilty plea is taken to demonstrate remorse whatever the offender's true state of mind. Limiting the procedure to first convictions carries forward the policy of creating a predictable and coherent structure of formal interventions for youth offending, initiated in the procedures for reprimands and final warnings in the Crime and Disorder Act 1998, ss. 65 and 66. When both Acts are fully operative, the sequence of formal interventions for a repeat young offender should be as follows: first offence dealt with by reprimand; second offence by warning; third offence to be prosecuted and if a guilty plea is made to receive a sentence of referral to a youth offender panel.

Notwithstanding the apparent coherence of the structure created, the new provisions may be criticised. First, it can be argued that it is wrong in principle to equate a bind over with a first conviction for the purpose of barring referral to the panel. Although a bind over may be imposed as a sentence, proof that a person has committed an offence is not a pre-condition. Thus, a bind over may be accepted in return for the dropping of charges which the defendant disputes. In some cases courts may bind over witnesses or complainants who are before the court but who do not face charges. In such cases the person against whom a bind over is sought must be permitted to address the court or, if proceedings are instituted under the Magistrates' Courts Act 1980, s. 115, is entitled to a full hearing. However, there is no requirement of proof in relation to past conduct before a bind over may be imposed. Whereas, it has been held that a bind over may be imposed only where the court is satisfied beyond reasonable doubt that a bind over is necessary to prevent a *future* breach of the peace (*Percy* v *Director of Public Prosecutions* [1995] 1 WLR 1382) that is very different from proof of a past crime.

The second ground of criticism is that the rigidity of the structure of interventions may lead to referrals to a youth offender panel for very minor offending and for offenders who do not need this level of intervention. This possibility is exacerbated by the rule which treats a conditional discharge as a conviction for this purpose. Thus, it might be possible for a young offender to receive a referral after three relatively minor incidents committed in a short space of time. This sort of situation might lead to panels being tied up with a mass of minor cases, thereby diluting the resources and energy which might be applied to more serious cases.

The third criticism is that the line which is drawn between those who may be considered for discretionary referral and those who may not is arbitrary. This may be illustrated by the following scenario. A youth is arrested late at night after an alleged street disturbance. He is willing to admit that he was drunk and noisy but strongly denies an allegation of threatening behaviour. If the youth is charged with threatening behaviour on its own and is convicted after pleading not guilty, he cannot be considered for a referral (under present arrangements). If however a charge of drunk and disorderly is added, to which the youth pleads guilty, he may be referred at the discretion of the court. As this example demonstrates, whether or not a young offender qualifies for a referral may depend upon a prosecutorial choice rather than any factor relating to the offence or offender.

The Government has reserved the power to amend the categories of offenders who qualify for either compulsory or discretionary referral. Whether or not this is done may depend upon the outcome of trials of the new sentence which are being held in advance of general implementation. The scheme may be extended if it appears to be particularly successful or if, as suggested above, the scheme is found to arbitrarily exclude some categories of young offender. The scope of the scheme may be reduced if panels become overloaded with referrals, although this prospect seems unlikely in view of the priority attached to the scheme by the Government. Any amendment to the qualifying criteria must be by regulations made by the Home Secretary, to be laid before Parliament and subject to the affirmative resolution procedure (s. 2(3); PCC(S)A 2000, s. 17(3)).

In exercising this power the Home Secretary apparently has complete discretion as to categories of offender to be included within the scheme; it is therefore perhaps odd that s. 2(4) (PCC(S)A 2000, s. 17(4)) lists matters which the Home Secretary may employ in redefining categories of eligibility. These matters are:

(a)   the offender's age;
(b)   how the offender has pleaded;
(c)   the offence (or offences) of which the offender has been convicted;
(d)   the offender's previous convictions (if any);
(e)   how (if at all) the offender has been previously punished or otherwise dealt with by the court; and
(f)   any characteristic or behaviour, or circumstances relating to, any person who has at any time been charged in the same proceedings as the offender (whether or not in respect of the same offence).

THE REFERRAL AS THE SOLE SENTENCE OF THE COURT

The referral order is seen as a distinct step in the hierarchy of formal interventions in relation to offending, lying between the diversionary procedures of reprimand and warning and the ordinary sentencing powers of the court. In line with this policy, the referral will normally be the sole sentence of the court and must not be combined with other sentences. Thus, where a referral order is made, the court is barred from also imposing either a community sentence, a fine, a reparation order or a conditional discharge (s. 4(1), (2), (3) and (4); PCC(S)A 2000, s. 19(1), (2), (3) and (4)). It should be noted that this prohibition does not include ancillary orders, which are technically not sentences. Such ancillary orders include forfeiture orders relating to property associated with the offence, confiscation orders, compensation orders and exclusion from football matches or other sporting events.

In relation to any associated (or connected) offence(s) (i.e., those which fall to be dealt with at the same time), the court is limited to either making a referral order or awarding an absolute discharge (s. 4(3); PCC(S)A 2000, s. 19(3)). The court imposing a referral order is also barred from binding over the offender or imposing a parental bind over under the Criminal Justice Act 1991, s. 58 (PCC(S)A 2000, s. 150), or a parenting order under the Crime and Disorder Act 1998, s. 4(5) (PCC(S)A 2000, s. 19(5)).

The exclusion of parental bind overs and parenting orders requires an explanation in view of the emphasis which was placed in the White Paper *No More Excuses* on parents taking responsibility for their children's offending. The explanation is that a referral, and the contract which results from it, will require participation by parents and it was considered that it might be counter-productive to subject parents to too many and possibly conflicting demands. The option of parents undertaking the classes or counselling involved in a parenting order on a voluntary basis remains however a possibility, and the Home Office has indicated that this should be encouraged locally (*The Referral Order: Guidance for Youth Offending Teams* (Home Office, 2000, para. 3.20).

The restrictions on sentencing powers which accompany a referral are contingent on the offender's co-operation with the referral order. If the young offender fails to agree a contract or fails to perform his obligations under a contract, he may be referred back to the court, which may quash the referral order and re-sentence him for the offence, exercising any of the sentencing powers which would have been available to the original court but for the referral order (sch. 1, para. 5; PCC(S)A 2000, sch. 1, para. 5).

THE TERMS OF THE REFERRAL ORDER

Under s. 3(1) (PCC(S)A 2000, s. 18(1)), a referral order must:

(a)   specify the youth offending team responsible for implementing the referral (which must be the YOT for the area in which the young offender lives: s. 3(2); s. 18(2));

(b)   require the young offender to attend each meeting as required by the panel; and

(c)   specify a period between three and 12 months during which the contract between the young offender and the panel is to run.

As indicated above, where a court imposes a referral order in respect of one offence, any associated (or connected) offence dealt with at the same time must be either subject to a further referral or to an absolute discharge (s. 4(3); s. 19(3)). Where the former occurs and two or more referrals are imposed at the same time, each referral must be to the same panel and each must specify the period for which it is to run (s. 3(5); s. 18(5)). These periods may be ordered to be either concurrent or consecutive, but in either case the total period must not exceed 12 months (s. 3(6); s. 18(6)).

Parental involvement

Where a referral order is made in relation to an offender who is aged under 16, the court must require at least one person who is a parent or guardian, or if the child is in local authority care, a representative of that authority, to attend meetings of the youth offender panel (s. 5(2); PCC(S)A 2000, s. 20(6)). In relation to offenders aged 16 or 17, the court has a discretion whether to require one or more parent or guardian to attend panel meetings (s. 5(1); s. 20(1)). The court should not however make an order requiring a parent or guardian to attend if it is satisfied that it would be unreasonable to do so, or to the extent that it would be unreasonable to do so. Typically, this will apply where a parent is in ill health, or working away during the week, or living separately from the child and at a distance. It may be anticipated that some parents will have difficulty attending because of child care responsibilities.

If one of the purposes of parental attendance is to enlist parents in the cause of preventing further offending, a more constructive approach to encourage parental attendance would be for the YOT to find funds to help with child care for the parent. It might be counter-productive if parents with such difficulties are simply required to attend and left to resolve child care problems from their own resources and at their own expense. As with other mechanisms for imposing parental responsibility for children's offences, it will be relatively responsible parents who are making some efforts to care for their children who will carry the burden which absent parents, already shirking their responsibilities, will escape.

Where a parent, guardian or local authority representative who is required to attend panel meetings is not present in court at the time when the order is made, the court must send a copy of the order to the parent, guardian or relevant local authority (s. 5(7); s. 20(7)). Where a parent or guardian who has been required to attend fails to do so, this may be dealt with by the court under the Magistrates' Courts Act 1980, s. 63 which provides a power to fine or imprison for default in respect of court orders. Under this power the court can act of its own motion or by complaint; presumably in this case, the complaint is to be made by the YOT.

Power to vary the referral order

A referral order may be varied where, because the offender has moved residence or is going to do so, the YOT originally specified in the order is no longer appropriate (s. 6(5); PCC(S)A 2000, s. 21(5)). In this case the court should amend the order to specify the YOT with responsibility for the area in which the offender will live as the team responsible for implementing the order and for establishing a youth offender panel. If this occurs after a contract has been agreed with the initial panel, then this contract should continue as if it had been agreed with the new panel (s. 6(6)(c); s. 21(6)(c)). However, if the move occurs before a contract has taken effect, the new YOT not only has responsibility for establishing a panel but must also arrange for the first meeting of that panel for the purpose of agreeing a contract with the young offender (s. 6(6)(b); s. 21(6)(b)).

PANEL MEETINGS

Having established a panel for a particular offender and arranged its first meeting under s. 6 (PCC(S)A 2000, s. 21), the YOT must notify the offender, and any parent, guardian or local authority representative who has been required to attend, of the time and place of the meeting (s. 7(1); s. 22(1)). Current guidance to YOTs issued by the Home Secretary emphasises the need for speedy progress with the implementation of referral orders and suggests that first meetings should be held within 15 days of the making of the referral, and that the offender and other parties required to attend should be notified within five working days of the referral. At this stage the YOT should be gathering any reports made available to the court relating to the young offender and any other reports, for instance from social services or school. In order to avoid doubt about the matter, the Crime and Disorder Act 1998, s. 115 provides that it is lawful for the police, local authorities, health authorities and probation committees to pass such information to YOTs for the purpose of providing youth justice services.

The YOT should also be considering what other persons should be invited to attend the first and/or subsequent meetings of the panel. Section 7(4) (s. 22(4)) specifically mentions victims and persons who appear to the panel to be capable of having a good influence on the offender as persons who might attend, although neither is given a right to do so. Under current guidance issued by the Home Secretary, victims must be contacted within five days of making the order and will normally be given an opportunity to attend, and prior to the panel meeting should be provided with information about the purpose of the meeting. Victims should also be invited to indicate whether or not they would accept reparation from the young offender. A victim who attends has a right to be accompanied by one person; that person may be chosen by the victim with the agreement of the panel (s. 7(5); s. 22(5)). Other examples of persons who might be allowed to attend are grandparents, teachers or religious leaders, where it is thought that they might be able to exert a positive influence on the child. Additionally, the child may choose one person who, with the agreement of the panel, shall be entitled to accompany the offender to any panel meeting; it need not be the same person who attends every meeting in this capacity (s. 7(3); s. 22(3)). Interestingly, the draft Home Office Guidance indicates that young people will not be legally represented at panel meetings 'as this could seriously hinder the process of the panel' (para. 3.32).

Under the current version of Home Office Guidance to YOTs it is recommended that panel meetings should be held in informal settings other than homes, close to where the offender lives, and that they should normally be held in the evening or at weekends to ensure that volunteer panel members, parents and others are able to attend. The draft guidance envisages rather different roles for the professionals and volunteers from the community. It is suggested that the panel should be chaired by a volunteer who would take the lead in interacting with the youngster (para. 3.51) and negotiations concerning the contract will be chiefly between the community panel members and the young person (para. 3.55). The role of professional members would be to focus on advising and providing information.

Recent studies of juvenile justice, notably the Audit Commission report *Misspent Youth*, have focused on the lack of meaningful involvement of young offenders in the processes to which they are subject. This problem is addressed in current Home Office

Guidance which emphasises the need for active involvement of the young offender at panel meetings. Thus, the Chair must 'facilitate an exploration of the causes of the offending behaviour through personal statements from the young person' (para. 3.52) and the panel must 'encourage the participation of all parties' and 'facilitate exchanges between parties' (para. 3.53).

There is a potential conflict within the current procedures which may become apparent as the pilots progress. The admirable emphasis on responding quickly to the offending may be defeated by the difficulty of arranging meetings where so many parties are involved.

THE FIRST MEETING: AGREEING THE CONTRACT

At the first meeting of a youth offender panel, the primary objective will be to reach agreement with the young offender on a programme of behaviour with the aim of preventing re-offending (s. 8(1); PCC(S)A 2000, s. 23(1)). The language of contract and the emphasis in the statute (s. 8(4); s. 24(4)) and in the Home Office Guidance on the young offender's consent to the programme is undermined by the sanctions imposed if the young offender fails to agree a contract acceptable to the panel. If there is a failure to agree at the first meeting, the panel may either arrange a further meeting to consider the issue (s. 10(1); s. 25(1)) or, if there appears to be no prospect of reaching agreement, refer the offender back to court (s. 10(2); s. 25(2)). The normal consequence of being referred back will be re-sentencing for the original offence (sch. 1, para. 5). Similar powers apply if the offender simply does not attend the first panel meeting (s. 7(2); s. 22(2)) or if, following the reaching of an agreement, the offender unreasonably refuses to sign a record of the agreement (s. 10(3); s. 25(3)).

Section 8(2) (s. 23(2)) lists a number of activities and requirements which may be provided for in the programme of behaviour agreed between the young offender and the panel. These are:

(a) financial reparation or other reparation to any victims or others affected by the offences for which the offender was referred;

(b) mediation sessions between the offender and victim;

(c) carrying out unpaid work or service in or for the community;

(d) being at home at specified times;

(e) attendance at school, other educational establishment or place of work;

(f) participating in specified activities such as those designed to address offending behaviour, those designed to offer education or training or those assisting with drug or alcohol rehabilitation;

(g) presenting himself to specified persons at times and places specified in or determined under the programme;

(h) staying away from specified places and/or persons;

(i) supervision and recording of the offender's compliance (or otherwise, presumably) with the programme.

Specifically excluded from the agreed programme are electronic monitoring and physical restrictions on the offender's movements. These measures are excluded in order to distance the agreed programme from traditional punitive sentences and to encourage the offender to see the programme as being of positive benefit to him rather than detrimental. This reasoning is rather unconvincing in view of (d) and (e) above which may involve a curfew and considerable restrictions on the offender's freedom of movement.

Although reparation is not a compulsory element, ministers shepherding these provisions through Parliament laid great stress on the reparative element. This is reflected in the current Home Office Guidance: 'The contract should always include some element of direct or indirect reparation ...' (para. 3.56). Notwithstanding the mention of financial reparation in s. 7(1)(a), the Guidance recognises that generally money compensation would not be appropriate from a young offender and that victims should be counselled not to have unrealistic expectations of the process in which they are involved. Reparation is most likely to take the form of an apology, work to make good any damage, work for the community or victim/offender mediation. It is recognised that mediation is a difficult process and the Guidance emphasises that it should not be embarked upon without a very careful assessment of the needs and abilities of the victim and offender (paras. 3.66 to 3.69).

Where a programme of behaviour is successfully agreed, it is the duty of the panel to make a written record of it in language capable of being readily understood or explained to the offender (s. 8(5); PCC(S)A 2000, s. 23(5)). The agreement, to be described as a 'youth offender contract', takes effect once a copy has been signed by the offender and a member of the panel (normally the Chair) (s. 8(6); s. 23(6)). The contract will run from that time for the period specified in the original referral order or orders (s. 9; s. 24). Where there is more than one referral order, the duration of the contract will depend upon any court order under s. 3(6) (s. 18(6)) concerning whether the orders should be additional to each other or whether they should run consecutively (s. 9(4); s. 24(4)). The ultimate length of the contract period may also be extended where a court dealing with a further offence by the young offender, committed either before or after his original referral, exercises its powers under sch. 1, para. 11 or 12 to extend the period of the order (s. 9(5); s. 24(5)). The period of the contract expires where the contract is revoked by the court for non-compliance under sch. 1, para. 5, or for further convictions under para. 14 (s. 9(6)).

PROGRESS MEETINGS

At any time during the continuance of a youth offender contract, the panel may hold a progress meeting if it appears expedient to review the offender's progress in relation to the agreed programme of behaviour or in relation to any other matter arising out of the contract (s. 11(1) and (2); PCC(S)A 2000, s. 26(1) and (2)). Under s. 11(3) (s. 26(3)), the panel must hold a progress meeting in three cases: where the offender wishes to seek a variation in the terms of the contract; where the offender wishes to be referred back to court to request the revocation of the order on the ground of a significant change of circumstances; and where it appears to the panel that the offender is in breach of any of the terms of the contract.

At a progress meeting, the panel may review the offender's progress, discuss any breaches of the contract and consider any requests to vary the terms of the contract or refer the offender back to court (s. 11(4); s. 26(4)). Where an apparent breach of contract is discussed, the panel and the offender may agree that the contract should continue to apply, possibly with an agreed variation, or the panel may decide that the offender should be referred back to court (s. 11(5); s. 26(5)). A variation agreed after discussion may include any term which could have been included in the original contract (s. 11(9); s. 26(9)). Where such a variation is made, the panel must produce a written record, in language capable of being understood by or explained to the offender (s. 11(6); s. 26(6)). Any such variation will take effect once signed by the offender and a member of the panel (s. 11(7); s. 26(7)). If, however, the offender unreasonably refuses to sign the agreed variation, the panel may end the meeting and refer the offender back to court (s. 11(8); s. 26(8)). The offender may also be referred back to court if the panel accepts that as a result of a significant change of circumstances continued performance of the contract would be impractical (s. 11(10); s. 26(10)). In any case in which the offender is referred back to court, procedures set out in sch. 1 must be followed (s. 13; s. 29).

FINAL MEETING

Towards the end of the period during which a youth offender contract runs, the panel must hold a final meeting (s. 12(1); s. 27(1)) for the purpose of reviewing the offender's compliance with the terms of the contract and deciding whether he has satisfactorily completed the contract (s. 12(2); s. 27(2)). The offender should attend this meeting and, if he does not do so, he may be referred back to court or the meeting may be adjourned under s. 7(2)(a) (s. 22(2)(a)). It is not permissible to adjourn beyond the time for compliance with the contract (s. 12(6); s. 27(6)) and if there is no opportunity to hold another meeting within the contract period the only option for the panel will be to refer the offender back to court. However, it is not necessary to refer the offender back to court where the panel is satisfied that the contract has been completed satisfactorily (s. 12(5); s. 27(5)). The decision of the panel must be written down and given to the offender. Where it is decided that the offender has satisfactorily complied with the terms of the contract, the referral order will be discharged as from the end of the contract period (s. 12(3); s. 27(3)). If such a positive decision is not made, the offender will be referred back to court (s. 12(4); s. 27(4)) to be dealt with under procedures in sch. 1.

THE CONSEQUENCES OF DISCHARGE OF A REFERRAL ORDER

The sentence of referral to a youth offender panel is seen as being a positive measure to help the youngster avoid further offending. The process itself embodies the practices of reparation and the ultimate aim is re-integration into the law-abiding community. It is consistent with this that where a convicted offender receives a referral order, the period after which the conviction is spent for the purposes of the Rehabilitation of Offenders Act 1974 will be the period set by the court for the duration of the referral order or until the contract is revoked. Where a referral order is made, but no contract ever takes effect (e.g., where the offender does not attend or the parties are unable to reach an agreement), the conviction will be spent after the end of the period during which a contract would have run had one been made. Thus, for the purposes of rehabilitation, where no contract is made under the order, the offender is treated in exactly the same way as if a contract had been made and run its normal course. These rules are found in the Rehabilitation of Offenders Act 1974, s. 5(4B) and (4C), inserted by sch. 4, para. 6.

REFERRALS BACK TO COURT FOR NON CO-OPERATION: sch. 1, part I

In a number of circumstances, generally involving non co-operation, an offender subject to a referral order may be referred back to court under sch. 1. As noted above, sch. 1 is in almost exactly the same terms for both the 1999 Act and the PCC(S)A 2000. The circumstances in which the offender may be referred back are:

(a)   failure to attend meeting (s. 7(2); s. 22(2));
(b)   no prospect of agreeing a contract (s. 10(2); s. 25(2));
(c)   failure to sign agreement (s. 10(3); s. 25(3));
(d)   breach of terms of agreement (s. 11(5); s. 26(5));
(e)   failure to sign agreement as to variation (s. 11(8); s. 26(8));
(f)   change of circumstances renders performance impractical (s. 11(10); s. 26(10));
(g)   failure to complete contract satisfactorily (s. 12(4); s. 27(4)).

When the offender is under 18 at the time when he will first appear before the court on the reference back, the relevant court will be the youth court for the petty session area in which he lives. Where the offender will be 18 or over at the relevant time, the reference will be to the magistrates' court for that area (para. 1). The reference must be accompanied by a report prepared by the panel indicating the reasons for it (para. 2).

Having received such a report, the court may secure the attendance of the offender by summons, or if the report is substantiated on oath, by warrant for arrest (sch. 1, para. 3(2)). Such a warrant may be executed in Scotland as well as in England and Wales (sch. 1, para. 3(4); PCC(S)A 2000, s. 159). Offenders under 18 who are arrested may be detained under the Children and Young Persons Act 1933, s. 107 in a place of safety for up to 72 hours but must be brought before a youth court within that period; in the event that the offender turns 18 while being detained, he should be brought before a magistrates' court (para. 4(1)(b)). Where the court before which the offender is brought is not the appropriate court for receiving the reference back from the youth offender panel, the court actually dealing with the offender is given powers to remand on bail or in custody. In relation to a child under the age of 18, remand must be to accommodation provided by the local authority in whose area he appears to reside (para. 4(2), (3), (4) and (5)).

Once the offender is before the appropriate court to deal with the reference back, that court must review the decision of the panel which resulted in the reference back. If it is proved to the satisfaction of the court that any finding of fact on which the court based its decision was a finding which the court was entitled to make, and that any discretion exercised by the panel was reasonably exercised, then the court may revoke the referral order (para. 5(1) and (2)). This revocation will include any order extending the referral order under para. 11 (for further offences committed pre-referral) or para. 12 (for further offences after referral) (para. 5(3)). If the court wishes to exercise the power to revoke, it may do so only if the offender is present (para. 5(6)). The power to revoke may be exercised even though the period for which the contract has effect has expired (para. 5(6)).

This procedure leaves a number of questions unanswered. It is not clear how the court is to make its determination and in particular whether it must hear evidence or whether it can simply rely upon the panel's report. The Act makes no mention of the offender having a right to be heard, although this would presumably be implied as a matter of natural justice. Burdens and standards of proof are not specified. Although it was probably the intention to make this a relatively straightforward procedure, it might fall foul of the right to fair trial under Article 6 of the European Convention on Human Rights and of the Human Rights Act 1998 from October 2000. It is arguable that the proceeding is criminal in nature because it involves a determination that a person has done wrong (e.g., breached a duty under the contract) and could lead to a significant punishment which otherwise would not have been received. If it would be so classified as a criminal proceeding, the summary nature of the procedure might be found to contravene Article 6.

Consequences of revocation

Where a referral order is revoked, the court may deal with the offender in any manner in which he could have been dealt with when originally sentenced, apart from the power to refer the offender to a panel under s. 1 (para. 5(4) and (5)(a)). Any sentence awarded may be appealed to the Crown Court (para. 6). In sentencing an offender following revocation, the court shall have regard to the circumstances of his referral back to court and, where a contract has taken effect between the offender and the panel, the extent of the offender's compliance with the contract (para. 5(5)(b)).

In the analogous situation where an offender is re-sentenced following breach of a community sentence under the Criminal Justice Act 1991, sch. 2, the extent to which he has complied with the sentence prior to breach may be taken into account to reduce sentence. This suggests that where the court considers the extent of the offender's compliance with the contract this may operate to reduce sentence, for instance where some required activities under the contract have been completed.

It is less clear whether the sentence could be increased where the young offender has behaved badly, for instance by disrupting panel meetings. Again, drawing an analogy, where a community sentence has been breached without reasonable excuse the court has a number of options among which are to impose a fine, a new community service order or an attendance centre order (Criminal Justice Act 1991, sch. 2; PCC(S)A 2000, sch. 3). This may suggest that, where a court is exercising re-sentencing powers following revocation of a referral order, it is permissible to punish any breach which led to the revocation. There are however two important differences between the referral order procedure and that relating to community sentences. The court's sentencing powers following breach of a community sentence are provided by law and when imposing a community sentence the court must explain the possible consequences of breach to the offender (see, for example, PCC(S)A 2000, ss. 37(1), 41(7) and 46(1)). In relation to breaches of referral orders it would be unfair for the conduct amounting to the breach to exacerbate the sentence without clear legal provision for this and fair warning to the person concerned. A safe approach for courts would be to consider the offender's behaviour to the extent that it indicated his attitude towards his original offending but to avoid the temptation to punish the offender for his poor conduct in relation to the referral.

As indicated above, where an offender is referred back, the court must make a judgment on whether the panel were entitled to make any findings of fact on which they based their decision and exercised any discretion reasonably (para. 5(1)). If having considered these issues, the court is not satisfied as to these matters then the offender will remain subject to the referral order or orders (para. 5(2)). Where a contract has taken effect between the offender and the panel, this will continue in force and will run until its normal expiry date. Where a contract has not taken effect, then the panel must proceed with further meetings with the object of agreeing a contract. Where a contract has run its full course and expired by the time the court considers a reference back then, if the court is not satisfied with the correctness or reasonableness of the panel's decision to refer the offender back, it must discharge the referral order or orders (para. 7(3)).

The court also has a power to discharge an order where the panel has referred an offender back to court under s. 12(4) (PCC(S)A 2000, s. 27(4)) on the ground that he has not completed the contract satisfactorily. If the court, having reviewed the panel's decision, decides that the offender's compliance with the terms of the contract amounts to satisfactory completion of it, the referral order must be discharged (para. 8). Where a court has extended the period of a referral order under powers in sch. 1, para. 11 or 12 (discussed below), such extension orders will be automatically discharged at the same time as the referral order to which they relate (para. 9).

FURTHER CONVICTIONS DURING REFERRAL: sch. 1, part II

The referral to a youth offender panel is conceived as the key stage in a young offender's criminal career at which relatively intensive intervention may be effective in preventing re-offending. It was recognised that the salutary effect of the order would be lost if repeat referrals were possible and it were to become seen as a routine 'let off'. Accordingly, a referral is a once only opportunity for a young offender which, as described above, may be abandoned if it appears to be failing in its aims.

In view of the policies which inspired the order, a further conviction during the currency of the order is problematic. On the one hand, the conviction may indicate that the order has failed and should be abandoned; on the other hand, to abandon the order half way through may be considered a wasted opportunity to influence the young offender.

The problem of further convictions is tackled by sch. 1, part II which is in almost identical terms under both the 1999 Act and the PCC(S)A 2000. Part II seeks to achieve a balance between the competing considerations noted above. Those who re-offend while still under 18 may be given a second chance. Thus, where a further conviction relates to offences committed prior to the referral, the order may continue subject to an extension. Where further minor offences are committed during the currency of the order, the order may be terminated, but in some cases it may be continued and extended where the court is satisfied that this is likely to help prevent re-offending. For more serious offences, the offender should be sentenced in the normal way and the order revoked. The detailed scheme is set out below.

Extension for pre-referral offending

Paragraph 11 deals with the situation where an offender aged under 18 (para. 10(1)), who is already subject to a referral and who has not been sentenced (apart from absolute discharge (para. 13(6)) or bound over (para. 13(7)) on any other occasion, falls to be sentenced for an offence (or offences), all of which were committed prior to the referral. In these circumstances, provided that the offence (or offences) are ones which would have qualified for a referral if prosecuted earlier, the court may sentence the offender by extending the period of the referral order. Offences qualify for a referral where the court is proposing neither a custodial sentence nor an absolute discharge and the sentence is not fixed by law (s. 1(1); PCC(S)A 2000, s. 16(1)). It is made clear that any extension should not extend the compliance period of the order beyond 12 months (para. 13). Consistent with this, no extension is permitted where 12 months was set as the compliance period for the original referral order (para. 10(2)).

Although the structure of para. 11 suggests a presumption of extension for pre-referral offending, the court clearly has a discretion not to do so. This may be exercised where the court feels that the later offence adds little to the offences which prompted the original order or where the original referral was for the maximum 12 months. In these cases an absolute discharge might be appropriate. Equally, a court may exercise its discretion against extension where, having received a report from the relevant panel, it appears that the order is not working as hoped.

Extension for post-referral offending

Paragraph 12 provides for the sentencing of an offender under 18, who is already subject to a referral, but who has not been sentenced (apart from absolute discharge) or bound over on any other occasion, and who is subsequently convicted of an offence (or offences) committed after he was referred to the panel. In this case an extension to the referral period is possible, but only if the court is satisfied that extending the compliance period is likely to help to prevent further re-offending (para. 12(2)). Before making such a determination, the court must consider a report from either the relevant youth offending panel or, where a contract has yet to take effect between the offender and the panel, the relevant YOT (para. 12(3)). Where the court exercises its discretion to extend an order in such circumstances, it must announce in open court that it is satisfied that it will be likely to help prevent re-offending by the offender, and also why it is so satisfied (para. 12(2)(b)).

General provisions relating to extensions to referral orders

Where the court exercises its discretion under paras 11 or 12 to extend the period for compliance with a referral order, its sentencing powers are restricted as they are when a referral order is first made (para. 13(2) to (5)). Thus, in relation to any associated (or connected) offence, the court's powers are limited to either extending the original referral order, in which case the two extensions may be concurrent, or ordering an absolute discharge (para. 13(4)). Specifically, the court may not impose any of the sentences listed in s. 4(4) (PCC(S)A 2000, s. 19(4)) or the associated orders listed in s. 4(5) (s. 19(5)). The Home Secretary retains a power to amend by regulation the categories of offender for whom the referral order period may be extended (para. 13(8)).

Revocation of the referral order following re-offending

Where an offender falls to be sentenced for a further offence whilst subject to a referral order and the sentencing court neither imposes an absolute discharge nor extends the original order under para. 11 or 12, whatever other sentence is imposed will have the effect of revoking the referral order (para. 14(1) and (2)). When this occurs, the sentencing court has a discretion to deal with the offender in relation to the offence for which the now-revoked referral was made (para. 14(3)). This power should be exercised only 'if it appears to the court in the interests of justice to do so'. In exercising this discretion the court should receive a report from the panel and is under a duty to take into account the extent of the offender's compliance with the contract agreed between himself and the panel (para. 14(4)). It would clearly be unjust to re-sentence for the earlier offence where the period of the contract has almost run and the offender has substantially complied with its terms. Similarly, where a court decides to re-sentence for the earlier offence, partial compliance with the contract would serve as mitigation.

The categories of offenders whose orders will be revoked under para. 14 are:

(a)   offenders whose later offence warrants custody;
(b)   offenders in relation to whom the court exercises a discretion not to extend the referral order;

(c)   offenders who received a maximum 12 month referral when first sentenced; and

(d)   offenders who are over 18 when they appear to be sentenced for the second offence.

In these circumstances the revocation is automatic and there is no power of appeal as there is where revocation follows a court determination against the offender under para. 5(2). In relation to categories (c) and (d) the decision to revoke may be arbitrary, in the sense that it is not based upon a judgment about the offending behaviour or the offender's conduct under the youth offender contract. Where an offender is doing well under his contract but does not qualify for an extension because he is already subject to a 12-month order or has turned 18, the court can avoid revoking the order by imposing an absolute discharge.

Chapter 3
The Case for Special Measures

OVERVIEW

Special measures available to witnesses under the Act

The special measures which the Act contains are derived from the recommendations
of *Speaking Up For Justice*, the Report of the Interdepartmental Working Group on
the Treatment of Vulnerable or Intimidated Witnesses in the Criminal Justice System
(Home Office, 1998). Witnesses may be eligible for the measures on grounds of youth
or incapacity, or because of the fear or distress they are likely to suffer in giving their
evidence. (Eligibility is dealt with in Chapter 4.) The measures available under the
1999 Act to assist eligible witnesses are:

(a)   screening the witness from the accused (s. 23);
(b)   giving evidence by live link (s. 24);
(c)   ordering the removal of wigs and gowns while the witness testifies (s. 25);
(d)   giving evidence in private (in sexual cases and cases involving intimidation)
(s. 26);
(e)   video recording of evidence in chief (s. 27);
(f)   video recording of cross-examination and re-examination (where evidence in
chief is so recorded) (s. 28);
(g)   examination through intermediary (for young or incapacitated witnesses)
(s. 29);
(h)   provision of aids to communication (for young or incapacitated witnesses)
(s. 30).

The provisions of the 1999 Act regarding special measures are not in force at the time
of writing. According to Action for Justice: Implementing the Speaking Up for
Justice Report in England and Wales (Home Office, 1999) the intention is that
most of the measures will become available in the Crown Court and Youth Courts
from the end of 2000, except for ss. 28 (pre-recorded cross-examination) and 29
(intermediaries) which are not scheduled to be brought into force until Autumn 2001.

In Magistrates Courts it is intended that the measures be available in Spring 2003 before magistrates courts are equipped with the technology to make the special measures work in summary trials.

It does not follow that witnesses are for the time being deprived of all assistance while giving evidence, for most of these measures are not new. The Criminal Justice Act 1988, s. 32 already permits live link for child witnesses in certain cases and the evidence in chief of a child witness may in some circumstances be given in the form of a video recording under s. 32A of the 1988 Act (added by the Criminal Justice Act 1991). There exists also a little-used statutory power to clear the court in certain cases (Children and Young Persons Act 1933, s. 37) and any court has the power to order the use of screens (*X, Y and Z* (1990) 91 Cr App R 36) and the modification of court dress (see, e.g., *Practice Direction (Crown Court: Young Defendants)* [2000] 1 WLR 659). At common law evidence may be received through an intermediary (*Duffy* [1999] 1 Cr App R 307) or with the help of an aid to communication such as an alphabet board (acknowledged by Lord Williams, House of Lords Report Stage, *Hansard*, 2 March 1999, col. 1608). The only measure that is entirely novel and untried, therefore, is the pre-recorded cross-examination.

It has already been noted (see p. 3) that the *Report of the Advisory Group on Video Evidence* (Home Office, 1989), chaired by Judge Pigot, suggested that changes originally made to benefit child witnesses should be extended to vulnerable adult witnesses in due course. In making a wider range of witnesses eligible for special measures, the Act reflects an ongoing concern that there are witnesses besides children who require the assistance that special measures can provide (*Speaking Up For Justice*, para. 3.7). The object of this chapter is to consider the principles which have led to the decision to create special measures, and to give a flavour of the research which has been undertaken with regard to the efficacy of special measures where children testify.

THE ACT AND THE 'BEST EVIDENCE' PRINCIPLE

Central to the case for making special measures available to assist some witnesses to give their evidence in court is the proposition that the traditional criminal trial, with examination in chief and cross-examination conducted in open court by trained advocates, may disable some witnesses from giving their best evidence. The question that is then posed is whether traditional procedures should bend to accommodate the needs of individual witnesses, with a view to improving the quality of the evidence the witness is able to give. The reforms contained in the Criminal Justice Acts 1988 and 1991 were clearly predicated on the notion that the trial process should be flexible enough to accommodate the needs of child witnesses, and the same supposition informs the approach taken in the 1999 Act:

> In introducing the Bill, the Government recognise that in the past the criminal law and the criminal justice system have not always got it right. All too often, witnesses have not been able to give of their best in court, for a variety of reasons. The

measure is designed to protect the public interest and thus the interests of justice, striking a proper balance between the interests and rights of the defendant and those of the victim. That demands that the best evidence possible be laid before the jury. Fear, intimidation and the vulnerability of age or incapacity can militate against witnesses giving their best evidence. The proposal will ensure that the best evidence comes before the jury ... (Paul Boateng, Minister of State for the Home Office, House of Commons Standing Committee E, *Hansard*, 17 June 1999)

The term used in the Act itself to reflect this 'best evidence' principle is 'quality'. The procedure for making a special measures direction in s. 19 (see p. 45) requires the court to focus on whether there are special measures which would improve the quality of the evidence and, if there are, to determine which of the measures (together or in combination) would maximise the quality of that evidence. Quality is defined as 'quality in terms of completeness, coherence and accuracy' (s. 16(5)). Essential to the case for reform is that all witnesses should be given the opportunity to give evidence that is the best they can provide. In order to afford this opportunity, the philosophy of the Act is that it is justifiable to employ special measures which depart from the traditional model for the presentation of evidence in court.

Special measures may relieve stress

The traditional trial may inhibit witnesses from giving their best evidence by putting the witness under an unacceptable degree of stress. The atmosphere of a courtroom, the form of dress adopted by judges and advocates, and the very formal nature of the trial itself are intended to inspire awe and a respect for the solemnity of the occasion in the ordinary adult witness, and to deter the giving of false or unconsidered testimony. For children in particular, and also for some other witnesses, such formality may simply be intimidating, and may make it impossible for them to provide their best evidence, notwithstanding that they may be telling the truth. (See J. Spencer and R. Flin, *The Evidence of Children*, 2nd ed., Blackstone Press (1993), Ch. 13.) Also stressful for many witnesses is the prospect of being brought face to face with the accused person, particularly where the witness is alleged to have been the victim of sexual abuse or violence. One reason for the adoption of special measures to protect children from confrontation with their alleged abuser at trial was the regularity with which children who had been through the traditional trial process reported that it was worse than the original abuse. Such feelings were compounded by the sort of difficulties which frequently beset witnesses at trials, such as being kept waiting at court, and being unable to give evidence at the time, or on the day, originally anticipated (see, e.g., J. Chandler and D. Lait, 'An analysis of the treatment of children as witnesses in the Crown Court' in *Children in Court* (1996) Victim Support Research Study 1, Victim Support).

The special measures in the Act can reduce stress for the witness in a variety of ways. The unease which children in particular may feel in consequence of the unfamiliarity of court dress can be relieved by removing wigs and gowns while a witness testifies. The use of a screen or other similar arrangement in court prevents the element of direct confrontation with the accused while making the witness available to give evidence in the traditional way. The live link provides a similar facility, but with the witness at a distance from the courtroom. The power to order evidence to be given in private in sexual cases and cases involving witness intimidation, while not itself preventing the witness from seeing the accused, removes the stress involved in giving evidence in front of spectators who may be motivated in the one case by indecent motives and in the other by the desire to put improper pressure on the witness to retract. In addition, in sexual cases, the witness may be spared the embarrassment of speaking about intimate matters in front of strangers.

The use of pre-recorded testimony may also have a significant part to play in reducing the stress caused by confrontation with the accused and by the formality surrounding the process of questioning in the courtroom. Pre-recorded evidence in chief is conducted in a deliberately informal setting by skilled interviewers, not by advocates. Pre-recorded cross-examination and re-examination, which is a process adopted for the first time by the 1999 Act, may of necessity have a greater air of formality about it, as a judge or magistrates will be involved in this stage of proceedings and the questions will be chosen by advocates (although they may be put through an intermediary). Even so, such a process may be markedly less stressful than the traditional cross-examination at trial. The witness whose examination in chief and cross-examination are video recorded is not brought into confrontation with the accused during the process, and is also spared the anxiety of being kept waiting at the trial for his turn to testify.

Special measures may improve recall and communication

Speaking Up For Justice noted that a witness's functions include providing a clear, full and truthful account of relevant matters and responding to questions about them, which requires an ability to understand and recall events which may have occurred some time in the past (para. 3.3). The ability to perform these tasks may be affected by a variety of circumstances. The problem of recall is likely to be greater where there is a long wait for the trial. A recent research study found that the average time it took for child abuse prosecutions to come to trial in the Crown Court was 57.5 weeks, and this notwithstanding provisions in the Criminal Justice Act 1991, s. 53 designed to 'fast track' such cases (G. Davis, L. Hoyano, C. Keenan, L. Maitland and R. Morgan, *An Assessment of the Admissibility and Sufficiency of Evidence in Child Abuse Prosecutions* (Home Office, 1999)). If the witness's long-term memory is poor, a much fuller and more detailed account may be forthcoming if his evidence in chief can be pre-recorded soon after the event. Accuracy and completeness are matters which, under the Act, are expressed to contribute to the 'quality' of a witness's evidence (s. 16(5)), so that the problems such a witness might encounter at trial are indicative of the need to resort to the pre-recording of his evidence. The pre-recording of cross-examination may also have some advantages in terms of capturing a fresher account, but the gain is unlikely to be significant as the cross-examination will not take place much in advance of trial. This is because the defence case takes time to prepare, and the process of disclosure of evidence which precedes the trial may also be a lengthy business, particularly in sexual cases. The main advantage of the pre-recorded cross-examination lies, then, in the reduction of stress for the witness.

Special measures can also assist a witness to communicate more effectively. A child, or a witness who has an incapacity that affects his powers of communication, might be unable to give effective evidence without resort to an intermediary or a physical aid to communication such as an alphabet board. The view taken by the Act is that special measures may improve the quality of a witness's evidence in terms of coherence as well as completeness and accuracy; an extreme but nevertheless plausible example is that of a witness who without the provision of some form of aid to communication would be adjudged incompetent to testify at all (see further Chapter 9).

The quality of a witness's account may also be very much affected by the way in which he is questioned. Where the witness is a child, or has a learning disability or a mental illness, a questioner who is trained to accommodate the witness's special needs is likely to elicit a far more satisfactory account than a lay person, or even an advocate with no such insight into the needs of the witness. A witness who pre-records his evidence in chief will be questioned by a specially trained interviewer, who will be guided by the provisions of the *Memorandum of Good Practice*. This document, the full title of which is currently the *Memorandum of Good Practice on Video Recorded Interviews with Child Witnesses for Criminal Proceedings* (Home Office and Department of Health, 1992), is being revised to take account of the wider range of eligible witnesses and special measures available under the 1999 Act. It must be envisaged that it will emerge with a somewhat different name, but the central principles of interviewing are likely to remain constant. Thus, for example, the *Memorandum* states that the effective pre-recorded interview is one which is tailored to the witness's particular needs and circumstances. It also phases the interview in such a way as to enable a rapport to be built up before the alleged offence is discussed. The part of the interview in which the offence is disclosed is carefully structured so as to encourage the witness to provide as full an account as he can in his own words and in his own time. Questioning is regulated by rules designed to ensure that unreliable information is not elicited; the rules being grounded in psychological research about, for instance, the very limited value which may attach to the answers to leading questions. The net result of this accumulation of expertise is likely to be an interview that is of better 'quality', in all of the senses in which that term is used in the 1999 Act, than an exchange conducted in the form of an examination in chief in court.

THE ACT AND THE 'CROSS-EXAMINATION' PRINCIPLE

The second plank in the Act's strategy is that any variations on traditional methods of presentation of evidence must not sacrifice the rights of the party seeking to test the strength of the evidence (normally the accused) to do so in a proper manner. As has already been noted (see p. 4), the Interdepartmental Group responsible for *Speaking Up For Justice* was specifically required to have regard to the interests of justice in developing its proposals, and to balance the rights of the defendant to a fair trial against the needs of the witness 'not to be traumatised or intimidated by the criminal justice process' (*Speaking Up For Justice*, para. 1.14). The preservation of the right to cross-examine is regarded as essential to the maintenance of a healthy balance, even though the use of special measures may mean that the cross-examiner's questions are put in a non-traditional way, such as through an intermediary or at a pre-recorded cross-examination in which it is not essential that the witness sees the person by whom the questions are put. A court making a special measures direction is bound to consider whether the use of a measure would 'tend to inhibit' the evidence being 'effectively tested' by a party to the proceedings (s. 19(3)(b): see p. 47). The only case in which the Act explicitly departs from the rule is where a video recording may be given as evidence in chief in circumstances where the witness is not available to be cross-examined, but this is primarily intended for cases where the parties are agreed that this is an appropriate course to take (s. 27(4): see p. 66).

It was part of the Government's argument in favour of special measures that the 1999 Act was superior to other provisions under which the evidence of some vulnerable or intimidated witnesses can currently be received. Lord Williams (House of Lords Committee Stage, *Hansard*, 1 February 1999, col. 1376) pointed out that 'there is already a provision for the admissibility in evidence, *without cross-examination in some circumstances*, of statements made by those who are too terrorised or afraid to come to court'. Such statements would normally be admitted under the Criminal Justice Act 1988, s. 23, which permits a document to stand as evidence of facts stated in it where, *inter alia*, the statement is made to an investigator in the proceedings and the maker does not give oral evidence through fear. The provision is broad enough to admit a pre-recorded interview or a witness statement, but the court must consider that it is in the interests of justice to do so. It is an important part of the thinking behind the 1999 Act that a witness who is provided with special measures may not only be helped to provide a better examination in chief, but may also be enabled to cope with cross-examination. Once the new provisions are in place, it is likely to be more difficult to invoke s. 23 of the 1988 Act. For example, where a witness who has been intimidated claims to be too afraid to give oral evidence, the court is unlikely to be satisfied that it is in the interests of justice to admit the witness's pre-trial statement unless his fear cannot be assuaged by special measures such as pre-recorded evidence or the use of screens or live link in court.

Where a witness who is subject to a special measures direction is subject to cross-examination there is, despite the careful way in which the Act has been constructed in order to hide it, something of a conflict of ideologies. The Act is there to help the witness give his 'best' evidence; this strategy is exemplified by the use of psychological research to aid in the construction of the pre-recorded interview which may replace evidence in chief, where the concern of the interviewer is to enable the witness to maximise his potential to give a coherent, complete and accurate account. If the function of the cross-examiner were limited to *exposing* those respects in which the account is incoherent, incomplete or inaccurate, then it could be said that there is a consistency of ideology: the examiner in chief brings out the best possible account from the witness; and the cross-examiner teases out the weak points. However this, though an important aspect of cross-examination, is not its only function. Cross-examiners do not simply question: rather they seek to persuade the court to accept the version of events being advanced by the party they represent. It is a matter of constructing a reality, or telling a story, in antithesis to the account advanced by the other side:

> The main way for an advocate to tell his story is through his own witnesses, but he should also seek confirmation and support by constructive forms of cross-examination or by destructive challenges to the competing story. Cross-examiners should do more than just score isolated points; they should be promoting their whole version of the facts wherever they can. (M. Stone, *Cross-Examination in Criminal Trials* (1988))

The cross-examiner's armoury includes a range of techniques which, when turned upon a vulnerable witness in order to promote the cross-examiner's version of the facts, may produce an effect which undermines the apparent credibility of the evidence in the eyes of a jury or magistrates without actually impacting adversely on its coherence, completeness or accuracy. A good example would be where a witness with a learning disability such as Down's Syndrome has a tendency to seek to please any person in authority. The interviewer conducting a video recorded examination in chief would seek to avoid the use of any questions which might trigger this reaction, so that the evidence is, so far as possible, uncontaminated by any desire the witness may have to please the interviewer. If the cross-examiner, in roundly asserting a contrary view of events, manages to procure the witness's assent, such a departure might be of very little real value — yet it might well seem to be meaningful to a jury. Techniques adopted in cross-examination may frequently have a distorting effect of this kind on witness testimony, particularly where the witness is vulnerable (see, e.g., L. Ellison, 'The Protection of Vulnerable Witnesses in Court: an Anglo-Dutch Comparison' [1999] 3 *E&P* 29). The way forward would seem to lie in the tighter control by the court of the cross-examination of vulnerable witnesses. An important document in the training of advocates preparing cases involving child witnesses is 'A Case for Balance' (NSPCC, 1997), which accompanies a training video approved by the Judicial Studies Board. This suggests:

> The prosecution advocate should shield the child witness from unnecessary or unfair attack by drawing the judge's attention to questioning which is inappropriate in tone or content or which is framed as an assertion or which is clearly repetitive.

The judge in the training video is seen laying down limits as to the style of questioning that he is prepared to permit in relation to a young witness with a degree of learning disability. It is also suggested that judges and prosecution advocates need to be alert to such matters as 'questions taken literally but mistakenly' and 'multiple questions or questions combined with assertions'. To the extent that this level of control may be thought to provide a challenge to the autonomy of the cross-examiner it may be said that it is a necessary infringement if the Act is to work so as to enable many witnesses who qualify for special measures to give their best evidence. The style and content of cross-examination will in future have to be closely monitored in relation particularly to adults with a learning disability, but witnesses with mental illness and physical disability, and those who are eligible for special measures on grounds of the fear and distress they are likely to suffer in giving evidence, may also require special consideration in this regard. With this in mind, *Speaking Up For Justice* recommended that the Lord Chief Justice should be invited to consider issuing a practice direction giving guidance to barristers and judges on the need to disallow 'unnecessarily aggressive and/or inappropriate cross-examination' (Recommendation 43).

THE ACT AND THE 'LIMITED ELIGIBILITY' PRINCIPLE

Although it is a fundamental of the Act that special measures should be allocated on the basis of the individual's need, this is predicated on the basis that the witness falls within a class described by the Act. The classes selected are witnesses who are vulnerable as a result of the personal characteristics of youth and incapacity, who may qualify for the full range of measures, and witnesses who are, for a variety of reasons, likely to suffer undue fear or distress if they give evidence in the traditional manner, who may qualify for a slightly more limited choice of measures. Not only will there be some witnesses who fall within the groups but for whom special measures are not suitable (many witnesses with physical disability will fall into this category), but also there may be some who might benefit from special measures but who fall outside the assigned categories. Such witnesses can be assisted to a limited degree by the court's inherent powers, which are preserved by s. 19 (see p. 48). (Eligibility is dealt with in detail in Chapter 4.)

THE ACT AND THE 'WITNESS PREFERENCE' PRINCIPLE

The Act incorporates two devices for taking account of the witness's preferences in relation to special measures. The first is to require the court, when determining the eligibility of incapacitated, fearful or distressed witnesses, and when selecting appropriate special measures, to take account of any views expressed by the witness (ss. 16(4), 17(3) and 19(3)(b)). The second is to give the witness the power to opt out of certain provisions. In relation to sexual cases, an adult complainant may decline eligibility on this ground alone (s. 17(4)) and a child witness may opt out of a pre-recorded cross-examination which is otherwise provided for by a statutory presumption (s. 21(7)(b)). These provisions help to advance the 'best evidence' principle by giving the witness some say about the level of assistance he feels he needs. Unfortunately the formula employed where the first device is adopted does not require the court to ascertain what views the witness holds, only to take account of any views the witness has expressed. The formula adopted in relation to the second device explicitly places the onus on the witness to inform the court that he does not wish to take advantage of the measure. It would, it is submitted, be good practice and would also reflect the spirit of the Act if the advocate who is to rely on the witness's evidence ensures that the witness's views have been sought before the relevant decisions are taken.

ARE SPECIAL MEASURES JUSTIFIED?

The framework adopted by the Act of making special measures available to defined classes of witnesses where to do so would improve the quality of their evidence is generally to be welcomed, as are the safeguards which are designed to ensure that the process is driven by the needs of the witness as ascertained by the court, not simply by the wishes of the witness, and that the party seeking to challenge the evidence enjoys a full and fair opportunity to do so. Nevertheless it appears that, in order to fulfil the Act's commitment to the quality of the evidence to be given by the witness, there will have to be further inroads into the traditional principles which govern the cross-examination of witnesses in court, so as to ensure that the testimony which the witness gives is not distorted or its true value misrepresented.

PILOTING SPECIAL MEASURES: CRIMINAL JUSTICE ACTS 1988 AND 1991

The remainder of this chapter is concerned with the case for including in the special measures menu the options of giving evidence by live link, and of giving evidence in chief by means of a video recording. These two measures, which have been in existence for some time as a result of earlier statutory reforms in relation to children, have been the subject of various evaluative studies. In this section the advantages and disadvantages of the use of live link and video to present witness's evidence will be considered. In the course of the discussion it will be convenient to speak of the measures in the older legislation in the past tense although they remain in force at the time of writing, because they will be superseded when the special measures provisions of the 1999 Act are brought fully into effect.

THE 1988 AND 1991 ACTS AND LIVE LINK

The statutory framework

Section 32 of the Criminal Justice Act 1988, as amended by the Criminal Justice Act 1991, permitted a child witness to give evidence through a live television link in certain cases. The provision applied only to trials on indictment or in youth courts of sexual offences or offences of violence or cruelty. Differential age limits applied: children aged under 17 could benefit from the provision in sexual cases, but in the other cases to which the section applied the child had to be under 14. Leave of the court was required before evidence could be given in this way, but the statute provided no guidance as to the circumstances in which leave should be given or withheld.

The effect of the provision in operation was, according to *Speaking Up For Justice*, that the child usually sat in a separate room in the court building, linked by live closed-circuit television to the courtroom where the judge and prosecution and defence counsel were able to view the witness on the TV monitor. The child, however, was able to see only the person asking the questions on their own monitor (para. 8.3). The advantage of the measure was said to be:

> the witness avoids the trauma of sitting in the court room facing the defendant and being overlooked by the defendant's supporters who may be in the public gallery. At the same time, the defendant's rights to see the witness's demeanour (on a TV screen) and to test the evidence by cross-examination are not infringed. (*Speaking Up For Justice*, para. 8.4)

Advantages and disadvantages of the live link

Speaking Up For Justice was of the opinion that the live link 'could greatly assist some vulnerable or intimidated witnesses give best evidence in court' (sic) (para. 8.6). No disadvantages are noted. The leading study (G. Davies and E. Noon, *An Evaluation of the Live Link for Child Witnesses* (Home Office, 1991)) concluded that the measure had met with a favourable reception, and that it appeared to improve the confidence of children who gave evidence using it. Children did not have to observe the accused during their evidence, nor were they subjected to the 'alien and sometimes oppressive atmosphere of the courtroom itself'. Minor hitches were found in high initial levels of equipment malfunction and the problems reported by advocates unfamiliar with the technology in establishing the normal level of rapport with witnesses, but these were teething troubles. The only substantial concern which was cited to the researchers by some practitioners, but with which they did not agree, was that a witness who appeared in this way had less immediacy for, and made less emotional impact on, the jury than the same witness appearing live. As the authors of the study say, a conviction achieved at the expense of the exploitation of a child's vulnerability and stress seems a 'somewhat dubious procedure', but they remained unconvinced that the concern could be substantiated. In a later study by one of the authors (G. Davies, 'The Impact of Television on the Presentation and Reception of Children's Testimony' (1999) 22 *International Journal of Law and Psychiatry*, p. 241), no evidence was found to support the contention that the reception of children's evidence on video had either a positive or negative effect on jury verdicts, while the availability of the measure clearly did allow younger and less assertive witnesses to testify in court.

Not every witness who uses the live link will be telling the truth, of course, and it is arguably harder to expose a liar without some element of physical confrontation. The literature review published as an Annex to *Speaking Up For Justice* (R. Elliott, 'Vulnerable and Intimidated Witnesses: A Review of the Literature' p. 124) notes the view of the Law Commission that, while it may be easier to tell a lie about a person behind his back than to his face, the desirability of confrontation may be outweighed by other factors such as the effect on the ability of the witness to give his best evidence (Report No. 245, *Evidence in Criminal Proceedings: Hearsay and Related Topics* (1997) at para. 3.35). On balance, the argument for the extension of the use of live link to cases beyond the limited range included in its original, very narrow remit for vulnerable children seems to have been made out.

THE 1991 ACT AND VIDEO RECORDED EVIDENCE IN CHIEF

Statutory framework

Section 54 of the Criminal Justice Act 1991 (which inserted a new s. 32A into the Criminal Justice Act 1988) made provision for the use in evidence in sexual cases and cases involving violence and cruelty of a pre-recorded interview between an adult and a child witness. The same differential age limits applied as to live link (see p. 34) and, again as with live link, the provision applied only to trials on indictment and in youth courts.

Where it was received in evidence, the interview took the place of the child's evidence in chief, and the child was then precluded from giving evidence in chief on any matter which, in the opinion of the court, was adequately dealt with in the recorded testimony. This provision was a deliberate compromise, in that the child still had to appear at the trial as a witness for the party relying on the tape and had to be available for cross-examination by the other parties to the proceedings. Provision was, however, made for a live television link to be used for the purposes of such a cross-examination, so as to spare the child the need to appear in the courtroom itself (1988 Act, s. 32(1)(b), as amended). In a technical sense, the recording was admitted as hearsay evidence, to the extent that the court was being asked to rely on the out-of-court statement of the witness; however the traditional objection to hearsay, that the statement was not subject to cross-examination, was removed. Thus the recording could be said to be on a par with a traditional examination in chief in court, and s. 32A(6) laid down that statements in a recording which was received in evidence were to be treated as if given by the witness in direct oral testimony.

A serious fault in s. 32A, from the point of view of the witness, was that attendance at the trial was likely to be a stressful experience, and the fact that the child's first experience of being questioned at the trial would be of cross-examination arguably made matters worse than when the child was able to be 'warmed up' by the examiner in chief taking him through his evidence. Waiting for the trial was also stressful for the child and, despite measures designed to 'fast-track' cases involving child witnesses, the wait for trial was often a lengthy one. (See G. Davis, L. Hoyano, C.

Keenan, L. Maitland and R. Morgan, *An Assessment of the Admissibility and Sufficiency of Evidence in Child Abuse Prosecutions* (Home Office, 1999).) Other adverse consequences might also flow from the delay: if the child needed therapy, for example, there was a risk that it might be withheld, lest going over relevant events with the therapist might corrupt the child's account.

Section 32A was introduced as an optional method of presenting a child's evidence. There was nothing in the legislation to indicate that it was the preferred method or to stop advocates changing their minds about the best way to present an individual child's testimony at trial. This created enormous difficulty in the preparation of child witnesses for trial, as it was impossible to give a child any assurances as to what would be expected of them in court (J. Plotnikoff and R. Woolfson, 'Evaluation of Witness Service Support for Child Witnesses' in *Children in Court* (Victim Support Research Study 1, 1996)). A process whereby binding rulings could be made in favour of pre-recorded evidence in chief was introduced by the Criminal Procedure and Investigations Act 1996, s. 62, a step in the right direction which has formed the template for the special measures direction in the 1999 Act.

The Pigot Report: a more radical proposal

The Pigot Report (*Report of the Advisory Group on Video Evidence* (Home Office, 1989)) had recommended that the adverse effects on children of appearing as witnesses in cases involving abuse (whether of a sexual or a violent nature) were such that they 'ought never to be required to appear in public as witnesses in the Crown Court, whether in open court or protected by screens or closed circuit television, unless they wish to do so' (para. 2.26). Pigot proposed a pre-trial 'preliminary hearing' at which the child's evidence could be taken in full. A pre-recorded interview with the child would have been admissible as part of the examination in chief, but provision would also have been made for further examination in chief, for cross-examination and re-examination, in informal surroundings but under the control of the trial judge. The accused would have been watching and listening, and able to communicate with his representatives, but would have been unable to be seen or heard by the child. A recording of the preliminary hearing would then have been available to be shown at the trial.

The Pigot recommendation, by removing the necessity for the witness to appear at the trial, would have avoided the problems which afflict the compromise adopted in s. 32A. The Criminal Justice Act 1991 adopted a more limited scheme whereby only evidence in chief could be pre-recorded (sometimes called 'half-Pigot') because of the difficulties that the defence would have encountered in preparing for and executing the cross-examination of an important prosecution witness prior to the trial. This was still a not insignificant gain, however, having among its advantages the production of a fuller and more detailed account than might be forthcoming at trial; the avoidance of any doubt as to how the witness would 'hold up' in examination in chief; the production of an admissible document that could be evaluated by the prosecutor when deciding whether to proceed with the case, and the gathering of information while it was still relatively fresh in the child's mind.

Memorandum of Good Practice

Section 32A contained a requirement that leave of the court be sought to admit a recorded interview. One of the grounds for refusing leave was that 'in the interests of justice' the recording ought not to be admitted. In order to maximise the chances that recordings of interviews with children would be admissible under s. 32A, the Home Office and the Department of Health published the *Memorandum of Good Practice on Video Recorded Interviews with Child Witnesses for Criminal Proceedings* (Home Office and Department of Health, 1992). The Memorandum was directed at police officers and social workers who, when working together in the course of an investigation into whether a child had been the victim of abuse, were the most likely people to be called upon to conduct a video recorded interview which might at a later stage be put in evidence in a criminal trial.

The Memorandum helped the interviewer in two main ways. It gave advice on the sort of interviewing practice which is regarded by experts in the field as most likely to produce the fullest and most dependable account from the child. It also suggested ways of keeping the interview within the bounds of the rules of evidence, particularly rules appertaining to leading questions, hearsay, and the accused's bad character.

The Memorandum itself attracted some criticism, particularly with regard to its preference for conducting the interview within a single session of about an hour's duration (paras. 1.7 and 2.17) — such an interview being intended as roughly the equivalent of a witness statement or first detailed account. These constraints were particularly difficult to satisfy where the child was very young, disabled or traumatised. The interviewer was also in a difficult position in seeking to produce a single recording that was in effect both the witness's first full statement and the witness's final statement on the subject, whereas an advocate conducting an examination in chief in court would be dealing with a witness who had already been through his account, perhaps on a number of occasions. The Memorandum discourages holding a supplementary interview to elicit further information, except where absolutely necessary (paras. 1.11 and 3.41).

There is to be a new Memorandum to cover the wider range of special measures and eligible witnesses who may qualify for their use under the 1999 Act. It is expected that it will be completed by the end of September 2000, in time for the coming into force of the bulk of the special measures including the new provisions for pre-recording examination in chief (*Action for Justice: Implementing the Speaking Up For Justice Report in England and Wales* (Home Office, 1999)).

Advantages and disadvantages of recorded testimony

Section 32A and the *Memorandum of Good Practice* were evaluated in a number of studies. An important early study by G. Davies, C. Wilson, R. Mitchell and J. Milsom, *Videotaping Children's Evidence: An Evaluation* (Home Office, 1995), found that the new measures had met with a broadly favourable response from many of the professionals involved in the criminal justice system, including judges, who considered that there would be a degree of reduction in the stress suffered by child witnesses, but that there was scepticism about a number of matters, including the reduced impact of a recording compared to a child giving evidence live and the problems posed by the child going 'cold' into the cross-examination stage at trial.

Serious practical disadvantages were revealed by a more recent study (A. Wade, A. Lawson and J. Aldridge, 'Stories in Court — Video-taped Interviews and the Production of Children's Testimony' (1998) 10 Child & Family Law Quarterly 179). This found that recordings often lacked specificity in important aspects of the evidence and tended to produce a disjointed narrative compared to the structured and linear examination in chief. If the recording was used in evidence, the defects could be remedied only to the limited extent permitted by s. 32A of submitting the child to examination in chief at trial on matters not adequately dealt with in the recording. This would appear to be a direct consequence of the dual use of the interview as an investigative and as an evidential document. Wade *et al.* also noted that the use of lengthy and unedited recordings in evidence placed increased demands on the attention of those who were required to watch them in the course of the trial: again, the fact of the matter is that examination in chief can be streamlined in a way that a recording frequently cannot.

Among the advantages noted in the Wade study was that the first or 'rapport' phase of a Memorandum interview, where the child is put at ease without being asked to discuss the offence, often made the child seem 'real' in court, and the second or 'free narrative' phase in which the child is encouraged to provide an account of events in his own words was capable of producing a more convincing account than the more structured examination in chief.

The most extensive recent research was done by a team at Bristol University (G. Davies, L. Hoyano, C. Keenan, L. Maitland and R. Morgan, *An Assessment of the Admissibility and Sufficiency of Evidence in Child Abuse Prosecutions* (Home Office, 1999)), which is referred to below as 'the Bristol Research'. The study endorsed the early findings in *Videotaping Children's Evidence: An Evaluation* that s. 32A had bedded down fairly well and that trial judges approached cases involving children from the starting point that it was in the interests of justice to admit their videotaped interviews.

The Bristol Research also identified a number of problems arising out of the 'half-Pigot' compromise solution to the presentation of children's evidence adopted by s. 32A. Amongst these was the difficulty, noted by Wade *et al.*, of reconciling the interviewer's different roles of information-gatherer and preparer of evidence in chief. This tended to lead to the production of evidence which was incomplete, difficult to comprehend or inadmissible: all defects which might be difficult to remedy after the event given the limited scope afforded by the Memorandum for repeat interviewing and by s. 32A for supplementary examination at trial (a procedure which the researchers found was rarely used). The prolonged interval between examination in chief and cross-examination which characterises the 'half-Pigot' system was also said to be capable of undermining the integrity of the child's evidence, and the involvement of the child in the criminal justice system for a long period was regarded as potentially deleterious to his welfare.

In an article based on the Bristol Research (C. Keenan, G. Davis, L. Hoyano and L. Maitland, 'Interviewing Allegedly Abused Children with a View to a Criminal Prosecution' [1999] Crim LR 863), the authors stress that skilled interviewers could sometimes elicit an account from a child in circumstances where the same child would have been unlikely to have disclosed abuse if called upon to do so in court. One of the skills identified was the gentle persistence necessary to prise an account out of a child who might at the very least be diffident or embarrassed, or at the worst severely traumatised or intimidated. An interviewer conducting a Memorandum interview would not necessarily be deterred by a child's initial denial that abuse had occurred, but an advocate in court might find it impossible to persist with examination in chief in similar circumstances. Even where good interviewing practices were adopted, however, the authors found that the end-product was often a recording which was a less than satisfactory substitute for examination in chief given the difficulty of obtaining a complete account at the initial investigative stage and the obstacles in the way of supplementing the evidence at a later stage. The same conclusion is reached in the Bristol Research itself.

Conclusions

An important recommendation arising out of the Bristol Research was that a feature of any new statutory regime should be a degree of flexibility in the extent to which the pre-recorded interview forms the core of the child's evidence in chief. This was an aspect of the scheme recommended by Pigot whereby the interview could be incorporated into the child's evidence in chief without necessarily being the sole or main source. As we shall see, however, the 1999 Act has in fact adopted an approach that is even more inflexible than that of the 1991 legislation. Where an interview is used, the opportunities for supplementary examination in chief are reduced rather than enlarged by s. 27(5) (see p. 67), and the 'primary rule' imposed by s. 21 on the courts when making special measures directions in relation to child witnesses makes it harder to avoid the use of a recorded interview as evidence in chief, even if the recording is not a full or entirely coherent account (see p. 49). The 1999 Act thus imposes more pressure on the interviewer to provide a near-perfect recording at the first attempt, in the face of research findings which suggest that this is simply too much to expect.

For a detailed critique of the problems with the 'half-Pigot' scheme, and the particular difficulties faced by child witnesses, see L. Hoyano, 'Variations on a Theme by Pigot' [2000] Crim LR 252.

Chapter 4
Eligible Witnesses and Procedure for
Special Measures Directions

OVERVIEW

Chapter I of Part II of the Act, as we have already seen (see Chapter 3), makes available a variety of special measures to assist vulnerable and intimidated witnesses to give evidence to the best of their ability. It assists two groups of witnesses. The first group comprises witnesses who are eligible by reason of age or incapacity (s. 16). The second group comprises witnesses eligible because of the fear or distress they are likely to suffer in connection with giving their evidence (s. 17). The accused is specifically excepted from eligibility under either category.

In relation to the first group of witnesses, the special measures which may apply are: screening the witness from the accused; giving evidence by live link; ordering the removal of wigs and gowns while the witness testifies; (in sexual cases and cases involving intimidation) giving evidence in private; video recording of evidence in chief; video recording of cross-examination and re-examination (where evidence in chief is so recorded); examination through intermediary and the provision of aids to communication.

In relation to witnesses eligible only by reason of fear or intimidation, the last two measures are unnecessary and are therefore not made available (s. 18(1)(b)).

The Act provides a procedure (s. 19) for the making of a direction (a 'special measures direction') in relation to any eligible witness which will state which measure or measures are to be adopted. It is envisaged that the direction will be made, wherever possible, in advance of trial so that the witness may be reassured as to the manner in which his evidence will be given. Special measures directions are binding throughout the proceedings, although they may be discharged or varied as the interests of justice dictate (s. 20). Although the court enjoys a considerable measure of discretion in relation to adult witnesses, child witnesses are dealt with by special provisions under which the court is directed, with varying degrees of compulsion, towards specific combinations of measures for the witness. These complex provisions divide child witnesses into three categories, with the choice of the appropriate measure or measures being indicated by the type of offence charged (ss. 21 and 22). The procedures governing the making of special measures directions are not in force at the time of writing. They will be brought into force at the same time as the special measures begin to become available under the Act, i.e., from Autumn 2000 in the Crown Court and the youth court, and from Spring 2003 in the magistrates' courts.

ELIGIBILITY FOR SPECIAL MEASURES

Age and incapacity

Witnesses who are eligible for special measures by reason of their age must be under the age of 17 at the time of the hearing (s. 16(1)(a)). The 'time of the hearing' for this purpose is the time at which the court has to determine eligibility as a condition of the making of a special measures direction (s. 16(3) and 19(2)). Witnesses who are the subject of a special measures direction and who attain the age of 17 during the proceedings attract special provisions (s. 21(8): see p. 53) as do witnesses who are not eligible at the time of the hearing but who made a video-recording of an interview when under 17 (s. 22: see p. 52)).

The first set of witnesses who may qualify on grounds of incapacity are those suffering from mental disorder or otherwise having a significant impairment of intelligence and social functioning (s. 16(2)(a)). The court may not find that a witness falls within this category without first considering any views expressed by the witness (s. 16(4)), as the issue is obviously one on which sensitivity is required. 'Mental disorder' is defined by the Mental Health Act 1983, s. 1(2) to mean mental illness, arrested or incomplete development of mind, psychopathic disorder and any other disorder or disability of mind. The second set of witnesses qualifying on grounds of incapacity are witnesses with a physical disability or disorder (s. 16(2)(b)). Again, any views expressed by the witness must be taken into account before deciding that a witness falls within this category. Advocates who are planning to rely on the evidence of witnesses who may be the subject of a special measures direction should inform themselves of the witness's preference in advance of any hearing at which the issue of special measures might arise (see p. 44).

Eligibility in relation to both types of incapacity arises only where the court considers that the quality of evidence given by the witness is likely to be diminished by reason of the incapacity if no assistance is provided. 'Quality' for this purpose refers to quality in terms of completeness, coherence and accuracy. 'Coherence' refers to a witness's ability in giving evidence to give answers which address the questions put and which can be understood both individually and collectively (s. 16(5)). Although the Act does not expressly say so, it must contemplate the use of special measures where the alternative is that the witness would not be able to give any evidence at all. Some witnesses will not be competent to give evidence without the assistance of an intermediary or an alphabet board, and it is clearly intended that the Act can be invoked in this situation (see p. 139). A more straightforward example of a diminution in quality would be where a competent witness who has a relevant disability might be better able to give a full account of events if, for example, the live link is employed to relieve the anxiety of appearing in court or if pre-recording is used to capture the evidence in full as soon as possible after the events which are the subject of the trial.

Fear and distress

Eligibility may also be established on the ground that the court is satisfied that the quality of evidence given by the witness is likely to be diminished by reason of fear or distress 'in connection with' testifying in the proceedings (s. 17). The causal link required between the fear or distress and the prospect of testifying may be established in any number of ways according to the circumstances of the case. The witness might be concerned at the prospect of confronting the accused, because the crime itself was a shocking one or because the evidence he must give is embarrassing.

Section 17(2) lists a range of circumstances which the court must take into account in deciding eligibility. These include the nature and circumstances of the offence, the age of the witness, and such of the following matters as the court considers to be relevant:

(a)   social and cultural background;
(b)   ethnic origins;
(c)   domestic and employment circumstances;
(d)   religious and political beliefs; and
(e)   any behaviour towards the witness by the accused or those associated with him, including anyone else likely to be an accused or a witness in the case.

The list is not exhaustive. Section 17(2) says that the court must *in particular* take the listed matters into account, but it does not preclude the consideration of other matters. It is still useful, however, in that decisions based on the listed circumstances will not be subject to challenge on the ground that irrelevant matters have been considered. Section 17(3) also requires the court to have regard to any views expressed by the witness.

A recurring theme in the debates on the Act was that, although everyone finds giving evidence stressful, it is not intended that s. 17 should be available to all. The intention behind the provision is not to facilitate a mass exodus from the witness box of every witness who is affected by a measure of apprehension, even though it can, with some justification, be said by every witness that the quality of his evidence in terms of the stipulated matters of coherence, completeness and accuracy (s. 16(5)) might improve if he were allowed to take advantage of one or more of the special measures. It remains to be seen how selective it is possible to be, given the inclusive terms in which the section is couched.

Because it will be at least arguable that s. 17 applies in many (if not all) cases, the implications in terms both of expense and forward planning are enormous. On the positive side, it may facilitate the prosecution of cases in which witnesses in fear currently decline to attend the trial altogether, and where the prosecution is enabled to continue, if at all, only by reliance on pre-trial statements admissible under the hearsay provisions of the Criminal Justice Act 1988, s. 23. If such witnesses can be persuaded, by the availability of special measures, to undergo cross-examination (whether behind a screen, in a cleared court, on video or by live link), a resultant conviction will be more likely to be appeal-proof than one obtained in reliance on the 1988 Act, under which there is no cross-examination as such (see p. 30). If the witness's evidence is unsupported, there is even a possibility that the use of s. 23 contravenes Article 6 of the European Convention on Human Rights (*Thomas* [1998] Crim LR 887).

Complainants in respect of sexual cases (defined by s. 62) enjoy a presumption of eligibility under s. 17. This reflects a view that it will always be reasonable to assume that a high level of apprehension and distress is involved in giving evidence in such circumstances. The presumption applies 'in relation to ... proceedings' where the witness is testifying in relation to 'that offence and any other offences' (s. 17(4)). Thus, for example, if the witness is testifying about an indecent assault alleged to have been committed against her and also another offence such as false imprisonment, her eligibility extends to her evidence in relation to false imprisonment. It does not seem to matter if she is not the alleged victim in relation to the further offence. If the indecent assault charge is reduced to common assault, the presumption does not operate at all. The witness can inform the court that she prefers not to be regarded as eligible by virtue of the presumption. Where such a preference is expressed, it would appear that the court should still consider whether the witness is eligible without it, but in most cases the outcome is likely to be that no special measures direction is made.

Other witnesses

Not every witness who may be assisted by special measures will necessarily qualify for them. It may be hard, for example, to stretch the statutory words so as to invoke special measures for an elderly and somewhat confused resident of a nursing home who is not suffering any specific mental disorder and who is not particularly upset at the prospect of coming to court. This is so even if it is clear that her evidence is likely to be of better quality if a special measure, such as the pre-recording of her evidence in chief, is employed. The enhancement of the quality of a witness's evidence if special measures are available is a necessary but not a sufficient condition for the use of such measures by adult witnesses under the Act.

The accused

The accused is the only witness excluded from consideration in each of the categories of eligibility (ss. 16(1) and 17(1)). The reasons given in *Speaking Up For Justice*, the Report of the Interdepartmental Working Group on the Treatment of Vulnerable or Intimidated Witnesses in the Criminal Justice System (Home Office, 1998) are unconvincing. The Report states (para. 3.28) that the accused has the protection of other measures, such as the right to special safeguards at interview, and the right to legal representation and to refuse to testify at trial. However, he has no equivalent assistance to that afforded by special measures directions to help him to give the best evidence at his trial, which was the object of the exercise in relation to other witnesses. Nor is it good enough to state, as the Report goes on to do, that 'many of the special measures' are designed to protect witnesses from intimidation by the accused, who is not likely to require protection from anybody else in court. This does not explain why the accused cannot avail himself of pre-recorded evidence, the advantages of which go far beyond such protection and include the preservation of recollections which are fresh in the mind, and the reduction of the stress associated with giving evidence in court (see pp. 28–29). The decision of the European Court of Human Rights in *T* v *UK and V* v *UK* [2000] Crim LR 187 makes it likely that the Act will have to be amended so as to make special measures available to young defendants, but change should not stop there. If A and B both have a learning disability, and B's answer to a complaint of sexual assault made by A is that A was the aggressor and he the victim, why should A be the only one to benefit from special measures simply because it has been decided to prosecute B? If the Act is serious in its desire to ensure that evidence given in court is of the best possible quality, it is utterly invidious to exclude the accused from access to special measures.

AVAILABILITY OF SPECIAL MEASURES

It was always envisaged that special measures would be phased in. In *Speaking Up For Justice* the suggestion was made that certain special measures could be made available to witnesses with incapacity on the same terms as they are currently available to children, and that they could then at a later stage be extended to fearful and intimidated witnesses (para. 8.48). Instead the legislation covers all three classes of eligible witnesses, but s. 18(2) provides that courts must wait to be notified by the Secretary of State that a particular special measure is available in their area. This, according to the Explanatory Notes accompanying the Act, allows for 'phased implementation of the measures'. (The Notes accompanying the original Bill included a reference to the need for piloting too, but this appears to have been dropped.)

   Section 18(5) also allows the Secretary of State wide powers by order to alter the special measures available to eligible witnesses in any of the categories, either by modifying the provisions relating to the measure itself (s. 18(5)(a)), or by making a measure available to one category that is currently available only to another (s. 18(5)(b)(i)). It is also possible for an entirely new measure to be brought on stream in this way (s. 18(5)(b)(ii)) or for an existing one to be removed (s. 18(5)(c)). Thus there is considerable scope for modifying the statutory scheme that appears on the face of the Act, and which may never be brought into force, for all courts, in the form it currently takes. The Act does not give the Home Secretary power to add to the classes of eligible witness so that, for example, a decision that the accused should no longer be excluded from eligibility would have to be expressed in amending legislation.

SPECIAL MEASURES DIRECTIONS

The expression 'special measures direction' means a direction under s. 19 of the Act (s. 19(5)). The direction is the vehicle for making a particular measure or measures applicable to an eligible witness. It may come about as a result of an application by a party (s. 19(1)(a)) or because the court of its own motion has raised the issue (s. 19(1)(b)). Rules of court may be made to prevent the renewal of unsuccessful applications except where there has been a material change of circumstances (s. 20(6)(b)). In the case of an adult witness, the court's discretion is broad and is essentially constrained only by the need to hold a balance between the needs of the witness and of the party for the benefit of whom cross-examination is conducted (s. 19(2) and (3)). In the case of a child, the special provisions in s. 21 (see p. 48) come into play and point the court in the direction of suitable measures. The measures which s. 21 deems to be appropriate are then regarded, by virtue of s. 21(2), as measures which the court has itself selected using the criteria identified in s. 19(2), and the court incorporates them in the direction it makes under that provision.

Section 20(6) permits rules of court to be made to provide, *inter alia*, for expert evidence to be received in connection with an application for special measures (s. 20(6)(c)) and for the way in which confidential or sensitive information is treated in connection with an application for special measures and in particular its being disclosed to, or withheld from, a party to the proceedings (s. 20(6)(d)).

The making of the direction involves a formal process. The direction itself must specify particulars of the provision made by the direction in respect of each special measure which is to apply to the witness's evidence (s. 19(4)). It would seem to follow that the direction must be in documentary form. When a special measures direction is given, or an application for a direction is refused, the court must state its reasons for doing so in open court and a magistrates' court must enter those reasons in the register of its proceedings (s. 20(5)).

Venue

In the Crown Court, it is envisaged that an application for special measures would be considered at a plea and directions hearing or at a separate hearing following shortly afterwards (*Speaking Up For Justice*, para. 7.7). In magistrates' courts a similar procedure for pre-trial hearings will need to be developed, possibly out of the existing procedure for pre-trial review. Procedures are already in place in the Crown Court for dealing with the special measures made available to children under earlier legislation (see p. 33). These procedures are rightly regarded as of great importance in focusing the attention of the relevant professionals on any special needs a witness may have. The training package 'A Case for Balance', prepared by the NSPCC and approved by the Judicial Studies Board, includes a video which demonstrates the need for careful planning not only in relation to the sort of provisions which will in future amount to 'special measures' under the Act, but also with regard, for example, to the witness's need for planned breaks while giving evidence.

The same approach is advocated in the *Young Witness Pack* which helps children prepare for court under the previous legislation to assist them in giving their best evidence. This includes the handbook *Preparing Young Witnesses for Court (A Handbook for Child Witness Supporters)* (1998), which is produced by Childline and the NSPCC; this stresses 'the need for greater certainty in planning how the child will give evidence'. It encourages those who support child witnesses through the trial process to 'encourage as many issues as possible to be resolved at the plea and directions hearing', on the ground that '[d]ecisions delayed until the trial make it impossible to describe to the child with any certainty what is going to happen at court'. In addition to the cluster of issues surrounding special measures, the handbook instances as possible matters which require forward planning:

(a) refreshing the child's memory of his or her statement or video taped interview;
(b) minimising the child's waiting time at court;
(c) co-ordinating arrangements at the court building;
(d) deciding the order of witnesses;
(e) anticipating the need for breaks in the child's testimony;
(f) anticipating whether the child may be asked to demonstrate intimate touching on his or her body, and providing an alternative method of demonstration;
(g) withholding the child's address from being given in open court.

Under the 1999 Act the wider range of potentially eligible witnesses will generate still more issues of this kind, which are relevant to the special provision to be made for a witness without themselves being 'special measures'. Insofar as some of the decisions surrounding issues of this kind will require the involvement of the court, it would seem sensible to dispose of them at the same time as the making of a special measures direction is under consideration. The current version of the *Plea and Directions Hearing: supplementary pre-trial checklist for cases involving young witnesses (Archbold*, Appendix C-2) provides a list to assist the judge in dealing with such matters as the use of video evidence, memory refreshing, preparation of the witness for court, planned breaks for the witness while giving evidence, court visits and case management. The judge cannot complete the checklist without first being satisfied that all relevant information has been made available, and the checklist says that it is 'vital' that advocates come to the hearing with full instructions including all relevant information from and about the young witness. This procedure, or something very similar, is bound to have to be adapted for the adult witnesses who qualify for special measures under the 1999 Act, and it is vital to the success of the Act's overall strategy that decisions made in relation to vulnerable and intimidated witnesses at the preliminary hearing are well-informed.

The Code of Conduct for the Bar of England and Wales (1998) states (Annex F, para. 14.2) that, if properly remunerated, the barrister originally briefed in a case should attend all plea and directions hearings. If this is not possible, he should take all reasonable steps to ensure that the barrister who does appear is conversant with the case and prepared to make informed decisions affecting the trial. The lack of proper funding for advocates at the hearings has been a bone of contention in the past, but it is to be hoped that the 1999 Act will not be prevented from achieving its aims for want of funding.

It may be that there is no objection from any of the parties to the proceedings to the use of special measures to assist a witness in giving evidence. In such a case, and provided that no other measures of the type considered above by which witnesses may also be supported are likely to be controversial, there is no need for a hearing. Section 20(6)(a) therefore provides that rules of court may make provision for uncontested applications for special measures to be determined without a hearing.

Adult witnesses

The court in effect has to determine two preliminary issues:

(a)   is the witness eligible under s. 16 or s. 17?
(b)   is the special measure available under s. 18?

Assuming that these conditions are satisfied, the making of a special measures direction requires the making of two further decisions:

(a)   Would the measure, on its own or in combination with other special measures, be likely to improve the quality of the witness's evidence (s. 19(2)(a))?
(b)   If so, which measures, or combination, would be likely to maximise the quality of that evidence (s. 19(2)(b))?

The court is then bound to give a direction under s. 19 providing for the measures thus identified to be applied to the evidence given by the witness. In deciding both what would improve and what would maximise the quality of the witness's evidence, the court is bound to take account of any views expressed by the witness (s. 19(3)(a)) and also of whether the measure or measures might tend to inhibit the evidence being effectively tested by a party to the proceedings (s. 19(3)(b)). The last concern requires some elaboration, for the Act cannot be taken to suggest that the use of a special measure could without more be an obstacle to effective cross-examination. Although all the measures to an extent affect the conditions under which cross-examination takes place, equally all are designed to preserve the essentials of a proper challenge to a witness's evidence. Thus it cannot be good enough simply to say that a screen or live link removes the element of confrontation with the accused, that the use of an intermediary or an alphabet board impedes the normal flow of question and answer or that pre-recorded cross-examination means that the witness will never be seen by the jury. There would have to be some reason why the measure, applied to a particular witness, would give rise to some specified difficulty over and above that which may be said to be inherent in its use in every case and which cannot be regarded as an inhibition for this purpose. Previous attempts to introduce pre-recorded cross-examination foundered because of concerns that the defence case would not be sufficiently developed for the witness to be effectively cross-examined in advance of trial (see pp. 34–35). If those concerns now resurface as arguments that pre-recorded cross-examination inhibits effective testing, the option to use the new provision will be stifled.

Preserved powers of the court

Section 19(6) preserves the court's power to make orders or give leave otherwise than by virtue of the Act. Where the witness is not eligible for special measures, the full powers of the court are preserved (s. 19(6)(a)). The accused is one such witness, at least until the anomaly identified above is rectified, so recourse must be had to the court's powers outside the Act to provide such assistance as the court considers it appropriate for him to receive. Once the provisions of the Act are up and running for other witnesses, judges might decide to take steps of their own volition to make orders for the use of the Act's special measures by the accused in appropriate cases and this might fairly be described as within the court's inherent powers. If this is wrong and the Act cannot be plundered to assist an accused person in this way, the court must at least have inherent jurisdiction over those measures previously regulated by the common law, such as the use of screens and intermediaries. This would not, however, give access to live link or to pre-recorded testimony, which have always been regulated by statute.

Where the witness *is* eligible for special measures, s. 19(6)(b) applies. This provides that the Act's provisions in relation to special measures do not affect the powers of the court to make an order or to give leave of any description in relation to an eligible witness where 'the order is made or the leave is given otherwise than by reason of the fact that the witness is an eligible witness'. The Act provides an example of what is meant. A foreign language interpreter may be required for an eligible witness, and the powers of the court to involve the services of such a person are not affected by the Act.

Child witnesses

Section 21 divides child witnesses into two basic categories:

(a)   child witnesses 'in need of special protection';
(b)   all other child witnesses.

Child witnesses in need of special protection are divided into two subcategories according to whether the proceedings relate to any of the following offences:

(a) offences within s. 35(b) to (d) (kidnapping, false imprisonment, an offence under the Child Abduction Act 1984, s. 1 or the Children and Young Persons Act 1933, s. 1 or any other offence involving an assault on, or injury or a threat of injury to, any person);

(b) sexual offences within s. 35(3)(a) (any offence under the Sexual Offences Acts 1956 and 1967, the Indecency with Children Act 1960, the Criminal Law Act 1977, s. 54 or the Protection of Children Act 1978).

Child witnesses not in need of special protection: primary rule and exceptions

Child witnesses who are not in need of special protection are subject to the 'primary rule', which means that the court must give a special measures direction providing:

(a) for a video recording made with a view to its admission as evidence in chief (a 'relevant recording' to be so used) (s. 21(3)(a)); and

(b) for any evidence given by the witness otherwise than by means of a video recording (whether in chief or otherwise) to be given by means of a live link (s. 21(3)(b)). (In rare cases where the parties agree to admit the video recording without cross-examination under s. 27(4)(ii) there is no evidence given by the witness which is not video recorded, so that the second part of the primary rule has no application to such cases.)

The primary rule is subject to three limitations:

(a) the special measure in question must be 'available', in the sense that the Secretary of State has notified the court under s. 18(2) that arrangements have been made for its use in the area where the proceedings are likely to take place (s. 21(4)(a));

(b) a video recording cannot be used if it is not in the interests of justice to admit it (ss. 21(4)(b) and 27(2): see p. 63);

(c) the rule does not apply to the extent that the court is satisfied that compliance with the primary rule would not be likely to maximise the quality of the witness's evidence so far as practicable (whether because the application to that evidence of one or more other special measures available in relation to the witness would have that result or for any other reason) (s. 21(4)(c)).

The third limitation is of particular interest in cases where the video recording is not the best evidence a child might be able to give, perhaps because it is disjointed or because relevant questions have not been put. Research suggests that these are common failings of video recorded interviews, and that in consequence it is undesirable to restrict a prosecutor to presenting evidence by video alone (see G. Davis, L. Hoyano, C. Keenan, L. Maitland and R. Morgan, *An Assessment of the Admissibility and Sufficiency of Evidence in Child Abuse Prosecutions* (Home Office, 1999) at p. 84). Section 21(4)(c) ensures that the court's hands are not tied if the recorded evidence fails to live up to expectations. If, on the other hand, the video recording is one on which the prosecution is content to rely, s. 21 does not deny the court the flexibility to go further than the primary rule requires. Pre-recorded cross-examination might be a superior alternative to live link in cases where the witness fears coming to court, or where there is a real risk that the witness's recollection of relevant events will have faded by the time of trial.

Nothing in the primary rule prevents the court from directing in favour of other compatible measures to accompany the specified measures, for example to use of an intermediary or the provision of aids to communication.

Child witnesses in need of special protection: offences within s. 35(b) to (d)

Where a child witness is in need of special protection because the offence is one involving an assault or one of the other offences specified in s. 35(b)–(d) of the Act, s. 21(5) provides that the court may not invoke the third exception to the primary rule. The result is that the evidence of a child witness in an assault case *must* be given by video recorded evidence in chief, provided only that such a video exists, the measure is available and it is not contrary to the interests of justice to use it. Any cross-examination or re-examination must be by live link unless the measure is unavailable or the court has ordered in favour of pre-recorded cross-examination.

It is not possible to list with any certainty all of the offences to which this rule may apply. This is because the offences in this category include those in s. 35(3)(d) ('any offence which involves an assault on, or injury or a threat of injury to, any person'), so that all of the problems identified in relation to 'threat of injury' in the context of s. 35 apply (see p. 83). The difficulty arises because the courts, when construing this phrase in judgments dealing with the Criminal Justice Act 1988, ss. 32 and 32A, declined to limit it to offences where a threat is part of the *actus reus*. Instead, threat was said to be used in the sense of risk, as in 'there is a threat of rain this afternoon' (*Lee* [1996] 2 Cr App R 266). In this sense, almost any offence may, depending on the circumstances in which it is committed, pose a threat of injury. In *Lee* itself, a child witnessed an act of arson by his father, by which the safety of the son was endangered. The expressed policy of the courts in these earlier decisions was that measures which sought to protect children should be given a broad, inclusive reading (*McAndrew-Bingham* [1999] 1 WLR 1897). Because s. 32 and 32A, which governed the power of the court to permit a child to give evidence by live link or by pre-recorded evidence in chief, were of very limited application, the effect of *Lee* and *McAndrew-Bingham* was that children who might otherwise have had no access to special measures were given the opportunity to use them. It by no means follows that the same broad reading should be given in the context of s. 21(5) of the 1999 Act. The effect would only be to bring more children within the 'special protection' category, for no obvious benefit; particularly as the person who must be exposed to the 'threat of injury' by the offence does not have to be the child or even anyone known to the child. The court has the *power* to make the same measures available to a child who is *not* in need of special protection so, given that the statutory words are unclear, it might be better to give 'threat of injury' a narrow meaning. This would enable the court to adopt the 'primary rule' (see p. 49) in relation to the child witness, which allows more flexibility.

Child witnesses in need of special protection: sexual offences within s. 35(3)(a)

Where a child witness is in need of special protection because the case is a sexual one, not only does s. 21(4)(c) prevent the court from invoking the third exception to the primary rule, but also s. 21(6) requires the court, if it gives a direction to admit a video recording as evidence in chief, to direct that pre-recorded cross-examination and re-examination (special measures under s. 28) shall also apply, subject to availability (s. 21(7)(a)). The exception is where cross-examination will be by the accused in person.

It thus appears that a child who has witnessed a minor indecent assault on a stranger is to be accorded a higher level of automatic protection than a child who witnesses the murder of a close relative. Of course, in the indecency case the child might not be an obvious candidate for a video recorded interview, and if no such interview takes place then pre-recorded cross-examination is not an option: it can be resorted to only where evidence in chief is presented in the form of a recording (s. 21(6), and see also s. 28(1)). In the murder example, the court would not take much persuading to opt for pre-recorded cross-examination where appropriate.

A child who has witnessed or who is alleged to have suffered a rape or other sexual assault will not always wish to be released from the obligation to testify at trial. Section 21(7)(b) therefore provides a limitation on the duty of the court in s. 21(6), which is that the court need not direct in favour of pre-recorded cross-examination if the witness has informed the court that he does not want that special measure to apply to him. To allow a child to opt out of the provision makes good sense in that it gives the child a feeling of having some say in the allocation of measures which are ultimately for his or her benefit. However it is odd that the same child has no right to opt out of video recorded examination in chief, even if he would very much prefer to give evidence live in court, confronting the accused in the traditional way. If this is the child's preference then, particularly if it is thought that he would make a good witness, there does not seem any obvious reason for denying him this option.

Cross-examination by the accused in person is an exceptional case because the provisions for pre-recorded cross-examination stipulate that the recording be made 'in the absence of the accused' (s. 28(2)). Although provision is also made for the accused to follow the proceedings (s. 28(2)(b)), this is on the supposition that he will be represented rather than representing himself. It is far from apparent in what circumstances a child who attracts the special provisions of s. 21 might also fall to be cross-examined by the accused in person, given that the definition of 'sexual offence' is taken from s. 35, which prevents the accused from cross-examining a child complainant or witness in such a case (see p. 83).

Expiry of special measures directions in relation to children

The special provisions for children do not necessarily endure until the end of the proceedings in which the child is a witness. Section 21(8) provides that a special measures direction given in relation to a child witness who is an eligible witness by reason only that he is under the age of 17 ceases to have effect at the time when the witness attains that age, except where the child has already begun to give evidence in the proceedings. A further exception is provided by s. 21(9), which applies where the direction has provided for the admission of recorded evidence in chief or cross-examination. In that case, the direction continues to have effect in the normal way under s. 20(1) (see p. 53) until the proceedings are over or the court discharges or varies the direction. Under s. 21(9)(b), a witness whose cross-examination is pre-recorded cannot benefit from this provision unless he is still aged under 17 when the recording is made. Witnesses whose special measures directions come to an end before the proceedings are finished may be the subject of further directions as appropriate under s. 19 or, if they are 'qualifying witnesses' by virtue of being aged under 17 when their evidence in chief was recorded, under s. 22 (see below). The expiry of a special measures direction may, in some cases, result in a witness having to give evidence in a manner which he has not anticipated having to do or being left in doubt as to what will happen. The courts should strive as far as possible to ensure that the witness is given as clear an indication as possible about what will happen, and that any reasonable expectations he may have are not without good reason defeated.

Witnesses over 17: 'qualifying witnesses'

A witness who was under the age of 17 when his evidence in chief was recorded but who is over that age by the time of the hearing is termed a 'qualifying witness' (s. 22) and qualifies for much of the protection afforded to child witnesses by s. 21 (see p. 48). Section 16(3) applies, so the 'time of the hearing' for this purpose is the time at which a special measures direction is made under s. 19(2). Qualifying witnesses, like child witnesses, come in two basic categories: qualifying witnesses in need of special protection, and all other qualifying witnesses. The grounds for affording special protection are identical with those applicable to child witnesses (see pp. 48–49). The provisions are as follows:

(a)   For qualifying witnesses, the primary rule is that evidence in chief shall be given by means of the relevant recording (s. 22(2)(a)). However, no special provision is made for evidence given by a qualifying witness in the proceedings otherwise than by means of a video recording. Thus the court appears to have a discretion in the matter, whereas in relation to child witnesses the primary rule (see p. 49) requires the use of the live link. As to the use of the recording, the limitations in s. 21(4) apply to the same extent as with child witnesses, i.e., there are exceptions where the measure is unavailable, it is not in the interests of justice to admit the recording or the court is satisfied that to admit the recording would not maximise the quality of the qualifying witness's evidence.

(b)   For qualifying witnesses in need of special protection where the offence charged is within s. 35(b) to (d), the primary rule is again restricted to the requirement that a relevant recording be received: no special provision is made for cross-examination. As with child witnesses, the recording cannot be rejected on the ground that to admit it would not maximise the quality of the child's evidence. Qualifying witnesses in need of special protection where the offence charged is a sexual offence within the meaning of s. 35(3)(a) are subject to the same provisions as for child witnesses, i.e., evidence in chief should be by means of a video recording and cross-examination and re-examination should also be pre-recorded, subject to the exceptions already stated in relation to children (which include the right of the witness to opt out of pre-recording of cross-examination).

Binding effect of special measures directions: s. 20(1)

The normal rule is that a special measures direction has binding effect from the time it is made until the end of the trial (s. 20(1)). If there is more than one accused, the direction endures until the proceedings in relation to each of them are over, whether by being determined or abandoned. The normal rule does not apply to a direction which ceases to have effect during the proceedings as a result of s. 21(8); this applies where a witness, eligible by virtue only of his youth, attains the age of 17 without having begun to give his evidence.

Variation and discharge

Section 20(2) gives the court an ongoing power to discharge or vary a special measures direction on the grounds that it is in the interests of justice to do so. A party can apply for variation or discharge of the direction, but must show that there has been a material change of circumstances since the direction was made, or since the last application under s. 20(2). The court is not so restricted, and can vary or discharge of its own motion at any time. However, the powers of the court will not be exercised lightly: the special measures direction is intended to create a measure of certainty for vulnerable and intimidated witnesses, so there is a strong 'interest of justice' in maintaining the status quo once a direction has been given.

The rule-making provisions of 20(6)(a) and (b) (see p. 45) apply to the procedure for variation and discharge as they apply to the original application, with the result that rules of court may make provision for uncontested applications to be disposed of without a hearing, and for preventing the renewal of an unsuccessful application except where there has been a material change of circumstances. The rule-making provisions with regard to evidence also apply, with the result that rules can be made to allow for the reception of expert evidence and the reception of sensitive material (s. 20(6)(c) and (d)).

The sections of the Act dealing with the special measures of live link, pre-recorded evidence in chief and pre-recorded cross-examination each contain specific and limited powers to vary the effect of a special measures direction which stipulates for the use of the particular measure. Section 24(2) and (3) allows the court, where a special measures direction has provided for the witness to give evidence by live link, to grant permission for a witness to give evidence in some other fashion. Section 27(4) to (7) provides a mechanism for excluding a video recording after a special measures direction has been made which provides for it to be admitted as evidence in chief (see p. 66). Section 28(4) to (6) provides a similar mechanism for excluding a recording of a cross-examination which is the subject of a special measures direction (see p. 73). In relation to these three sets of provisions, s. 20(4) provides that nothing in any of them affects the overarching power of the court to vary or discharge the original special measures direction. Thus the court, faced with circumstances which in its opinion make it undesirable in the interests of justice to continue in the fashion dictated by the original direction, may have more than one route open to it to arrive at a more satisfactory conclusion. Section 20(4) forestalls the argument that the court should content itself with the limited powers conferred by ss. 24, 27 and 28; if it is minded to change the original direction, the option is always open. If, however, the court prefers the more specific power, it is not clear what the impact of this course of action is on the original direction. The granting of permission under s. 24(2) for a witness to give evidence otherwise than by means of the live link appears, in substance if not in form, to be a variation of the original direction.

Section 20(5) provides that the court must state its reasons in open court when varying or discharging a direction, or when refusing an application for variation or discharge, and a magistrates' court must cause the reasons to be entered in the register of its proceedings. The same duty applies when a special measures direction is first made or an application refused (see p. 45).

Warnings

Where evidence is received in accordance with a special measures direction, the judge must give the jury such warning (if any) as he considers necessary to ensure that the accused is not prejudiced by the fact that the direction was given (s. 32). Such warnings are commonplace in relation to the use of video, live link and screens for children (see *X, Y and Z* (1990) 91 Cr App R 36 at p. 40). The judge generally points out that it is the practice to adopt such methods in order to prevent the witness being intimidated by the surroundings and that the jury should not hold it against the accused. If, however, the measure has specifically been adopted in order to minimise the distress experienced by a witness who is fearful of confronting the accused, or who claims to have been intimidated, a different, and particularly careful, form of words may be required.

Chapter 5
The Eight Special Measures

OVERVIEW

As explained in Chapters 3 and 4, the Act lists eight measures in respect of which a special measures direction may be made.

For all eligible witnesses

The following measures are available for all eligible witnesses:

(a)   screening the witness from the accused (s. 23);

(b)   giving evidence by live link (s. 24);

(c)   ordering the removal of wigs and gowns while the witness testifies (s. 25);

(d)   (in sexual cases and cases involving intimidation) giving evidence in private (s. 26);

(e)   video recording of evidence in chief (s. 27);

(f)   video recording of cross-examination and re-examination (where evidence in chief is so recorded) (s. 28).

For witnesses eligible on grounds of youth and incapacity only

The following measures are available only for witnesses eligible on the grounds of youth and incapacity:

(a)   examination through intermediary (s. 29);

(b)   provision of aids to communication (s. 30).

General

Each of the eight sections identified above describes the special measure to which it applies, and also lays down any special conditions applicable to the selection of that measure over and above the general considerations of eligibility, availability and the maximisation of the quality of the evidence which the court has to consider when making a special measures direction (see Chapter 4).

This chapter examines the content of these eight sections and related provisions, and some of the advantages and disadvantages of selecting each of the measures. It should not be forgotten that some of the measures can be combined (for example, the removal of wigs and gowns could be combined with the use of a screen) while others represent alternatives (for example, a screen is an alternative to the live link). When making a special measures direction, s. 19 directs the court to select the measure or *combination* of measures which it considers most likely to maximise the quality of an eligible witness's evidence (see p. 47).

SCREENS: s. 23

Section 23(1) stipulates that a special measures direction may provide for the witness, while giving testimony or being sworn in court, to be prevented by means of a 'screen or other arrangement' from seeing the accused. Whatever arrangement is adopted, however, s. 23(2) provides that it must not prevent the witness from being able to see, or from being seen by, whoever is trying the case (including, if there is one, the jury), legal representatives acting in the case and any interpreter or other person appointed to assist the witness (which would include an intermediary: see p. 75). Section 23(3) provides for the situation where a party has more than one legal representative and stipulates that it is enough that the witness is able to see and be seen by one of them. In a trial involving a number of defendants, this may still pose logistical problems in smaller courtrooms.

When is a screen appropriate?

Screens have been in use for some time as a measure to protect child witnesses from eye-contact with the accused. It appears that they were first used by Judge Pigot QC at the Old Bailey in 1987 (J. Spencer and R. Flin, *The Evidence of Children: The Law and the Psychology* (Blackstone Press, 2nd ed. (1993) at p. 100) and were approved by the Court of Appeal in *X, Y and Z* (1990) 91 Cr App R 36. In that case, the defence had consistently objected to the screens as being prejudicial to the accused. Lord Lane CJ held:

> The learned judge has the duty on this and on all other occasions of endeavouring to see that justice is done. Those are high-sounding words. What it really means is, he has got to see that the system operates fairly: fairly not only to the defendants but also to the prosecution and also to the witnesses. Sometimes he has to make decisions as to where the balance of fairness lies. He came to the conclusion that in these circumstances the necessity of trying to ensure that these children would be able to give evidence outweighed any possible prejudice to the defendants by the erection of the screen. This court agrees with him in that view.

At common law it was also possible for screens to be used to protect vulnerable adult witnesses, although the authorities conflicted as to the basis on which this could be achieved. In *Foster* [1995] Crim LR 333 the Court of Appeal applied essentially the same test as in *X, Y and Z*, while in *Cooper and Shaub* [1994] Crim LR 531 the court's preference was for the use of screens for adults only in 'the most exceptional cases' because of the risk of prejudice involved. In *Speaking Up For Justice*, the Report of the Interdepartmental Working Group on the Treatment of Vulnerable or Intimidated Witnesses in the Criminal Justice System (Home Office, 1998), the Working Group, having considered the authorities, recommended that screens be available on a statutory basis to assist all vulnerable and intimidated witnesses (Recommendation 38, para. 8.17).

Under the 1999 Act, the court has much the same role to play as that assigned to it in *X, Y and Z*. The witnesses in respect of whom the measure is sought are under the new regime unlikely to be children, given the presumptions in favour of pre-recorded evidence and live link in s. 21 (see p. 49). Adult witnesses most likely to benefit from screening are those who claim to have been intimidated by the accused or to have suffered a particularly distressing crime at his hands. A screen may also be the best way of enabling a witness to give his best evidence if he has a disability and there is particular concern about the likely effect on him of a confrontation with the accused. The judge or magistrates hearing the application for special measures should take account of the 'balance of fairness' referred to in the judgment of Lord Lane CJ when weighing the positive effect the screen may have on the quality of the witness's evidence against any risk that the screen might inhibit the effective testing of the witness's evidence (s. 19(3)).

The 'possible prejudice' to the accused to which Lord Lane CJ referred is not confined to the testing of the evidence, of course, but may be said also to arise if the jury concludes that the judge has ordered the screen because the accused is a bad man who may behave improperly towards the witness. The use of a screen in a jury trial is likely to be accompanied with the warning which s. 32 requires to be given to ensure that the accused is not prejudiced where evidence has been given in accordance with a special measures direction (see p. 54).

'Other arrangement'

Section 23 contemplates the use of some 'arrangement' other than a screen to prevent the witness seeing the accused. In the old case of *Smellie* (1919) 14 Cr App 128, S's daughter was called to give evidence of ill-treatment by her father. S was ordered to sit on the stairs leading out of the dock, out of sight of the child, while she gave her evidence. Although the Court of Criminal Appeal held that there was no objection to this procedure in any case where the judge considered that the presence of the accused would intimidate a witness, it is clearly potentially a more prejudicial course of action than the erection of a screen. Not only does it focus the attention of the jury on the accused as the likely source of the witness's discomfiture, it also prevents them from assessing his reaction to the evidence the witness gives and (potentially at least) makes it harder for the accused to have proper contact with those responsible for representing him without drawing attention to himself in a way which appears to run counter to the notion of hiding him in the first place. In *T* v *UK and V* v *UK* [2000]

Crim LR 187 the European Court of Human Rights considered that the inability of a young defendant to participate effectively in his trial was a breach of Article 6 of the Convention, and that the fact that V's legal representatives were 'within whispering distance' was of no avail if the defendant felt too inhibited, in the tense atmosphere of the courtroom and under public scrutiny, to communicate with them. One can imagine that the accused might also feel considerably inhibited by being placed out of sight of the witness, though much might depend on the layout of the court. Ordering the accused to move no doubt counts as an 'arrangement' to which s. 23(1) applies, so that a court has power under the Act to resort to such a measure. Nevertheless it is submitted that it should be seen as a last resort.

Screens versus live link

The use of screens pre-dates the introduction of the live link. It may be that the eventual introduction of live link equipment in all courts (including magistrates' courts which have not so far been able to utilise live link) will mean that the use of screens can be phased out. It appears that screens were originally regarded as a temporary measure pending the full implementation of the live link (J. Morgan and J. Plotnikoff, 'Children as Victims of Crime: Procedure at Court' in J. Spencer, G. Nicholson, R. Flin and R. Bull (eds) *Children's Evidence in Legal Proceedings: An International Perspective* (Cambridge, 1989)). On the other hand, the screen allows the magistrates or jury a greater measure of contact with the witness and many advocates subscribe to the theory that this encourages the establishment of a rapport in a way which the live link does not. It may be that this is not, by itself, a matter which should count for much in deciding between screen and live link: it will be remembered that the research evidence which was considered in Chapter 3 did not support the theory that live link impairs communication. A screen may, however, be the better method in any case where the trier of fact needs a clear impression of the size and bearing of the witness. This was particularly relevant in the past with regard to children, but might continue to be of significance where the witness is alleged to have been easily intimidated, or where the crime is a sexual one and it is alleged that the complainant was overpowered by the accused. If an advocate feels that the jury will receive a more accurate physical impression of the witness as the result of the use of a screen rather than live link this is pertinent to the question, posed by s. 19(2), of which measure or measures are most likely to maximise the quality of the witness's evidence. (It may be that the witness will also express a view on the subject, which is likely to be an important consideration.) In *Speaking Up For Justice*, the Working Group noted that the main advantages were that screens are flexible, easy to use and permit both the witnesses and the defendant to stay in court. It may therefore be that they will continue to be used as an alternative to live link.

Confrontation and the right to a fair trial

It must follow from the approval in *X, Y and Z* (1990) 91 Cr App R 36 of the use of screens where the balance of justice so requires that there is no right in English common law for the accused physically to confront his accusers. Whether the fair trial provisions in Article 6 of the European Convention on Human Rights are capable of accommodating s. 23 is a different matter, although the indications are positive. In *Doorson* v *Netherlands* (1996) 22 EHRR 330, the European Court of Human Rights accepted the need to develop principles of fair trial that balance the interests of the defence against those of witnesses or of victims who give evidence. The European Commission specifically accepted the need to screen intimidated witnesses from the accused in *X* v *UK* (1992) 15 EHRR CD 113, provided that the witness could be seen by the accused's legal representatives. In Canada, a rights-based analysis of the use of special measures to protect vulnerable witnesses has also led to the conclusion that screens are acceptable in child witness cases (*Levogiannis* [1993] 4 SCR 475) and that 'the evidence of all those involved in judicial proceedings must be given in the way that is most favourable to eliciting the truth'. Screens are also permitted by statute in proceedings in Scotland (Prisoners and Criminal Proceedings (Scotland) Act 1993, s. 34).

LIVE LINK: s. 24

Meaning of live link

Section 24 largely replicates the provisions of the Criminal Justice Act 1988, s. 32, under which live television links were made available to child witnesses in prosecutions for sexual offences and offences of violence and cruelty (see p. 35). Section 32 will be superseded when the new provision is brought into force. In current parlance live link connotes a closed circuit television link between the courtroom and another room, usually within the precincts of the court, and the 1988 Act applied specifically to a 'live television link'. A 'live link' under the 1999 Act may include more. The Explanatory Notes accompanying the 1999 Act note that s. 24 has been drafted sufficiently widely to include any technology with the same effect within its meaning.

Section 24(8) defines live link to mean:

> a live television link or other arrangement whereby a witness, while absent from the courtroom or other place where the proceedings are being held, is able to see and hear a person there and to be seen and heard by the persons specified in section 23(2)(a) to (c).

The persons who must be able to see and hear the witness are thus the same as those where a direction is made to screen the witness from the accused, i.e., those trying the case (including the jury), at least one of each of the parties' legal representatives and any interpreter or other person appointed to assist the witness, such as an intermediary (see pp. 75–77).

Continuing use of live link

Under s. 24(1), a special measures direction may provide for the witness to give evidence by means of live link. Section 24(2) provides that where a direction to this effect has been made, the witness may not give evidence in any other way without the permission of the court. This effectively creates a presumption that a witness who has given any evidence by live link shall continue to do so throughout the proceedings. The court's permission to change the method of giving evidence can be obtained either on application by a party on the grounds of a material change of circumstances, or by the court initiating the process of its own motion. In both cases it must appear to the court that the interests of justice require the permission to be given (s. 24(3)), and if a material change of circumstances is asserted it must have occurred since the direction was given or, if a previous application has been made, since that application (s. 24(4)). It is not clear how this differs from the more general power to vary a special measures direction contained in s. 20(2), which appears to operate on the same principles. It may be that Parliament has simply re-enacted the provisions of s. 32(3)(c) to (e) of the 1988 Act, and that the possibility of jettisoning these provisions in the light of the generality of s. 20(2) was not considered.

Special provision for magistrates' courts

Section 24(5) confers a power to appoint a place to be used for magistrates to receive evidence by live link in circumstances where there are no suitable facilities in a petty-sessional court-house in which the court could (apart from the power) lawfully sit. Very considerable expense is involved in the plan to extend live link facilities from Crown Courts and the youth court to all courts and this provision is one way of reducing the financial burden without depriving vulnerable witnesses of important facilities.

EVIDENCE GIVEN IN PRIVATE: s. 25

Trials where the measure applies

Unlike the other special measures, the power in s. 25 to order that evidence be given in private applies only to a limited range of offences. Section 25(4) restricts the powers of the court to make a special measures direction excluding the public to:

(a)   proceedings relating to a sexual offence; and
(b)   cases where it appears to the court that there are reasonable grounds to believe that a person (other than the accused) has sought, or will seek, to intimidate the witness in connection with testifying in the proceedings.

Speaking Up For Justice explains that the principle of open justice normally dictates that trials take place in open court, however intimidating that may be for the witnesses, but that a narrow exception can be justified in sexual cases and in cases involving intimidation. A wider exception might bring the Act into conflict with Article 6 of the European Convention on Human Rights.

Who may be excluded

Section 25(1) allows a special measures direction to provide for the exclusion from the court, during the witness's evidence, of persons of 'any description specified in the direction'. Section 25(2) contains the exceptions: the accused, legal representatives acting in the proceedings, and any interpreter or other person appointed to assist the witness, such as an intermediary, may not be excluded by such a direction.

The Explanatory Notes accompanying the Act state that 'the direction will describe individuals or groups of people, rather than areas of the court, and will mostly affect those in the public gallery and the press gallery'. However, special measures directions providing for representatives of news-gathering or reporting organisations to be excluded must be expressed *not* to apply to one named person who is a representative of such an organisation and who has been nominated for the purpose by one or more such organisations (s. 25(3)). The effect of this provision is to ensure that, provided a member of the press has been duly nominated for the purpose, the court will be obliged to allow at least one person to be present to report the proceedings. The exclusion of a member of the press from the courtroom under s. 25 does not of itself affect his freedom to report the proceedings, although a reporting restriction may be imposed separately (see Chapter 8). Proceedings held in private under s. 25 are deemed to be held in public should the question arise of any privilege or exemption arising out of the making of a fair, accurate and contemporaneous report of legal proceedings held in public (s. 25(5)). Section 14 of the Defamation Act 1996 provides an absolute privilege in respect of such a report, and s. 4 of the Contempt of Court Act 1991 recognises that the publication of such a report in good faith does not amount to a contempt under the strict liability rule.

REMOVAL OF WIGS AND GOWNS: s. 26

Section 26 simply states that a special measures direction may provide for the wearing of wigs or gowns to be dispensed with during the giving of the witness's evidence. *Speaking Up For Justice* noted that courts have traditionally exercised a discretion to dispense with the wearing of formal garb, particularly where child witnesses are concerned. It was thought advisable to put the power on a statutory basis so that it was clear that it could be made available to vulnerable adult witnesses (Recommendation 49, para. 8.80), but the Working Group wisely noted that some witnesses might prefer the judge and counsel to be attired in the traditional manner, particularly if they were familiar with courtroom dramas on television. When making a special measures direction, the court is always required to consider any views expressed by the witness (s. 19(3)(a)), but under s. 26 it is likely that the witness's views will be decisive: this would appear to be one special measure which can be entirely driven by the wishes of the witness.

VIDEO RECORDED EVIDENCE IN CHIEF: s. 27

In Chapter 3 an account was given of the history of video recorded evidence in chief, which was introduced for child witnesses in 1991 by the Criminal Justice Act 1988, s. 32A. Section 32A was a complex provision whereby the child had access to the measure only in relation to particular offences (sexual offences and offences of violence and cruelty) where the trial took place in the Crown Court or the youth court. Section 27 of the 1999 Act is modelled on the old s. 32A, which will be superseded when the new provision comes into force, but its ambit is much wider in that it will be open to all eligible witnesses, whatever the offence alleged and wherever the proceedings take place. Children will still be dealt with differently to adults, because of the presumptions in favour of video recorded evidence in chief which apply when a child testifies (see p. 49).

The conditions which s. 27 requires to be satisfied before a video recording can be given as evidence in chief substantially replicate those of s. 32A of the 1988 Act, but with some important changes. In particular:

(a)   it is no longer necessary for the witness to be available for cross-examination, provided that the parties are agreed;

(b)   the conditions under which supplementary examination in chief are permitted are more stringent;

(c)   the previous requirement to obtain the leave of the court is replaced by the procedure for obtaining the special measures direction itself.

'Interview'

Section 27(1) provides that a special measures direction may provide for a video recording of an interview of the witness to be admitted as the witness's evidence in chief. Under the superseded s. 32A of the 1988 Act there was some further definition of the interview, the main purpose of which was to stipulate that the interviewee had to be a child who was not the accused. As the eligibility criteria no longer confine the measure to children (see p. 40), the first stipulation no longer obtains and, as the accused is excluded from eligibility by ss. 16 and 17 (see p. 40), the second is unnecessary.

Exclusion of video recordings from special measures directions: s. 27(2)

Before making a special measures direction providing for a video recording to be admitted as a witness's evidence in chief, the court is directed by s. 27(2) to consider whether it is in the interests of justice that the particular recording should be so admitted. If it is *not* in the interests of justice that the recording, or a given part of it, should be admitted then the court *may not* make a special measures direction to provide for the recording (or the offending part of it) to be admitted. In so providing, the 1999 Act is more clearly proscriptive than its predecessor, s. 32A of the 1988 Act.

Under s. 32A, leave of the court was required to admit the recording, but such leave had to be given unless, *inter alia*, the court was of opinion that it was not in the interests of justice to admit the recording. This left open the theoretical (and admittedly highly unlikely) possibility that the court retained the discretion to grant leave in a case in which it had decided it was not in the interests of justice to admit the evidence.

Section 27(2) clearly contemplates that any objections to the admissibility of the whole or part of a recording tendered in evidence under the 1999 Act will be made at the pre-trial stage, when the court is considering which special measures are most likely to maximise the quality of the witness's evidence (see p. 49). It would be inappropriate for an objection to be held back until after the use of a video recording had been selected as the appropriate special measure and then voiced at the trial stage. The current pre-trial checklist for cases involving young witnesses (*Plea and Directions Hearing: Supplementary Pre-trial Checklist for Cases Involving Young Witnesses (Archbold,* Appendix C-2)) stipulates that objections to the admissibility of a young witness's video recorded examination in chief should not be left to be made at the trial in the absence of compelling reasons, and then only with the leave of the trial judge. The checklist is designed to be used where applications are made under s. 32A of the 1988 Act, but the more detailed special measures regime of the 1999 Act appears to lead to a similar result. The court can discharge or vary any special measures direction in the interests of justice and may do so at any time of its own motion, but a party cannot succeed in an application to do so unless there has been a material change of circumstances (s. 20(2): see p. 53). Thus an objection which could have been voiced before the direction was made is unlikely to succeed at a later stage of proceedings.

The 'interests of justice' and the 'fairness of the proceedings'

The 'interests of justice' test which applies under s. 27(2) overlaps with the general discretion of the court under the Police and Criminal Evidence Act 1984, s. 78 to exclude any prosecution evidence at trial on the grounds that its admission would have 'such an adverse effect on the fairness of the proceedings that the court ought not to admit it'. Section 27(2) operates more widely in that it may lead to the exclusion of a recording tendered by the defence, whereas s. 78 applies to prosecution evidence only. Insofar as there is overlap, s. 63(2) of the 1999 Act states that the provisions of Part II of the Act do not affect 'any power of a court to exclude evidence at its discretion', so that in theory the 'interests of justice' test and the 'fairness of the proceedings' test may both be invoked with regard to the same video recording tendered by the prosecution.

Is there any practical difference between the two tests? Section 27(2) substantially replicates the power of exclusion in s. 32A(3)(c) of the Criminal Justice Act 1988, which will be superseded when s. 27 is bought into force. The older power has been considered by the courts. In *G* v *Director of Public Prosecutions* [1998] QB 919 the Divisional Court compared the two powers of exclusion and decided that the

'interests of justice' test in the Criminal Justice Act 1988, s. 32A(3)(c) differs little
in practice from the 'fairness of the proceedings' test in s. 78 of PACE. In that case
the defence based its objection to the admissibility of video recordings tendered by
the prosecution on s. 78 of PACE, but the court did not suggest (as it might have been
expected to were there any reason to think that this was the case) that the result would
have been any different had the defence invoked the 'interests of justice' test.

Submissions to exclude video recordings in the interests of justice may be made
for a number of different reasons. Recordings may be of poor sound or picture quality.
Alternatively, objection may be taken to the quality of the interview itself. A common
failing of video recordings tendered under the 1988 Act is that questions are put by
the interviewer which infringe the guidelines laid down in the *Memorandum of Good
Practice on Video Recorded Interviews with Child Witnesses for Criminal Proceedings* (Home Office and Department of Health, 1992), currently being revised to take
account of the 1999 Act: see p. 37). For example, the Memorandum takes a strong
line on the use of leading questions, which it notes should not be used unless strictly
necessary (para. 3.54). Research conducted for the Home Office, however, discovered
that some 40 per cent of the interviews studied included impermissible questions and
it appears that a substantial number were leading questions (G. Davies, C. Wilson,
R. Mitchell and J. Milsom, *Videotaping Children's Evidence: An Evaluation* (Home
Office, 1995) at p. 21).

The defence objection to the use of the recordings in *G* v *Director of Public
Prosecutions* centred on the frequent use by the interviewer of leading questions, and
on his failure to make clear to the children being interviewed that they were entitled
to answer 'I don't know' when asked a question. Both transgressions were correctly
identified by the Crown Court (on appeal from a stipendiary magistrate) as breaches
of the Memorandum but the evidence was nevertheless admitted on the ground that
the faults were not, in the circumstances of the case, such as to justify exclusion. The
Divisional Court upheld this ruling as being one that the Crown Court was entitled
to make. Phillips LJ held that the question whether failure to comply with the
Memorandum should lead to exclusion of video evidence was to be determined by
considering the nature and extent of the breaches and the extent to which the evidence
affected by the breaches was supported by other passages of which no complaint was
made or by other evidence in the case. A court was thus entitled, in an appropriate
case, to admit evidence notwithstanding the existence of clear breaches of the
Memorandum. However, it was emphasised that it was of great importance that the
Memorandum should be followed and that the consequence if it is not may well be
that the evidence is excluded.

Although it will normally be the case that objections to the use in evidence of a
recording centre on the quality of the recording itself, a recording may be properly
conducted and provide a clear account of relevant events and still be excluded. In
Parker [1995] Crim LR 511 it was said to be an inappropriate exercise of discretion
for the trial judge to admit a video recording under s. 32A of the 1988 Act when it
was known that the child witness intended to retract what was said in evidence at trial.
The jury were said to have had their deliberations 'tainted' by seeing the tape.

Editing of recordings

Recordings are normally made at an early stage of the investigative process and it is not uncommon for them to require editing before they can be used at trial. Editing may be done to remove irrelevant or inadmissible material or to excise material which is admissible but which it is considered to be prejudicial or otherwise unfair to include. With regard to evidence tendered under s. 32A of the 1988 Act (the predecessor of s. 27 of the 1999 Act), the Crown Court Rules 1982, r. 23C provides a procedure under which decisions about the extent to which a recording should be admitted can be made before the trial. Because r. 23C deals only with evidence of children it will need to be revised to take account of the wider range of witnesses who may qualify for video recording under the 1999 Act. It must be envisaged, however, that some key features will remain. These include giving the other parties to the proceedings notice of the intention to rely on the recording, together with a copy of the entire interview. (Special safeguards apply to prevent an accused who is preparing his own defence from receiving a tape, although he is permitted to view it.) The court can then, by exercising its power to admit the recording in part only, direct that it be edited. *Practice Direction (Crime: Child's Video Evidence)* [1992] 1 WLR 839 provides that the party who made the application to admit the recording must then edit it in accordance with the court's directions and provide copies of the edited version for the Crown Court and the parties to the proceedings. The *Practice Direction* will also have to be amended or replaced to accommodate the wider range of witnesses who are eligible to give video recorded evidence under the 1999 Act. It is essential that the court, rather than the parties, controls the editing process as any editing has the power to distort the testimony of the witness.

Exclusion in part and the desirability of showing the whole recording: s. 27(3)

Section 27(3) preserves a related rule, previously contained in s. 32A(4) of the 1988 Act, which applies when the court is considering whether to exclude part of an otherwise admissible recording. In deciding whether it is in the interests of justice to exclude the relevant part, the court must consider whether any prejudice to the accused from showing the full recording is outweighed by the desirability of showing the whole, or substantially the whole, of it. Sometimes prejudicial material (such as references in the interview to other misconduct of the accused that is not admissible under the similar fact rule) can be edited out without detriment to the usefulness of the recording as evidence. If it cannot, s. 27(3) permits the court at one and the same time to decide that the relevant portion of the interview contains prejudicial material but that, on balance, the interests of justice (including, of course, the interests of the witness being interviewed) are best served if the recording is shown in its entirety. If prejudicial material is admitted in consequence of such a decision, it will be important to direct the jury (where there is one) to ignore the prejudicial parts.

A party against whom video evidence is being tendered may decide, as a tactical matter, not to object where a video contains some prejudicial material but it assists the party's case if the video is shown in its entirety. This might be so, for example, where it is the defence case that the witness's account has been moulded by the inappropriate use of leading questions. If the magistrates or jury are allowed to observe the impact of the offending questions on the witness at interview, the overall effect may well be that the defence case is thereby advanced.

Later exclusion of recording included in a special measures direction: s. 27(4)

In addition to the court's general power to vary a special measures direction in relation to a video recording (s. 20(2): see p. 53), s. 27(4) provides that, where a special measures direction has been made which provides for a recording to be admitted, the court may nevertheless subsequently direct that it is not to be admitted if it appears to the court that:

(a) the witness will not be available for cross-examination (whether in the ordinary way or in accordance with a special measures direction which provides for pre-recording) *and* the parties have not agreed that there is no need for him to be so available; or

(b) rules of court requiring disclosure as to the circumstances in which the recording was made have not been complied with to the satisfaction of the court.

Under the predecessor of s. 27 (s. 32A of the 1988 Act), there was no specific provision for video evidence to be admissible where the parties were agreed that there was no need for the witness to be cross-examined. Under s. 27(4), the parties may so agree. Such agreement may, for instance, be forthcoming where the main issue at trial is identification and the victim whose recording is tendered speaks only of the commission of the offence, the circumstances of which are not contested.

In the absence of agreement, or in the event of failure to comply with rules of court made under s. 27, the court has a discretion to exclude a recording but only, it seems, where the issue arises at some point *after* a special measures direction has been made providing for admissibility of the recording. It is unclear what the maker of the *original* special measures direction should do if it appears that the witness will not be available at trial: presumably this factors into the 'interests of justice' test in s. 27(2) (see p. 63).

The maker of the later decision under s. 27(4) is clearly given a discretion ('the court *may* nevertheless subsequently direct that [the recording] is not to be so admitted'), but it is not apparent in what circumstances such a discretion might be exercised in favour of admitting the recording in the face of an objection by the other party or parties to the proceedings. If the obstacle to the use of the recording is non-compliance with rules of court regarding disclosure then the outcome might turn on the extent to which another party will suffer prejudice. If the obstacle is the non-availability of the witness for cross-examination (otherwise than by agreement), it might be important that the witness has undergone cross-examination at some earlier stage of proceedings (for example, where the issue arises at a retrial or appeal by way of rehearing).

The rules stated in s. 27(4) in relation to the court's subsequent powers of exclusion apply to a recording in respect of which a special measures direction has been made admitting it in part, and references to the recording or to the testimony of the witness are to be read as references to the part which is to be admitted (s. 27(6)).

Calling the witness: s. 27(5)

In the absence of an agreement that the witness need not be available for cross-examination, the witness must be called by the party tendering the recording in evidence (s. 27(5)(a)). The exception is where a special measures direction provides for the witness's cross-examination to take place otherwise than by testimony in court (s. 27(5)(a)(i)). This would appear to be a reference to the power to video record cross-examination and re-examination under s. 28 (see p. 72). Where a special measures direction is made under s. 28, the witness is not 'called' as such: all his testimony is taken in advance of trial. The phrase 'otherwise than by testimony in court' is preferred to a direct reference to s. 28, but it is not clear what other form of special measures direction might have the effect of removing the need to call the witness.

Supplementary examination in chief

Supplementary examination in chief of a witness whose evidence 'is admitted' under s. 27 is permitted only in accordance with s. 27(5)(b). The restrictions contained in this provision contemplate the situation where the trial is already in progress at the time when the request for a further examination of the witness falls to be dealt with. The Act does not concern itself with the more common situation where the police, at an early stage of the investigation, seek a repeat interview with the witness, either because his disclosure is incomplete or because other matters, commonly matters raised by the accused, require to be dealt with. This is a matter currently regulated by the *Memorandum of Good Practice on Video Recorded Interviews with Child Witnesses for Criminal Proceedings* (Home Office and Department of Health, 1992), which is to be revised to accommodate the wider provisions of the 1999 Act. The Memorandum discourages repeat interviewing except where absolutely necessary (paras. 1.11 and 3.41). It may however be better for supplementary questions to be raised at the investigative stage than left until the point at which the witness is about to face cross-examination, by which time the coherence of the witness's narrative as a whole may be far harder to establish.

Where the recording is admitted under s. 27, the Act contemplates three possible cases in which further examination in chief may be undertaken (two explicitly and one implicitly):

(a)   If a matter has, in the opinion of the court, been 'dealt with adequately' in the recording, the witness may *not* give evidence in chief otherwise than by means of the recording on that matter (s. 27(5)(b)(i)). This replicates s. 32A(5)(b) of the 1988 Act (as amended), the forerunner of s. 27.

(b)   Where the matter is dealt with in the recording, but not adequately, the court may give permission for supplementary examination in chief (s. 27(5)(b)(ii)). The requirement for permission in this situation is new (L. Hoyano, 'Variations on a Theme by Pigot: Special Measures Directions for Child Witnesses' [2000] Crim LR 252). Under the 1988 Act such matters could as of right be followed up in a supplementary examination in chief.

(c)   Inferentially, where the matter is not dealt with at all in the recording the witness can be called for supplementary examination in chief and the permission of the court is not required.

Permission for supplementary examination

The procedure for granting permission under the second of the three situations identified above is governed by s. 27(7). The court must consider that it is in the interests of justice to give permission for the purposes of s. 27(5)(b)(ii). A party to the proceedings is limited in making an application for permission to cases where there has been a 'material change of circumstances since the relevant time' (s. 27(7)(a)). The relevant time is either the time of the last application under s. 27(7), or the time when the special measures direction was given (s. 27(8)). Because s. 20(4) provides that nothing in s. 27(5) is to be regarded as affecting the power of the court to vary or discharge the direction itself, the court would also have the option to change the terms of the original direction or even to discharge it (see p. 53).

Supplementary examination under s. 27(5)(b)(ii) may be conducted by means of live link (s. 27(9)) and the provisions permitting magistrates' courts to operate outside their normal geographical boundaries in order to take advantage of available live link facilities (s. 24(5) to (7)) apply.

No permission required

Assuming that it is a correct inference from the two cases expressly dealt with in s. 27(7) that a party may as of right supplement a witness's video recorded evidence by conducting a further examination in chief regarding matters which are not dealt with at all in the recording, it must further be supposed that the court is entitled to order that any such examination should be conducted using such special measures as would enable the witness to give his best evidence in court.

Supplementary examination of child witnesses

In cases where the prosecutor is forced to rely on s. 27 as the preferred, or the only permissible, method of presenting a child's evidence under the provisions of ss. 21 and 22 (see p. 49), it is crucial that there are pathways by which gaps in the evidence can be filled, as it is well documented that video recordings are often deficient in dealing with every matter about which the party calling the witness will wish to secure his testimony (G. Davis, L. Hoyano, C. Keenan, L. Maitland and R. Morgan,

An Assessment of the Admissibility and Sufficiency of Evidence in Child Abuse Prosecutions (Home Office, 1999), considered at pp. 38 to 39). It is, of course, contrary to the spirit of the special measures direction under which video recorded evidence may be received if the witness who has already provided a video recorded statement is then forced to endure the ordeal of going over matters a second time, particularly if this involves, as it may do, testifying at the trial. Those who are responsible for the making of recordings will not wish to fall back on the power to supplement a witness's evidence unless it is really necessary. The report by Davis *et al.* suggests (p. 60) that such examinations are rare at present and it is essential that they should continue to be resorted to only where there is no alternative.

The status and weight of recorded evidence

A statement made in a recording which is received in evidence under s. 27 is treated as if made while giving direct oral evidence in court (s. 31(1)) and is admissible as evidence of any fact of which the witness could have given evidence (s. 31(2)(a)). 'Statement' for this purpose includes any representation of fact, whether made in words or otherwise (s. 31(8)), so that it is clear that gestures which the witness makes on the tape, such as nodding or shaking the head, and which are intended to communicate facts are receivable.

Witnesses do not normally take an oath before making a recording even if their evidence at trial would be given on oath (as to evidence on oath, see Chapter 9). The fact that the recording is unsworn does not affect its reception as evidence of facts even though it is evidence which, if given by the witness at trial, would have been sworn (s. 31(3)). This accords with the general policy of the Act in eradicating the rigid distinction between sworn and unsworn evidence (see p. 139). However, it appears from the Explanatory Notes which accompany the Act that there may be an intention in future to administer the oath to witnesses who are about to make a recording:

> Witnesses aged 14 and over who make a video recording that is intended to take the place of their evidence in chief will either swear an oath at the beginning of the interview, if someone is available to administer the oath and they are capable of being sworn, or give evidence unsworn. (Note 117)

It is unlikely that it will be practical to administer the oath to a witness who may be making a recording at a very early stage of proceedings and it is unclear what advantage the procedure is thought to have, unless to deflect the suggestion that the evidence, being unsworn, is inferior. For most witnesses there will come a point at which they are cross-examined, either at the trial or (by virtue of s. 28) before it, and it would seem preferable for them at that stage to ratify on oath the evidence previously given unsworn. Ratification is not possible where the evidence previously given is inadmissible in consequence of being unsworn (*Simmonds* [1996] Crim LR 816: see p. 140) but that is not the case here.

The fact that evidence is not on oath may be a factor going to its weight as evidence: s. 31(4) permits any reasonable inferences to be drawn from the circumstances in estimating the weight which attaches to the statement. The process of drawing inferences as to the weight to be given to the evidence is the same as for evidence given in court, except that s. 31(4) imposes a statutory duty to have regard to all the circumstances from which an inference can reasonably be drawn. It is, of course, quite impossible to police such a provision where the inferences are to be drawn by a jury, but provisions of this type were included in the 1988 and 1991 legislation and are presumably considered by the draftsman to have some function.

The provision in s. 31(2)(b) as regards corroboration is also of little practical significance: it states in effect that video evidence given by a witness in accordance with a special measures direction cannot corroborate any other evidence he gives in the proceedings. Quite apart from the question whether a witness would be able to give any other evidence in the proceedings, applying the restrictive rules on supplementary examination (see p. 67), the circumstances in which a witness's evidence requires corroboration in law or where a corroboration direction is to be given as a matter of good practice are now very limited (see p. 141). It thus seems that s. 31(2)(b) would be of very limited effect even if there were not (as there is) a perfectly sound common-law rule that a witness cannot corroborate himself.

Although it is necessary sometimes to include provisions of this type out of an abundance of caution, it is hard to imagine that any court would have been in difficulty had s. 31(2)(b) and 31(4) never been enacted.

Perjury

Liability for perjury attaches to false statements made on oath which are received in evidence in pursuance of a special measures direction. Although the making of a recording is not itself a 'judicial proceeding' within the meaning of s. 1 of the Perjury Act 1911, s. 31(6) of the 1999 Act deems it to constitute part of the judicial proceeding in which it is subsequently received in evidence. Where a person wilfully makes a false statement otherwise than on oath in the course of a proceeding which is not, for the purposes of the 1911 Act, a judicial proceeding, and the statement is subsequently received in evidence under a special measures direction, then (provided that the statement is made in such circumstances that the maker would have committed perjury had it been given on oath in a judicial proceeding) the maker is guilty of an offence under s. 31(7) of the 1999 Act. He is liable to any penalty attaching to the giving of false unsworn evidence under s. 57(2) of the 1999 Act (see p. 142).

VIDEO RECORDED CROSS-EXAMINATION AND RE-EXAMINATION: s. 28

The Pigot Report

Video-recorded cross-examination and re-examination are entirely new measures. Their introduction follows the essence of a recommendation of the Pigot Committee

(*Report of the Advisory Group on Video Evidence* (Home Office, 1989): see p. 36) that the adverse effects on some vulnerable witnesses of a court appearance was such that they ought not to appear at trial at all. The Committee recommended a special procedure whereby a child witness would attend a preliminary hearing, held out of court in informal surroundings, at which he would be asked to adopt the recording which he had made as his evidence in chief. The child could then, after such examination in chief as was necessary, be cross-examined by the other parties. It was proposed that the accused would be present at the hearing, but would be able to view events only through a television link or a two-way mirror.

The Pigot proposal was not incorporated into the original video evidence reforms in the Criminal Justice Act 1991, but a similar measure was suggested for inclusion in the 1999 Act in *Speaking Up For Justice*. *Speaking Up For Justice* noted (paras. 8.55–60) that the introduction of new disclosure provisions in the Criminal Procedure and Investigations Act 1996 meant that there might be a lengthy delay between the making of the recording to be used in evidence in chief and the point in time at which the witness is to be cross-examined. Thus there would be only a limited prospect that pre-recorded cross-examination would take place while events were fresh in the witness's memory. The Report nevertheless concluded that children and some adult vulnerable witnesses would benefit from such a measure, and went on to recommend that it be available for a witness whose statement has been recorded on video and who could 'particularly benefit from cross-examination outside the courtroom'. The benefit, it must be assumed, flows primarily from being spared the gruelling experience of a court appearance and from the consequent reduction in stress which may otherwise threaten to spoil the quality of the witness's evidence (see pp. 26–27).

The 1999 Act incorporates the proposal of *Speaking Up For Justice* by providing for cross-examination and re-examination to be recorded and admitted in the proceedings. Little is said about the procedure to be adopted but it does not appear to be the intention that there should be a preliminary hearing of the type recommended by the Pigot Report at which the witness is given an opportunity in effect to present his evidence in chief, supplemented by his pre-recorded interview, before being cross-examined. Where a witness's evidence in chief is taken in advance of trial in the form permitted by s. 27, it is the recording which stands as his evidence and the opportunity for supplementary examination in chief under s. 27(5) is very limited (see p. 67). A more likely format for a s. 28 recording will be that the recorded examination in chief will first be shown to the witness, and any supplementary questions permitted by the court will be put, but the focus of the hearing will be simply to conduct the cross-examination.

The use of s. 28

The intention appears to be that, apart from the special provision for child witnesses in sexual cases (s. 21: see p. 51), the provisions for pre-recording cross-examination will be resorted to only sparingly:

The Government believe that video cross-examination should be reserved for witnesses who need the special protection of being kept completely out of a criminal trial ... [C]hild witnesses of sexual offences need that protection. Other witnesses will have to convince the court that video recorded cross-examination will improve the quality of evidence. (George Howarth, House of Commons Standing Committee E, *Hansard*, 22 June 1999)

The suggestion that pre-recorded cross-examination is some kind of 'special protection' reserved for unusual cases is not, however, reflected in the drafting of the Act, which gives the court an unfettered discretion in any case in which evidence in chief is to be given in the form of a recording to be admitted under s. 27.

Section 28(1) to (3): the statutory framework

Under s. 28(1), the pre-recording of cross-examination and of any re-examination which is to follow is an option only where a special measures direction provides for a video recording to be admitted under s. 27. Where such a direction is made, it may also provide for cross-examination and any re-examination to be by means of a video recording (s. 28(1)(a)), and for any such recording to be admitted as that witness's evidence under cross-examination or re-examination, as the case may be (s. 28(1)(b)).

The direction itself may provide a limitation on the persons present, as may rules of court, but subject to the minimum specifications in s. 28(2), which are similar in effect to those in the provisions relating to the use of screens, live link and intermediaries. Thus the recording must be made in circumstances where the judge or justices (or both) and at least one of each party's legal representatives acting in the proceedings can see and hear the examination of the witness and 'communicate with the person in whose presence the recording is being made' (s. 28(2)(a) and 28(3)). Rather surprisingly perhaps, it is not regarded as essential for the cross-examination in a Crown Court trial to take place in the physical presence of the judge, although he will be able to control it from whatever distance is imposed. The rules of court to be made in relation to pre-recording will presumably stipulate who is meant by 'the persons in whose presence the recording is being made', but the most obvious contenders are any intermediary or interpreter assigned to the witness. Although these are only minimum requirements, so that it may still be possible to have a recording made in circumstances that more closely replicates a traditional cross-examination, the other extreme contemplated by the Act is a cross-examination that takes place outside the courtroom, in a setting which is so private that the witness does not necessarily have to confront, or even be able to hear, the advocate who is putting the questions in cross-examination. This will provide an interesting challenge to advocates whose techniques in cross-examination have hitherto included the use of body language and vocal intonation to exert pressure on a witness to qualify or retract the evidence they have given in chief.

Special provision is made for the accused. Although the recording must be made in his absence (s. 28(2)), he must be able to see and hear the examination, and communicate with any of his legal representatives (s. 28(2)(b)). As occurs throughout the Act, the communication requirement is satisfied provided the accused can communicate with one of his representatives at all times (s. 28(3)). The Act appears to envisage an arrangement such as the use of the live link, by which the accused can follow proceedings and take an active part to the extent of prompting the defence questioning of the witness, but without being able to induce fear or stress in the witness by his physical presence in the room.

Exclusion of recordings: s. 28(4)

The court retains control over the use of any pre-recorded cross-examination produced under s. 28. It may exclude it if it fails to comply with the requirements in s. 28(2) as to the persons who may be present, if the terms of the special measures direction itself have not been complied with or if there has been a breach of rules of court (s. 28(4)). The fall-back position with most witnesses (subject to what is said below in relation to s. 28(5) and (6)) will be that cross-examination can take place at the trial itself. It is no objection to this that both counsel and the witness have had a dummy run at it, given that this may also happen in relation to retrials or appeals by way of rehearing. However, it is hugely undesirable that a vulnerable witness who believes that his contribution to the proceedings is over should be forced to relive the ordeal of cross-examination and no doubt the court will have this in mind when exercising its powers under s. 28(4).

It is not clear how s. 28(4) sits alongside the requirement in s. 21 relating to a child witness in need of special protection who is giving evidence in a sexual case (see p. 51). Such a witness must, if his evidence in chief is to be given in recorded form, be the subject of a special measures direction which provides for 'the special measure available under section 28 ... to apply' to recording of cross-examination and re-examination. By 'apply' one assumes that the Act intends that the child should give his evidence in the form prescribed by s. 28 but, as s. 28 also permits the recording to be jettisoned, it may be argued that the child could, in this case, be required to face cross-examination at trial. A better alternative, if time permits, might be to make a second recording which avoided the defects of the jettisoned one.

Supplementary cross-examination: s. 28(5) and (6)

The Youth Justice and Criminal Evidence Bill, as originally introduced into Parliament, took a very strong line on the issue of supplementary cross-examination, providing that it was to be permitted only where new matters came to light which were not reasonably discoverable at the time of the recording. This put the onus on the cross-examiner to get it right first time, but in the event of his failure to do so it was the defendant who shouldered the consequences. Concern that the outcome in such a case would be a trial which, judged by the measure of Article 6 of the European Convention on Human Rights, might be thought unfair, led to the introduction of a further qualification, namely that the court might permit a further cross-examination if it would be in the interests of justice to do so. This opens up the prospect of rather more frequent supplementary cross-examinations, depending on how the courts interpret the provisions. Given that the witness on the receiving end of this potentially uncertain process is by definition sufficiently vulnerable to require the making of a special measures direction to pre-record cross-examination in the first place, the courts will have an exceptionally difficult balance to strike when considering applications under these provisions.

The provisions work in the following way. Section 28(5) prohibits a witness in respect of whom a recording has been made in pursuance of s. 28(1) from being subsequently cross-examined or re-examined in respect of any evidence he has given, whether in an admissible recording or otherwise. The only exception is where the court gives a further special measures direction under s. 28(1)(a) and (b). Section 28(6) then provides that the court may make such a further direction only where it appears to the court that:

(a)   a party wishes to cross-examine as to a matter of which it is now aware but which it could not with reasonable diligence have ascertained at the time of the original recording (s. 28(6)(a)); or

(b)   it is for any other reason in the interests of justice to give such a direction (s. 28(6)(b)).

The form of the provision is not surprising in the light of the way in which the second ground came to be added to the statute, but the result is a provision in which the first ground is no more than one illustration of a general rule represented by the second. To have kept the two grounds separate in this way reflects a view that, except where fresh evidence comes to light, the court should be reluctant to grant leave. Introducing the amendment which is now s. 28(6)(b), Lord Williams of Mostyn said:

I hope that repeated cross-examinations will be rare. The kind of witness likely to be cross-examined on video before trial will be extremely vulnerable and repeated cross-examinations can be extremely distressing. Pre-trial video cross-examination should normally be the only cross-examination. Cross-examining parties will therefore be expected to exercise reasonable diligence to ensure that they cross-examine the witness on all relevant issues the first time round ... The amendment ... ensures that whenever it is in the interests of justice to allow further cross-examination, the judge will be able to allow it. I hope that the new provision will be relied on only occasionally, but it is a necessary safeguard to avoid unjust convictions resulting from witnesses not having been cross-examined on relevant issues at trial. (House of Commons, 3rd Reading, *Hansard*, 23 March 1999, col. 1188.)

Cross-examination by the accused

Section 28(7) provides that nothing in s. 28 applies to any cross-examination by the accused in person (in a case where the accused is able to conduct such a cross-examination). It follows that pre-recorded cross-examination and re-examination are not available options in such cases. Many witnesses who are in need of the protection which s. 28 provides will also fall within the provisions of s. 34 (which provides that the accused may not himself cross-examine the complainant in a sexual case) or s. 35 (which prevents the accused from cross-examining many child witnesses) (see Chapter 6). Section 28(7) does not bite on such cases. A problem may arise only where:

(a) the witness is vulnerable and in need of the protection afforded by s. 28;
(b) the accused is unrepresented and intends to cross-examine the witness himself; and
(c) nothing in s. 34 or 35 expressly prohibits him from doing so (this might, for example, arise where the accused is charged with offences involving the 'stalking' of an adult witness).

In such a case, the court should give serious consideration as to whether the conditions in s. 36 of the Act, under which it has a discretion to prevent the accused from cross-examining in person any witness not covered by s. 34 or 35, are satisfied (see p. 85). If, as seems likely to be the case, the conditions are satisfied, a s. 36 direction could be given which will then enable the provisions of s. 28 to be brought into play in a special measures direction.

Status and weight of evidence

A statement made by a witness in pre-recorded cross-examination or re-examination is treated as if made in direct oral testimony in court, and is thus evidence of any fact of which the witness could have given such oral evidence (s. 31(1)). The court is under a statutory duty to have regard to all the circumstances from which an inference (as to the accuracy of the statement or anything else which is relevant) can properly be drawn (s. 31(4)).

Perjury

False statements made on oath in a video recorded cross-examination which is subsequently received in evidence in pursuance of a special measures direction are regarded as having been made in a judicial proceeding, and fall within the domain of the Perjury Act 1911, s. 1 (s. 31(6)). Where the cross-examination which is received is not conducted on oath, s. 31(7) makes it an offence wilfully to make a false statement. The penalty is stated to be the same as for giving false unsworn evidence under s. 57(2) (see p. 142).

EXAMINATION THROUGH INTERMEDIARY: s. 29

A special measures direction may provide for any examination of the witness to be conducted through an intermediary (s. 29(1)). Special provisions apply where the

76 The Eight Special Measures

examination in question is an interview which is to be admitted under s. 27 as pre-recorded evidence in chief (s. 29(6)), as it is unlikely that a special measures direction will be sought prior to the making of such a recording.

The special measure in s. 29 can be made available only to witnesses eligible on grounds of youth or incapacity under s. 16: witnesses eligible only on grounds of fear or distress under s. 17 do not qualify (s. 18(1)(b)).

The intermediary

An 'intermediary' is described as an interpreter or other person approved by the court for the purposes of s. 29 (s. 29(1)). The function of such a person is to communicate to the witness the questions which are put, and to communicate to the questioner the answers which the witness gives in reply. The intermediary also explains the questions and answers, but only to the extent necessary to enable them to be understood by the witness or the questioner as the case may be (s. 29(2)). The most important use of the intermediary will be with regard to a witness with a form of learning disability which severely restricts his ability to communicate with others. To reduce questions into a form which such a witness can respond to will require a degree of special knowledge about the witness's individual level of comprehension and use of language. An example might be a witness who uses the word 'yesterday' to refer to all events in the past. When asked when the incident which is the subject of the trial occurred, the response 'yesterday' would seem entirely misconceived unless the intermediary was able to explain to the court what the witness understood by the term.

Some witnesses may require more than one intermediary: for example, a person with a hearing or speech impairment who also has a learning disability may require a person skilled in signing as well as a person who has an understanding of the limitations of the witness's understanding of language. The court will need to be well informed by expert evidence of the witness's special needs before making a special measures direction specifying the level of assistance the witness requires.

The Act does not descend to the level of detail of specifying who may act in the intermediary's role, though this issue may be addressed in rules of court to be made under the 1999 Act. Many people with a learning disability who have problems with communication are able to make themselves understood to a particular family member or support worker. That person might be ideal in the role of 'appropriate adult' where the individual is being interviewed, either as a suspect or as a witness, under PACE Code C (The Code of Practice for the Detention, Questioning and Treatment of Persons by Police Officers), because the role of the appropriate adult includes advising and being on the side of the person being questioned as well as assisting, where necessary, in communicating with him. But the intermediary's function is limited to communicating, in as objective a way as possible, with the witness, and any attempt to gloss or supplement his answers by reference to the intermediary's personal knowledge of relevant events, or of previous accounts given by the witness or others, must be avoided, as must any attempt to steer the witness towards, or away from a particular answer. It would be very hard for someone close to the witness, who may have formed a very clear idea about the circumstances of the offence which is the subject of the trial, to be so objective. A system of using only intermediaries who have not been closely involved with the witness would no doubt offer more in the way of reassurance to the court that the evidence of the witness was untainted in transmission, but might mean that, for some severely disabled witnesses, no intermediary could be found.

The intermediary's declaration and sanctions for perjury

There is a special declaration to be made by the intermediary (in a form to be prescribed by rules of court) that he will faithfully perform his statutory function (s. 29(5)). Any person acting as an intermediary is subject to the provisions of the Perjury Act 1911, s. 1 to the same extent as a lawfully sworn interpreter (s. 29(7)); thus he commits perjury if he wilfully makes a statement which he knows to be false or does not believe to be true. This sanction applies to intermediaries, whether or not the proceeding in which they assist are 'judicial proceedings' as defined by the 1911 Act, since s. 29(7) deems all the proceedings in which an intermediary acts to be part of judicial proceedings for this purpose. An intermediary who assists in court will presumably take the interpreter's oath, but one who aids in the making of a video recorded interview made to be shown as evidence in chief would not normally do so. Whether on oath or not, however, the effect of s. 29(7) is that the sanction of perjury applies. This is in contrast to the sanction which applies to the witness himself, who is not liable for perjury in respect of unsworn statements but for the lesser offences under the 1999 Act (ss. 31(7) and 57(2)).

Procedure where an intermediary is used

The persons who may be present when the intermediary is working with the witness can be limited by the special measures direction itself or by rules of court. Section 29(3) lays down the irreducible minimum requirements in terms which mirror those which obtain where screens and live link are used (see pp. 56 and 59) or where cross-examination is video recorded (see p. 72). The judge or justices trying the case must be able to see and hear the examination of the witness and communicate with the intermediary, as must the legal representatives acting in the proceedings (s. 29(3)). As with the other three measures, the requirement in relation to legal representatives is satisfied provided that one of a number of representatives of a particular party is accommodated in this way (s. 29(4)). The jury (if there is one) is also entitled to see and hear the examination, except where it is a video recorded examination (s. 29(4)). It is possible that some video recorded examinations, particularly cross-examinations, will take place after the jury has been empanelled, so that the exception is necessary to enable the procedure in s. 28 to work as intended.

The intermediary at the video recorded interview

Where the intermediary is called upon to assist at an interview which is to be video recorded with a view to being shown as evidence in chief, s. 29(6) provides that the gateway to admissibility is via s. 27 (see p. 62) not s. 29(1). This is because a special measures direction is likely to be made only after this recording is completed and tendered in evidence and the personnel who are required to watch the intermediary at work in a courtroom, or during a video recorded cross-examination, will not have been appointed to their various functions at the stage at which the interview is to be taped. The court may admit the recording under s. 27 provided that:

(a)   the intermediary made the necessary declaration before the interview began;
(b)   the court gives retrospective approval of the use of the intermediary before making the s. 27 direction.

The approval to be given is approval 'for the purposes of' s. 29, so that a person may not be approved to do the job of intermediary at the interview if he would be considered an inappropriate person to perform the same function in court. The Act thus provides a mechanism for retrospective approval. Interviewers will need to be alert to the need both to obtain the intermediary's declaration and to ensure that the person to whom the task is assigned is a proper person to perform the functions of the intermediary.

AIDS TO INTERPRETATION: s. 30

Section 30 permits a special measures direction to provide for a witness, while giving evidence, to be provided with 'such device as the court considers appropriate' to enable questions or answers to be communicated to or by the witness. The special measure in s. 30 can be made available only to witnesses eligible on grounds of youth or incapacity under s. 16: witnesses eligible only on grounds of fear or distress under s. 17 do not qualify (s. 18(1)(b)). Furthermore, as the purpose of s. 30 is said to be to enable the witness to overcome any 'disability or disorder or other impairment' which would otherwise inhibit effective communication, it is not apparent that a witness who is eligible only on grounds of youth could benefit. The section could certainly not be invoked if, for example, a rape complainant wanted her voice to be 'scrambled' to make her less easy to identify.

The sort of device contemplated for the use of s. 30 is an alphabet or sign board or a voice synthesiser or enhancer which may enable a disabled witness to respond to questioning. A special measures direction under s. 27 may be made in respect of the witness's evidence in court 'or otherwise', so that a witness undergoing a pre-recorded evidence in chief or cross-examination could presumably also benefit. On the other hand, there is unlikely to be a special measures direction in force at the time when an interview is recorded which may ultimately function as the witness's evidence in chief under s. 27. Interestingly there is no provision echoing s. 29(6) (see above) which effectively requires video recorded evidence in chief which is conducted through an intermediary to be dealt with by a special measures direction under s. 27 if the court at that stage retrospectively approves the use of the intermediary. Witnesses who need aids to communication will need them as much when pre-recording interviews as when giving evidence in court, so that video recordings admitted under s. 27 may well require the court in effect to ratify their use. Presumably the necessary degree of control can be achieved within the court's general duty under s. 27 to take account of all relevant circumstances when deciding whether the admission of a recording is in the interests of justice (s. 27(2)). The reason for the special provision with regard to s. 29 is the extra degree of control required to ensure that the intermediary who assists at a recorded interview complies with the requirement to make the statutory declaration (s. 29(5)).

Chapter 6
Protection of Witnesses from Cross-examination by the Accused in Person

OVERVIEW

Sections 34 to 39 make inroads into the right of an unrepresented defendant to conduct cross-examination in person. Section 34 prevents a defendant charged with a sexual offence from personally cross-examining the complainant. Section 35 replaces and extends the provisions of s. 34A of the Criminal Justice Act 1988 (which prohibits cross-examination in person of child witnesses in certain cases). Sections 36 and 37 give the court a power by direction to prohibit unrepresented defendants from cross-examining witnesses in some further cases in order to improve the quality of that witness's evidence. Provision is also made for ensuring the availability of a legal representative to conduct a necessary cross-examination (ss. 38 and 40) and for a suitable warning to be given to caution the jury against being prejudiced against the accused in consequence of the restrictions imposed upon him (s. 39).

These provisions were due to come into force in the Spring of 2000, according to *Action For Justice: Implementing the Speaking Up For Justice Report in England and Wales* (Home Office, 1999) but it was not until 4 September 2000 that ss. 34 and 35, together with the related provisions in ss. 38–40, were brought into force (SI 2000 No. 2091). Schedule 7, para. 4 provides that the new provisions do not apply to proceedings instituted before the commencement date, so that only proceedings begun on or after 4 September are affected. The commencement order makes no reference to the discretionary powers contained in ss. 36 and 37, and it is not clear why these provisions have not been brought into force at the same time as the others, as originally intended. Rules of Court have been promulgated to expand upon the procedure for the appointment of a legal representative to conduct a cross-examination which the accused is prevented from conducting himself by virtue of ss. 34 or 35 (SI 2000 No. 2093).

BACKGROUND

Any person accused of an offence normally has the right to conduct his own defence and, if he does so, to confront and cross-examine the witnesses against him. There is no obligation to be represented by a professional lawyer, as there is in some other systems (*Brown* [1998] 2 Cr App R 364). In certain cases, particularly those where the case against the accused is that he has intimidated his victim (rape being the most obvious example), there is a risk that he might seek to repeat the intimidation under the guise of cross-examination. Such intimidation might take many forms. The more obvious are prolonged questioning on upsetting or embarrassing topics or bullying the witness, although more subtle, but no less distressing, tactics include wearing the same clothes as on the occasion of the offence. It was the perceived misuse of the right by defendants charged with offences against children which led to the enactment of the partial prohibition in the Criminal Justice Act 1988, s. 34A (see p. 83). One of the main concerns which prompted the setting up of the Interdepartmental Working Group on the Treatment of Vulnerable or Intimidated Witnesses in the Criminal Justice System (which produced *Speaking Up For Justice*) was that the law was falling down in its duty to protect adult witnesses in similar situations. The trials at the Old Bailey of Ralston Edwards, and Milton Brown, widely reported in the press in 1996 and 1997, involved the lengthy and distressing cross-examination of women alleged to have been sexually assaulted by the accused. Sentencing Brown, Judge Pontius described his questioning of the victims as a 'merciless cross-examination designed only to intimidate and humiliate them'. Although instances of such conduct appear to be rare (the debates in Parliament on the 1999 Act were almost exclusively concerned with these two cases), the Government was concerned to reassure victims who might be deterred from coming forward by the prospect of cross-examination by their abuser. According to Lord Williams of Mostyn (2nd Reading, House of Lords, *Hansard*, 15 December 1998, col. 1305):

> What matters is the genuine fear that we have established ... that women are reluctant to go to court because they fear the consequences — not of proper cross-examination or of questioning in the interests of a defendant — but of what in the past has amounted to grotesque, humiliating bullying.

The common law affords a certain amount of protection from oppressive cross-examination, but the Government view was that this was insufficient. At the hearing of Milton Brown's appeal (*Brown* [1998] 2 Cr App R 364), Lord Bingham CJ stressed that the trial judge has a duty not only to ensure that the accused has a fair trial but also that witnesses who may be traumatised by giving evidence are properly protected and went on to state:

> Judges do not lack power to protect witnesses and control questioning. The trial judge is the master of proceedings in his court. He is not obliged to give an unrepresented defendant his head to ask whatever questions, at whatever length, the defendant wishes. In a case such as the present it will often be desirable, before any question is asked by the defendant of the complainant in cross-examination, for the trial judge to discuss the course of proceedings with the defendant in the absence of the jury. The judge can then elicit the general nature of the defence and

identify the specific points in the complainant's evidence with which the defendant takes issue, and any points he wishes to put to her. If the defendant proposes to call witnesses in his own defence, the substance of their evidence can be elicited so that the complainant's observations on it may, so far as relevant, be invited. It will almost always be desirable in the first instance to allow a defendant to put questions to a complainant, but it should be clear in advance that the defendant will be required, having put a point, to move on, and if he fails to do so the judge should intervene and secure compliance. If the defendant proves unable or unwilling to comply with the judge's instructions the judge should, if necessary in order to save the complainant from avoidable distress, stop further questioning by the defendant or take over the questioning of the complainant himself. If the defendant seeks by his dress, bearing, manner or questions to dominate, intimidate or humiliate the complainant, or if it is reasonably apprehended that he will seek to do so, the judge should not hesitate to order the erection of a screen, in addition to controlling questioning in the way we have indicated.

In the course of debates on the Act, Lord Bingham CJ suggested that, in the light of the guidance given in *Brown*, it would be wise to wait and see if a further remedy was required before making such significant inroads into the discretion of judges to control criminal proceedings (2nd Reading, House of Lords, *Hansard*, 15 December 1998, col. 1271). His plea fell on deaf ears, however, and it is clear that the changes brought about by the Act are intended not only to protect the witnesses to whom they apply from questioning in an improper manner (as *Brown* seeks to do) but to go further and relieve them of the trauma associated with the fact that it is the accused who is asking the questions. Under *Brown* this is possible only where the judge steps in and stops further questioning, by which time the damage might have been done. Under the Act, it will normally be possible for the witness to know in advance that cross-examination by the defendant is not an option. *Speaking Up For Justice* envisaged that the matter will normally be settled at a pre-trial hearing, although it is sometimes the case that the defendant decides to dispense with his legal representatives at a late stage of proceedings, necessitating a ruling in the course of the trial (para. 9.55).

SEXUAL CASES

Section 34 provides that no person charged with a sexual offence may cross-examine the complainant in person. The ban extends to questions about other offences with which the defendant is charged so, for example, a defendant facing charges of false imprisonment and rape could not cross-examine on either charge. In *Speaking Up For Justice* the view was taken that a mandatory ban offered the greatest reassurance and certainty to the witness, and was consistent with the approach adopted in respect of child witnesses. The Report further concluded, however, that the impact such a measure would have on the defendant's rights meant that the mandatory ban should protect adult witnesses only in those cases which had given rise to the greatest concern. Confining the ban to victims of alleged sexual assault ensured that those cases were covered which were likely to involve 'cross-examination of a personal and intimate nature which, if conducted by the defendant, is likely to be traumatic and distressing for the victim' (paras 9.37–8).

The definition of 'sexual offence' for this purpose is contained in s. 62. The main offences included are rape, burglary with intent to rape, various offences of unlawful intercourse, indecent assault and inchoate versions of these offences. Accomplice liability for such offences is also included, thereby protecting complainants from cross-examination by alleged secondary parties as well as principals. Some offences against children, such as the offence of incitement of a child aged under 16 to incest under the Criminal Law Act 1977, s. 54, are included, although a child giving evidence in such a case is doubly protected as s. 35 also applies. In this context, the significance of s. 34 will be to protect the adult who complains of an offence committed during her childhood.

CHILD COMPLAINANTS AND OTHER CHILD WITNESSES

Section 35 prohibits the cross-examination of a 'protected witness' by a person charged with an offence to which the section applies. Most of the witnesses protected by the provision are children, but witnesses who have given evidence in chief by means of a video recording made when a child, or who have had a birthday since examination in chief by virtue of which they have crossed the age threshold and are no longer children, are also covered (s. 35(2)(b)).

As with s. 34, the ban applies not only to cross-examination in relation to the offence which triggers the provision, but also in relation to any other offence with which the person is charged in the proceedings (s. 35(1)(a) and (b)). Section 35 follows the pattern of its predecessor, s. 34A of the Criminal Justice Act 1988, in protecting not only the child complainant who testifies but also any child 'alleged to have been a witness to the commission of the offence' (s. 35(2)(a)). The corresponding part of s. 34A of the 1988 Act, which refers to someone 'alleged to have witnessed the commission of the offence' has not been judicially construed, but appears to refer to first-hand eye-witnesses rather than to those called to provide, say, circumstantial evidence of the defendant's behaviour before or after the alleged offence.

The offences in respect of which protection is provided go beyond the list in the 1988 Act. The new offences are kidnapping, false imprisonment and offences under the Child Abduction Act 1984, s. 1 or 2 (s. 35(3)(b)). In *Speaking Up For Justice*, the only reason given for the extension was that such offences 'are often included on the same indictment as rape'. In itself this does not provide a justification in the context of the 1999 Act, which, as has already been stated, extends the protection to any offence charged in the same proceedings. False imprisonment charged with rape would thus be included in any event.

Offences which were previously covered by s. 34 of the 1988 Act, and which remain so, are:

(a)   the offences under the Sexual Offences Act 1956, the Indecency with Children Act 1960, the Sexual Offences Act 1976, the Criminal Law Act 1977, s. 54 and the Protection of Children Act 1978 (s. 35(3)(a));

(b)   offences of cruelty and neglect under the Children and Young Persons Act 1933, s. 1 (s. 35(3)(c)); and

(c)   any other offence which involves an assault on, or injury, or a threat of injury to, any person (s. 35(3)(d)).

Under the 1988 Act the words 'involving ... a threat of injury' were held to have a wider meaning than is at first apparent. In *Lee* [1996] 2 Cr App R 266, L was convicted of arson being reckless whether life was endangered. He set fire to clothing in a wardrobe belonging to his former cohabitee, an act witnessed by his six-year-old son. The issue was whether it had been correct to allow the boy to give his evidence in chief by means of a video recording under s. 32A of the 1988 Act: a facility available in respect of the same range of offences to which s. 34A of the 1988 Act applied. It was held that the Act was one involving a 'threat' of injury if any person was put at risk of injury by the defendant's conduct (as in the expression 'it is threatening to rain'). It was not necessary for L to make a deliberate threat (in the sense of a menace) to injure another. *Lee* was approved in *McAndrew-Bingham* [1999] 1 WLR 1897, also a decision on s. 32A, where the Court of Appeal considered that the statutory words required to be given a purposive construction so as to facilitate the protection of children by extending the use of video recording and the live link for the benefit of any child likely to be traumatised by confrontation with the accused. On such an approach, the offence of attempted child abduction under the Child Abduction Act 1984, s. 2 was an offence which came within the statutory words, although the court noted that the omission of the offence from the list of specific provisions might be considered an oversight if the object was to protect those children most likely to be traumatised by confrontation with the alleged offender. It would seem from the amended list in the 1999 Act that this observation was correct, as offences under the Child Abduction Act 1984, ss. 1 and 2 are now specifically included, and in consequence it is no longer necessary to stretch the notion of 'threat of injury' in abduction cases. Facts such as those in *Lee*, however, will only fall within s. 35 of the 1999 Act if that decision holds good in the context of the Act's scheme to protect witnesses from unnecessarily traumatic cross-examination in person. Arguably the existence of s. 36, which would give the court a discretion to prohibit cross-examination in person if this was necessary in the particular circumstances, might suggest that there is no need to adopt such a wide, purposive reading of s. 35. The overriding need is to balance the interests of the witness against those of the defendant and s. 36, it is submitted, provides the correct mechanism for doing so in all cases falling outside the normal meaning of ss. 34 and 35.

Section 35 omits specific reference to inchoate offences and offences alleged against secondary parties (compare s. 62, which makes provision for such offences in relation to s. 34 of the Act, and s. 32A of the Criminal Justice Act 1988, which made similar provision in relation to s. 34A of that Act). Accomplice liability is arguably included because a secondary party will be charged with the same offence as the principal, although a different mode of participation is alleged. Some forms of inchoate liability may be included, but only to the extent that they involve a 'threat of injury'. There is no obvious reason for the change of wording.

A complication which persists from the previous legislation is that 'child' is defined differently according to the offence in question. Where the offence is one of those defined by s. 35(3)(a) (i.e., it is sexual in nature), a child is a person aged under 17. If it is one of the offences in s. 35(3)(b), (c) or (d), the age limit is 14. There seems no obvious reason, other than tradition, to retain these differential limits. Of course, if one of the offences in (b), (c) or (d) is charged together with a sexual offence (rape and false imprisonment, say), the 16-year-old complainant will be protected in respect of both offences because the protection deriving from the rape covers all offences (of whatever nature) with which the defendant is charged in the proceedings. But it is not obvious why such a complainant is not deserving of protection when false imprisonment is the only offence charged. Section 36 could, however, be invoked to protect the complainant if this is considered to be necessary.

Under s. 35, a witness may be protected even though she is also on trial: s. 35(5) expressly includes a witness who is charged with an offence in the proceedings. This is in contrast to those provisions of the Act which make special measures available to assist vulnerable witnesses in giving their evidence and from which the accused is specifically excluded (ss. 16 and 17, considered at pp. 41–43).

DISCRETION TO PROHIBIT CROSS-EXAMINATION IN PERSON IN OTHER CASES

Section 36 contains a power to extend the prohibition on cross-examination by the accused to cases in which neither s. 34 nor s. 35 operates to provide an automatic ban. It follows that courts will have first to ascertain the ambit of the earlier provisions, taking account of the effect, if any, of *Lee* [1996] 2 Cr App R 266 (see above). If neither provision applies, s. 36(2) provides that the court may give a direction prohibiting the accused from cross-examining a particular witness if it appears to the court that the following conditions are satisfied:

   (a)   the quality of the witness's evidence is likely to be diminished if the cross-examination (or further cross-examination) is carried out by the accused in person;

   (b)   it would be likely to be improved if the direction is given; and

   (c)   it would not be contrary to the interests of justice to give such a direction.

'Quality' has the same meaning as that assigned for the purposes of s. 16(5) in relation to the allocation of special measures (see p. 41). Thus the court is concerned with the completeness, coherence and accuracy of the witness's evidence if it were to take place with, or without, cross-examination by the accused in person. A number of matters must, according to s. 36(3), be taken into account by the court in determining the quality issue. These are:

(a)   the views of the witness, particularly whether he is content to be cross-examined by the accused;

(b)   the nature of the questions likely to be asked having regard to the issues and the case for the defence;

(c)   the behaviour of the accused at any stage of the proceedings, whether generally or in relation to the witness;

(d)   any relationship between the witness and the accused;

(e)   whether s. 34 or s. 35 would or might have operated to protect the witness from cross-examination by a person other than the accused who is, or who has been, charged in the proceedings with an offence to which either of those provisions applies (thus, for example, if A is charged with a sexual offence it is a factor to bear in mind when deciding to allow B, his co-accused, to cross-examine in person even though B is charged with some other offence. It remains a factor (though the weight attaching to it may be less) if A ceases to be charged with that offence, or drops out of the proceedings altogether);

(f)   any special measures direction which the court has given, or proposes to give, to assist the witness.

Because s. 36(3) states that the court must have regard 'in particular' to the above matters, it would seem to follow that the court must also consider any other matters which it regards as relevant. No particular guidance is given to the court in relation to the 'interests of justice' aspect of the test. One matter which might be thought relevant to both issues which the court has to consider is the effect of the decision in *Brown* [1998] 2 Cr App R 364 (see p. 81) on any cross-examination which the accused is entitled to conduct in person. If concern is centred on the manner in which the questioning is likely to be conducted if the accused is allowed to undertake the task, the protection afforded by *Brown* may well be sufficient. If the court is more concerned about the effect on the witness of being confronted by the accused, it may not.

Offences which, it has been suggested, might require a direction under s. 36 are those, such as stalking, where it is foreseeable that a witness might be intimidated and distressed by cross-examination. It might also be the case that violence by a former partner could fall into this category. In the debates on the 1999 Act, Lord Williams also identified the case of abuse or harassment of an elderly person living alone, who might well not give his best evidence if interrogated by the alleged perpetrator. He further identified witnesses with learning disability as the possible beneficiaries of the discretion (House of Lords Committee Stage, *Hansard*, 8 February 1999, col. 115). In response, Lord Thomas of Gresford advanced the view that the provisions would 'cotton wool' witnesses from the ordinary and proper stresses of cross-examination, and that it would be too easy for a witness to secure the protection of the section. The example was given of a witness about to be cross-examined by his employer, on trial for fraud, and who claimed to feel 'a little uneasy' about his future employment prospects. If this is the only objection, it would seem that the interests of justice test cannot be met, as the witness's employment prospects are affected, if at all, by giving evidence against his employer rather than by facing him across the court for cross-examination in person. A court applying the 'interests of justice' test will also need to bear in mind the constraints imposed by the European Convention on Human Rights (see p. 89).

PROCEDURE FOR DISCRETIONARY DIRECTIONS

A direction under s. 36 can be made either as a result of the prosecutor's application or where the court has raised the issue of its own motion (s. 36(1)(a) and (b)). Such a direction normally has effect from the time it is made until the time the witness is discharged (s. 37(1)), except that the direction may itself be discharged by the court in the interests of justice (s. 37(2)). A party applying for such a discharge must show that there has been a material change of circumstances (s. 37(2)(a)), but the court may also discharge of its own motion, and is bound by no such consideration (s. 37(2)(b)). The reasons for granting or refusing any applications, whether for a direction or for its discharge, must be stated in open court and, in the case of a magistrates' court, entered in the register of its proceedings (s. 37(4)). Section 37(5) allows rules of court to be made *inter alia* to govern the manner in which confidential or sensitive information is to be treated in connection with an application, and as to its being disclosed or withheld from a party to the proceedings. Section 37(5) also allows rules to be made for expert evidence to be received in relation to an application for, or for discharging, a direction, presumably as to the impact which cross-examination in person is likely to have on a fragile witness. The practice of the courts has been to exclude expert evidence where the court considers that it may safely draw its own conclusions and this may be the most likely approach where the witness is an ordinary person who has been subject to extraordinary stress (the alleged victim of stalking, for example). If the witness suffers from a specific mental or physical condition which is relevant to the exercise of the discretion and beyond the normal experience of the court, expert evidence would clearly be required.

If applications are to be hotly contested they may be both protracted and costly, although unrepresented defendants are very much the exception rather than the rule.

REPRESENTATION FOR PURPOSES OF CROSS-EXAMINATION

If an accused is prevented by s. 34, 35 or 36 from cross-examining a witness in person, s. 38(2) obliges the court to invite the accused to arrange for a legal representative to cross-examine on his behalf and to set a date by which he should notify them of the arrangements which he has made. If nothing is heard, or if the accused states that he has made no such arrangements, the court must then consider whether it is 'necessary in the interests of justice' for the witness to be cross-examined by a court-appointed qualified legal representative (s. 38(3)). Section 38(4) empowers the court to make such an appointment, and s. 40 amends the relevant statutory provisions so that payment may be made out of central funds. A representative appointed under s. 38(4) is expressly stated not to be responsible to the accused (s. 38(5)).

The assignment of a court-appointed representative may work reasonably well where the accused is compliant, but, where he is not, the representative will obviously be somewhat handicapped. It may nevertheless still be possible to conduct a useful cross-examination on the basis of available documentation such as statements made by the witness or by the accused at an earlier stage of proceedings, and on expert medical reports and the like. But there is no guarantee that the account given by the accused in evidence if he testifies will match with his earlier statements, so that the court might have to contemplate the prospect of recalling the witness for further cross-examination (a point made by Lord Thomas, House of Lords Committee Stage, *Hansard*, 1 February 1999, col. 1387).

Section 34A of the 1988 Act made no provision for representation to be arranged by the court. Where an accused was unrepresented and prohibited by law from cross-examining a child witness in person, the Court of Appeal held, in *De Oliviera* [1997] Crim LR 600, that it was generally desirable for the trial judge to test the reliability and the accuracy of the witness's evidence, although he should not 'descend into the arena' on behalf of the defence. It was also open for the judge to ask an accused whether there were matters which he would like the judge to put to the witness on his behalf. In a case where the court decides not to appoint a representative, the guidance in *De Oliviera* still holds good. However, the problems faced by the judge who takes over the questioning of the witness are such that it would be preferable, where there are important matters in dispute, to appoint a representative.

JUDICIAL WARNING

In a jury trial in which the accused has been prevented by one of the provisions considered above from cross-examining a witness in person, s. 39 requires the judge to consider whether to warn the jury. It is a matter for the judge to decide what warning (if any) is required (s. 39(1)). The object of the exercise is to ensure that the accused is not prejudiced by adverse inferences that might be drawn from the fact that he has not cross-examined the witness in person or (where this is the case) from the fact that the witness has been cross-examined instead by a court-appointed legal representative (s. 39(1)(a) and (b)). A warning may also need to be given where the accused has conducted part of the cross-examination in person but has then been prohibited from continuing (s. 39(2)); that is a situation particularly likely to arouse prejudice, as it is likely only to arise where the accused has misconducted himself in some way that his cross-examination is discontinued. No doubt the Judicial Studies Board will formulate a standard warning for the purposes of s. 39.

Although s. 39 does not specifically require it, the judge may also have to caution the jury against drawing adverse inferences of another sort. If the cross-examination is incomplete (for example, because the accused has been prevented from proceeding with it and the court has not appointed a cross-examiner to complete it), it would normally be inferred that the evidence which has not been challenged is accepted. This may well not be the case, and a particularly careful direction to that effect may be required.

An accused who is aggrieved that he has been deprived of his 'normal' right to cross-examine may complain to the jury, saying of his court-appointed legal representative 'I did not want that man. He has not asked the questions that I wanted to be asked. He has had no instructions from me and my trial is therefore unfair'. (A case put by Lord Thomas of Gresford, House of Lords Committee Stage, *Hansard*, 1 February 1999, col. 1387.) The judge will have to decide whether to comment on such a grievance, given that the accused would have had the opportunity to instruct a legal representative of his choice.

COMPLIANCE WITH THE EUROPEAN CONVENTION ON HUMAN RIGHTS

The Government anticipates that the restraints on cross-examination in person will not conflict with the European Convention on Human Rights. Article 6(3)(c) of the Convention provides, in the context of the accused's general right to a fair trial guaranteed by Article 6, that an accused has the right 'to defend himself in person or through legal assistance of his own choosing'. An accused who is dealt with under the provisions of the Act may be prevented from 'defending himself' at the essential stage of cross-examining a key witness and may be represented at that point in the trial by a court-appointed advocate who is not 'of his own choosing'. However, the Act preserves the accused's right to choose his own representative in the first instance, appointing another representative only in cases of necessity and where the accused has failed to do so himself (s. 38(2) to (4)). This may be sufficient by itself to deflect criticism, unless the historic nature of the right to defend oneself in criminal cases renders the compulsory substitution of a legal representative (chosen or otherwise) objectionable in itself. The Convention does not however appear to give the accused the right to conduct his own case in circumstances where legal representation is more appropriate. In *Croissant* v *Germany* (1992) 16 EHRR 135 the European Court of Human Rights stated that a provision in the German Code of Criminal Procedure requiring that the accused be represented by counsel in all trials conducted in the Regional Court could not be deemed incompatible with the Convention, indeed the provision was stated to have parallels in the legislation of other Contracting States (para. 27). It might be argued that there is a difference between a general requirement of representation and the selective and potentially prejudicial provisions of ss. 34 to 36 of the Act, but it would seem that reliance in this context may be placed on *Doorson* v *Netherlands* (1996) 22 EHRR 330. That case was concerned with anonymity of prosecution witnesses at trial; the Court stated that principles of fair trial require that 'in appropriate cases the interests of the defence are balanced against those of witnesses or victims called upon to testify' (para. 70). It is clear that the Court had in mind the specific rights of the witness under the Convention to the protection of individual liberty and privacy, and the 1999 Act may be seen as an attempt to strike a balance of the sort to which *Doorson* refers. This is supported by the comments of Lord Lester (House of Lords Committee Stage, *Hansard*, 1 February 1999, col. 1397), who cited correspondence showing that the Government view that the Bill complies with the Convention is based on their interpretation of the two authorities cited.

Chapter 7
Sexual History Evidence

OVERVIEW

The sexual history of complainants has traditionally been a matter on which evidence has been adduced and cross-examination permitted in trials for rape and related offences. The harmful effect of this practice in terms of trauma for the complainant and discouragement for victims to report or follow through rape complaints was recognised in the Sexual Offences (Amendment) Act 1976, s. 2, which prohibited the admission of such material except where it was necessary to avoid injustice to the defendant. It was the view of the Interdepartmental Working Group on the Treatment of Vulnerable or Intimidated Witnesses in the Criminal Justice System (which produced *Speaking Up For Justice*) that s. 2 had failed to achieve its purpose. Section 41 of the 1999 Act is intended to set out more clearly than its predecessor the circumstances in which such evidence can be adduced, not merely in rape cases but in proceedings for sexual offences generally. Section 42 provides for the interpretation of s. 41 and specifies the types of proceeding to which the new rules apply. Section 43 lays down the procedure to be followed where the defence applies to adduce evidence or to ask questions about the complainant's sexual history.

These provisions were due to come into force by Spring 2000, according to *Action For Justice: Implementing the Speaking Up For Justice Report in England and Wales* (Home Office, 1999), but subsequent developments have led to a revised target and they are not likely to be implemented until late 2000. There are transitional provisions in para. 5 of sch. 7 to the Act to protect continuing proceedings in which leave to adduce evidence or to cross-examine about sexual history has already been given under the old law.

SECTION 2 OF THE SEXUAL OFFENCES (AMENDMENT) ACT 1976

History

Section 2 of the Sexual Offences (Amendment) Act 1976 came about as a result of the *Report of the Advisory Group on the Law of Rape* (Cmnd. 6352, 1975), by the

Heilbron Committee. Rape was at that time (and continued to be until the amendments effected by the Criminal Justice and Public Order Act 1994, s. 142) an offence which could only be committed against a woman. The Heilbron Committee pointed out that a number of old precedents under which sexual history evidence had traditionally been adduced appeared to be based on the assumption that a woman's sexual experience outside marriage was an indication of her unreliability and untruthfulness as a witness. Based on this anachronism, procedures had developed, particularly in regard to cross-examination, which were not only inimical to the fair trial of the essential issues, but which resulted in distress and humiliation to the complainant herself. At common law, evidence of sexual experience was considered to have a limited bearing on the issue of consent, although evidence showing that the complainant was a prostitute was admitted on the ground that it tended to show consent (*Clarke* (1817) 2 Stark 241), as was evidence that she had previously had a sexual relationship with the accused (*Cockcroft* (1870) 11 Cox CC 410). Questions about the complainant's relationship with other men were thought to stand on a different footing, however, and to be relevant, if at all, to her credibility as a witness (*Bashir* [1969] 1 WLR 1303). It was in relation to this last type of questioning in particular that the Heilbron Committee considered that the cross-examiner had traditionally been allowed too much latitude. Because such evidence was collateral to the issues in the case, the complainant's denial of any sexual experience put to her in cross-examination to test her credibility could not be contradicted and had to be accepted as final. But if a witness was forthcoming about her experiences, there was a risk that the jury would think less of her because of her lack of chastity. Even if the suggestion was denied, the mere putting of intimate questions might be enough to embarrass the witness and to confuse or even to prejudice the jury. In either case, the complainant was unnecessarily distressed, and the prosecution case quite probably unjustifiably weakened in the eyes of the jury.

The Heilbron Committee concluded that some curtailment of unnecessary cross-examination of complainants was urgently required, and suggested that the previous sexual history of the complainant with men other than the accused should be inadmissible except with the leave of the trial judge. This proposal became the backbone of s. 2 of the 1976 Act, with s. 2(1) providing that in a trial for a rape offence 'no evidence and no question in cross-examination shall be adduced or asked at the trial, by or on behalf of any defendant at the trial, about any sexual experience of a complainant with a person other than that defendant'. The Heilbron Committee also made specific recommendations as to the circumstances in which the judge might grant leave, but these were not enacted. Instead s. 2(2) required an assessment by the judge of whether it would be 'unfair to the defendant to refuse to allow the evidence to be adduced or the question to be asked'. Only if he was so satisfied could the jury be made aware of the matter. Although it was common practice to speak of the judge as having a 'discretion' in relation to s. 2, the Court of Appeal in *Viola* [1982] 1 WLR 1138 correctly stated that the true position was that the judge had to 'make a judgment as to whether he is satisfied or not in the terms of section 2', and, if so satisfied, to admit the evidence.

Interpretation

Section 2 has the appearance of being the ideal mechanism to hold the balance between the right of the accused to a fair trial and the right of the witness not to be subjected on tenuous grounds to upsetting and intrusive questions. It forces the defence to formulate an argument for admissibility with specific information or questions in mind and is a major improvement upon the common-law position. *Speaking Up For Justice* does not say that s. 2 is a bad provision, rather that the practice of the courts in interpreting it conflicts with the legislative purpose behind s. 2 (*Speaking Up For Justice*, paras. 9.56–72). The main difficulty which appears to have arisen is that the courts, contrary to the view expressed by the Heilbron Committee, have accepted that evidence of a complainant's sexual relationships with other men, falling short of prostitution, could be evidence bearing on the issue of consent. In *Viola*, V had knocked on the door of the complainant's home (ostensibly in order to enlist her help in finding his lost car-keys) and had stayed to have intercourse with her. On V's account, C consented to have intercourse with him on the basis of a very slight acquaintance, and on hers he forced himself on her, using violence to overcome her resistance. At V's trial, evidence was excluded of two incidents. One concerned the visit of two other men, friends of C's boyfriend but only remote acquaintances of hers, some two hours before the alleged rape. On finding the boyfriend to be elsewhere, the men stayed to drink a lot of alcohol with the complainant and claimed that she then made sexual advances to both of them, to which they did not respond. The other incident concerned the arrival of a female neighbour on the following morning, a few hours after the alleged rape, to collect C's child. It was not disputed that she discovered another man, naked except for his carpet slippers, asleep on C's sofa. The Court of Appeal held that both incidents:

> are matters which went to the question of consent and which could not be regarded as so trivial or of so little relevance as for the judge to be able to say that he was satisfied that no injustice would be done to the appellant by their exclusion from the evidence. This case differs from those to which we have been referred, because those to which we have been referred were cases where the questions sought to be put in were questions solely as to credit. These questions were not mere questions as to credit.

It is a question of logic, not of law, whether the evidence of the other incidents tended to support V's case that C consented. The Court of Appeal clearly thought that it did, and laid down a principle that evidence which does not go merely to credit but which is relevant to an issue in the trial, such as consent, should normally be admitted on the ground that to exclude it would be to prevent the jury hearing something 'which … might cause them to change their minds about the evidence given by the complainant'. This perhaps does not put the point as well as it might be put, for a jury might also be induced to change its mind by evidence or questions which are strictly irrelevant to any issue at the trial, yet such evidence does not thereby become admissible. But the court is clearly right to state that evidence which is relevant to consent, and which is likely also to be significant in a reasonable jury's assessment of the matter, should not be excluded. The key issue, however, is not whether such evidence should be excluded, but whether evidence of the type which was admitted in *Viola* falls within the category and has the relevance attributed to it by the Court of Appeal.

In the debates on the 1999 Act, Paul Boateng, for the Government, claimed that one aim of s. 41 was to overturn *Viola*. He said:

> The [judgment in] *Viola* in 1982, where it was ruled that the complainant's promiscuity was relevant to consent, will be overturned. It is our view that the fact that someone is or has been promiscuous does not take away that person's right to say no and to be able to draw on the full protection of the law to say no. We aim to overturn the judgment in *Viola*. (House of Commons Committee Stage, Standing Committee E, *Hansard*, 24 June 1999)

The Court of Appeal in *Viola* was not, of course, taking away C's right to say no, but clearly regarded it as necessary for the jury to know of C's attitude to intercourse with a near-stranger on the night in question. In crude terms, one interpretation of the evidence was that C was looking for sex and was not too particular where she found it. This does not mean that she did consent to V, but it makes his story of a very casual sexual encounter in a woman's own home far more believable than would otherwise have been the case. Whatever the Government's intentions, it may be the case that *Viola* survives the 1999 Act (see p. 99) but, if it does not, then a defendant in V's position might legitimately question whether he has received a fair trial.

Among the other precedents which, according to Paul Boateng, the Act is intended to overturn is the decision of the Court of Appeal in *SMS* [1992] Crim LR 310. S, a black man with one hand and a false eye, was accused of raping a 14-year-old white girl in a grubby flat in circumstances involving considerable indecency. The court thought that the jury, who were kept in ignorance of the girl's sexual history, would have assumed the girl to have been inexperienced and would have found it difficult to believe that she would have consented to her first act of intercourse with such a person and in such circumstances. It was held that evidence showing the girl to have had some sexual experience ought to have been admitted, as it was relevant to the issue of consent. Of this, Mr Boateng stated that, unless the prosecution had positively asserted that the girl was a virgin, it was not proper to extract from her the knowledge that she was not. He asked, rhetorically, 'How could the fact that she was not a virgin be relevant?' It is clear that the Government and the Court of Appeal are operating with very different notions of what relevance means in this context. In *Brown* (1989) 89 Cr App R 97 the Court of Appeal held that it was a question of degree, to be decided on the facts of each case, whether 'the complainant's attitude to sexual relations could be material upon which ... a jury could reasonably rely to conclude that the complainant may indeed have consented to the sexual intercourse on the material occasion'. Set next to this Mr Boateng's statements that 'We say that the complainant's attitude is not relevant to consent' and 'We must get away from the old-fashioned idea ... that a class of women exists who are of loose sexual morals and whose consent can therefore be assumed in all circumstances' and you have the essence of the disagreement. The purpose of s. 41 is to translate the Government's concept of relevance into a statutory rule.

THE NEW RULE OF EXCLUSION: s. 41

Complainants in sexual cases

Section 41(1) provides that where a person is charged with a sexual offence the leave of the court is required before there can be any evidence or questions 'by or on behalf of any accused at the trial' about 'any sexual behaviour of the complainant'. 'Complainant' for this purpose means a person against or in relation to whom the offence was, or is alleged to have been, committed (s. 63). It is necessary to avoid the stereotypical image of an adult woman complainant. The complainant may be male or female, adult or child. Likewise it is important to note that the rule is not confined to matters raised in cross-examination of the complainant. It is not even explicit in the definition of complainant that he or she is someone who gives evidence in the proceedings, although this may be implicit in s. 43(1) (see p. 103) and would certainly be the normal case. The formula for exclusion is clearly wide enough to cover all defence evidence, so that the accused cannot introduce the complainant's sexual history as part of his own testimony. The definition of 'sexual offence' which is adopted is that contained in s. 62, except that s. 42(2) confers a power on the Secretary of State, for the purposes of s. 41, to add or delete any offence to or from the offences there listed. Until such action is taken, the main offences in respect of which s. 41 comes into play are (by virtue of s. 62(1)) rape; burglary with intent to rape; various offences under the Sexual Offences Act 1956 including unlawful sexual intercourse, indecent assault and abduction; unlawful sexual intercourse under the Mental Health Act 1959, s. 128; indecency towards children under the Indecency with Children Act 1960, s. 1; and incitement of a child to incest under the Criminal Law Act 1977, s. 54. The protection of s. 41 also applies where the accused is charged with incitement, conspiracy, or attempt to commit any of the substantive offences in s. 62, or with aiding, abetting, counselling or procuring such an offence (s. 62(2)). Section 41 thus has a very much wider scope than s. 2 of the 1976 Act, which applied only to 'a rape offence'. Decisions of the Court of Appeal such as *Funderburk* [1990] 1 WLR 587 established that, in trials of offences such as unlawful intercourse to which s. 2 of the 1976 Act did not strictly apply, the trial judge should be astute to see that complainants were spared the ordeal of unnecessarily humiliating cross-examination: the mischief at which s. 2 was aimed should not, it was said, be perpetrated in other, related contexts. Because s. 41 is of more general application, it is unlikely to be necessary for the courts to develop parallel common-law rules applying the spirit of s. 41 in other contexts.

Section 41(1) applies wherever 'a person is charged with a sexual offence', but s. 41(7) makes provision for special cases. Where the prosecutor decides not to proceed in respect of the charge which has triggered s. 41, the protection ceases to apply (s. 41(7)(a)). But where the person charged pleads guilty to, or is convicted of, the charge, the protection continues to apply (s. 41(7)(b)). While the protection is in force, it applies to any accused at the trial, whether or not charged with a s. 62 offence (s. 41(1)).

The protection conferred by s. 41 applies not only to trials, but to committals, applications to dismiss charges under the Criminal Justice Act 1991, sch. 6 and the Crime and Disorder Act 1998, sch. 3, *Newton* hearings and appeals (s. 42(3)(a) to (e)). It follows that, as the circumstances dictate, a 'person charged' sometimes includes a person who has been convicted.

Sexual behaviour

Section 41 applies only to evidence and questions about 'any sexual behaviour' of the complainant. This is defined by s. 42(1)(c) as 'any sexual behaviour or other sexual experience, whether or not involving any accused or other person', except that it generally excludes anything alleged to have taken place as part of the event which forms the subject-matter of the charge. (Compare s. 2 of the 1976 Act, which excludes (and then admits with leave) questions/evidence about 'any sexual experience' of a complainant with a person other than the accused.)

The exact scope of the rule of exclusion, and therefore of the exception to it where leave may be granted, is unclear. It is obviously necessary to obtain leave before asking whether C has had intercourse with the accused on other occasions, and presumably also before asking whether they kissed intimately at the office Christmas Party a month before the alleged offence took place. Whether a peck on the cheek under the mistletoe at the same party constitutes sexual behaviour remains to be seen, but it may well do so. The fact that C has worked as a prostitute must be regarded as sexual behaviour for the purposes of the section, though whether posing for topless newspaper pictures or working as an erotic dancer falls into the same category is less clear. In some trials, it appears that young female complainants have been asked about their use of vibrators, or other objects with which penetration of the vagina may be achieved, on the ground that to do so may explain away a tear in the hymen or other apparent evidence of sexual experience linked by the prosecution to the offence committed by D. (See, for example, *Barnes* [1994] Crim LR 691, where it was held that the 1976 Act did not apply to such evidence.) Under s. 41, leave will have to be given before asking such personal questions: sexual behaviour or experience explicitly includes conduct not involving 'any other person'. But it would surely not be necessary to ask for leave before cross-examining a young girl about the sort of sanitary protection she is accustomed to using, if it is relevant to the state of her hymen at the time of the alleged offence.

Is it 'sexual behaviour' or 'sexual experience' to assemble a collection of pornographic literature, or to loiter outside a toilet which is a known pick-up point for gay men? It is easy to see how such proclivities might be exploited to the embarrassment of the complainant, but not entirely obvious that they fall within the section. If the defence to a charge of rape is that C consented, however, and the evidence offered in support is that her 'pillow talk' included boasting about her previous sexual conquests, that would seem to be evidence of 'sexual behaviour' on her part (which might well fall within the narrow exceptions regarding the consent defence considered below). Conversations between C and the accused were held capable of amounting to evidence of sexual experience for the purposes of s. 2 of the 1976 Act in *Hinds & Butler* [1979] Crim LR 111.

A rather different problem arises in connection with questions about C's medical history, including whether she has had an abortion or treatment for a sexually-related illness (other than as a result of the alleged offence). These presumably fall within the protection afforded by s. 41 on the basis that they could not be put without revealing something of C's sexual behaviour prior to the medical intervention in question, and are thus 'about' it in the sense required by s. 41(1). If this is right, however, the same must be true of the fact that C was once married to D, for that carries an inference that marital intercourse took place. (Although it is rather harder to see that such a question is 'about' C's sexual behaviour as such, it is likely to be put with the purpose of getting before the jury the previous sexual relationship between the parties.) An inference that previous sexual behaviour occurred does not necessarily follow from the fact that C was once the accused's boyfriend or girlfriend, although the purpose behind the line of inquiry might have to be ascertained in order to decide for sure whether leave is needed in order to pursue the matter. It will be apparent that the definition of sexual behaviour is by no means free of difficulty.

Evidence which relates to the reputation of the complainant, though it may be evidence about sexual behaviour, cannot be adduced under any of the exceptions to the rule which are considered below. This is because s. 41(6) provides that any question or evidence adduced under the exceptions must relate to a specific instance or instances of alleged sexual behaviour on the part of the complainant. Evidence such as that which was admitted in *Bogie* [1992] Crim LR 301 about the complainant's reputation for being 'a tart' and 'an easy lay' could not be brought within the 1999 Act (and was quite possibly not intended to be brought under the 1976 Act: cf. *Howes* [1996] 2 Cr App R 490).

Grounds for giving leave: the two conditions

Leave can be given to adduce evidence or to put questions only on an application made by or on behalf of an accused (s. 41(2)) where the court is satisfied that two conditions are made out. The first of these, considered in detail below, concerns the relevance of the evidence to the issues in the case, and may be established by showing that either s. 41(3) or s. 41(5) applies (s. 41(2)(a)). The second condition is that 'a refusal of leave might have the result of rendering unsafe a conclusion of the jury or (as the case may be) the court on any relevant issue in the case (s. 41(2)(b))'. A purist might argue that the satisfaction of the second condition should be enough by itself to secure leave, without any need for the legislation to specify the precise way in which the question or evidence relates to the issues in the case. This would be a valid criticism on the assumption that the Act follows the traditional approach whereby it is for the court to decide whether a question or an item of evidence is relevant to an issue in the case. Under s. 41, however, the only question or evidence to which relevance can be conceded is that which arises in relation to the issues identified in s. 41(3) and (5). In other words, the situations in which sexual history evidence may be relevant are defined not by the court's sense of logic but by Parliament's.

Issues relevant to the defence: s. 41(3)

In order for s. 41(3) to apply, the judge must make two findings. The first is that the evidence tendered, or the question sought to be put, is relevant to an issue in the case. This means (s. 42(1)) any issue falling to be proved by prosecution or defence in the trial, but excludes (s. 41(4)) evidence or questions in relation to which 'it appears to the court to be reasonable to assume that the purpose (or main purpose) for which it would be adduced or asked is to establish or elicit material for impugning the credibility of the complainant as a witness'. (The formula 'it appears to the court to be reasonable to assume' is unusual, and it is not clear how, if at all, it differs from the more common 'it appears to the court'.) The problem envisaged arises where the defence seeks to introduce evidence or questioning under s. 41(3) which the court considers is mainly directed at undermining the witness's credibility. The solution s. 41(4) provides is that the relevance of the evidence is not to be determined simply by reference to its tendency to prove or disprove the matter in question, but by reference to the purpose of the person putting the question. If a case arises where the evidence is relevant (in the sense of probative of one of the matters in s. 41(3)) and the exclusion of the evidence might have the result of rendering any conviction of the defendant unsafe, it appears the court is nevertheless obliged to exclude it if it is being put forward predominantly for the wrong reason.

The second finding required by s. 41(3) concerns the nature of the issue to which the question or evidence relates. The defence application must rest on one of the following three grounds:

(a) the evidence/question relates to a relevant issue which is *not* an issue of consent (s. 41(3)(a));

(b) the evidence/question relates to a relevant issue which *is* an issue of consent and the behaviour took place at or about the same time as the event which is the subject-matter of the charge (s. 41(3)(b));

(c) the evidence/question relates to a relevant issue which *is* an issue of consent and the behaviour is so similar to behaviour alleged to have been part of the event which is the subject-matter of the charge, or to any other sexual behaviour which is alleged to have taken place at or about that time, that the similarity cannot reasonably be explained as a coincidence (s. 41(3)(c)).

Not an issue of consent: s. 41(3)(a)

An example of an application falling within ground (a) would be a case of rape where D claims that no intercourse took place, or where he disputes the prosecution's evidence of identification. Also (and perhaps surprisingly) within (a) is a rape case where D says that, although he now realises that C was not consenting, at the time he honestly thought that she was (the *Morgan* defence, so called after the decision of the House of Lords in *Director of Public Prosecutions* v *Morgan* [1976] AC 182). This is because s. 42(1)(b) defines 'issue of consent' as any issue whether the complainant in fact consented, but as excluding 'any issue as to the belief of the accused that the complainant consented'.

In support of a contention falling within s. 41(3)(a), D may seek to rely on any relevant question or evidence about C's sexual behaviour, provided:

(a)   its main purpose is not to impugn her credibility (s. 41(4)); and
(b)   a refusal of leave might have the result of rendering D's conviction unsafe (s. 41(2)(b)).

If D's defence is actual consent, however, as distinct from the *Morgan* defence of belief in consent, such evidence could not be adduced except where the more stringent conditions in s. 41(3)(b) or (c) are made out. The reasoning behind this distinction is that the complainant's past behaviour may be relevant to the accused's honest but erroneous belief in consent in a way that it is not relevant (or not as relevant) to consent itself. So the fact that D and C were once lovers may explain why he thought C was responding to his advances on the occasion which forms the basis of the charge, even though it may have very little if any bearing on the question whether C actually did so. This is particularly the case because the *Morgan* defence does not require D's belief to be based on any rational grounds: the jury is concerned only with the question whether the belief is honestly held. If, therefore, D says that he believed C was consenting because she had slept with all his friends and he assumed that she would sleep with him, it may be necessary to admit the evidence. This is subject to what was said by the Court of Appeal in *Barton* (1987) 85 Cr App R 5, where O'Connor J correctly pointed out that there is a difference between thinking that a woman would consent if advances were made to her and actually thinking that she is consenting to intercourse at the time it takes place. As it is the latter belief with which the court is concerned, the accused's expectations or assumptions based on C's sexual history might be of insufficient relevance to be admitted. Despite the fact that Government assurances were given during the debates on the Act that its provisions could never be used to admit 'tittle-tattle, bar-room or cloakroom gossip or the suggestion that because the complainant had gone willingly with unnamed people in the past she was willing to go with the defendant', it is hard to see how there can be any rigorous policy of exclusion of such evidence if it is the contention of the defence that it in fact influenced his belief on the issue of consent at the time of intercourse.

Those who feel that the way in which the Act deals with the *Morgan* defence will inevitably pose a threat to the completeness of the protection afforded to the complainant may take consolation from the review of the law of sexual offences which is currently underway. There are some suggestions in the House of Commons Standing Committee which considered the 1999 Act that the *Morgan* defence will be on the agenda for discussion at that review, and might well be reformed so as to inject a requirement that the belief be based on reasonable grounds. A recommendation along these lines may be found in the recent consultation paper *Setting the Boundaries: Reforming the Law on Sexual Offences* (Home Office, July 2000) at 2.13.14. This would provide the required platform for excluding tittle-tattle and the like (House of Commons Standing Committee E, *Hansard*, 24 June 1999). In the meantime, complainants may find it hard to derive much reassurance from the protection conferred in relation to consent, given the comparative ease with which their past lives may be raked over to support a *Morgan* defence. As the two defences are often raised together, many complainants will not be significantly better off and will not be consoled by an assurance that (as is presumably the case) evidence which is admissible only on the *Morgan* defence cannot be used by the jury or magistrates in relation to a concurrent defence of consent.

Defence of consent: behaviour at or about the same time: s. 41(3)(b)

Ground (b) applies where the issue is one of consent and the sexual behaviour of the complainant which it is sought to raise took place 'at or about the same time as' the event which is the subject-matter of the charge against the accused. The behaviour in question might, of course, be behaviour with D himself, as where a couple between whom rape is said to have occurred are seen apparently enjoying a kiss and an embrace shortly before, or after, the relevant act of intercourse. Or it might be behaviour with another, although it must be remembered that the philosophy of the Act is that consent is consent to a person and not to a circumstance, and the fact that C was willing to have, or indeed had, sex with Tom and Dick at noon does not mean that she consented to Harry at the quarter-hour. Nevertheless it is hard to escape the conclusion that, if the facts of *Viola* [1982] 1 WLR 1138 (see p. 92) were to recur, defence counsel would feel bound to submit that C's conduct with the other men, being so close in point of time to the intercourse with the accused, had a bearing on the issue of her state of mind at the relevant time. Finally, the behaviour might not involve any other person at all, as where it is alleged that C was performing a striptease at her open window in response to which D, a total stranger, climbed through the window and had consensual intercourse with C.

The first draft of the Bill confined the period within which relevant sexual behaviour had to take place to the 24 hours before and after the event which is the subject-matter of the charge. Such a specific rule would have been a nightmare to operate: one has only to imagine a case where C and D cannot agree the time at which intercourse took place, and on C's account the behaviour to which D wishes to refer is outside the 24-hour period, whereas on D's account it falls just within it. The 'at or about the same time' formula, though arguably narrower, at least permits the court some leeway in deciding what sort of behaviour connects sufficiently with the event.

Defence of consent: behaviour strikingly similar: s. 41(3)(c)

The third and most difficult ground, ground (c), applies where the defence is in effect claiming that there is similar fact evidence about C's behaviour at another time which is suggestive of consent. Again, this qualification was not included in the original Bill, which limited the field of inquiry to 24 hours before and after the event in all circumstances. The amendment was largely due to the persuasiveness of Baroness Mallalieu, who related the tale of a man accused of rape who claimed that C had invited him to her home to re-enact the balcony scene from Romeo and Juliet. Having done so, they then engaged in consensual intercourse. D subsequently discovered that this was a favourite ploy of C, and that other men had fallen (or rather ascended) into her arms in similar circumstances (though not within 24 hours of D's ascent). Such behaviour, as Baroness Mallalieu pointed out, has no value in support of a *Morgan* defence, as D could not claim to have known about it at the time. In support of a defence of consent, however, it effectively changes what sounds a most far-fetched story into a plausible account. Baroness Mallalieu's narrative echoed one of the proposals of the Heilbron Committee, which was that evidence of C's previous behaviour with other men might be admitted where it was 'strikingly similar to her alleged behaviour on the occasion of, or in relation to, events immediately preceding or following the alleged offence'. This recommendation has clearly formed the template for s. 41(3)(c).

The Heilbron Report borrowed 'striking similarity' from the decision of the House of Lords in *Director of Public Prosecutions* v *Boardman* [1975] AC 421, which deals with the the the use of similar fact evidence against the accused as part of the prosecution case, but it has since been recognised that 'striking similarity' is only one of a number of ways in which similar fact evidence may display the exceptional degree of probative value that the law requires of it. Thus two robberies might be linked by striking similarity (as where the robber on both occasions commits the crime wearing the ceremonial headdress of a Red Indian chief) or by other factors including time and circumstance (the same car is used on both occasions and the robberies occur within minutes of each other and a short distance apart). As Lord Mackay LC said in *Director of Public Prosecutions* v *P* [1991] 2 AC 447:

> the essential feature of evidence which is to be admitted is that its probative force in support of the allegation that an accused person committed a crime is sufficiently great to make it just to admit the evidence, notwithstanding that it is prejudicial to the accused in tending to show that he was guilty of another crime. Such probative force may be derived from striking similarities in the evidence about the manner in which the crime was committed ... But restricting the circumstances in which there is sufficient probative force to overcome prejudice of evidence relating to another crime to cases in which there is some striking similarity between them is to restrict the operation of the principle in a way which gives too much effect to a particular manner of stating it, and is not justified in principle.

Although s. 41(4)(c) does not use the expression 'striking similarity', it appears that it is intended to embody the narrow, *Boardman* approach to similar fact rather than the wider, modern formula in *P*. In *Boardman*, Lord Salmon, speaking of striking similarity, commented that 'the similarity would have to be so unique or striking that common sense makes it inexplicable on the basis of coincidence'. This seems to be the source of the form of words in the Act. It may follow (though it is a question for construction by the courts) that where the evidence which it is sought to introduce about the complainant is cogent because of what Lord Mackay in *P* terms 'relationships in time and circumstances' rather than striking similarity, it will fall to be excluded unless the link in time is so proximate that the evidence falls within s. 41(3)(b).

Consent, credibility and previous false complaints

Both grounds (b) and (c) can only be relied on to the extent that the purpose for which the evidence is tendered or the question is sought to be put is to address an issue in the case and not simply to impugn the credibility of the complainant as a witness. A particularly difficult issue arises with regard to a previous false complaint of rape by the complainant against a third party. The Explanatory Notes to the Act assert that 'it is not envisaged that evidence that seeks to do no more than show that the complainant has a history of making unproved complaints of sexual offences would be treated as evidence of sexual behaviour'. This is a plausible analysis where the defence case is that the complainant is a serial fabricator of events that never took place: in other words that the complaint does not in fact relate to any sexual behaviour or experience at all. The way is then clear to admit the evidence, to the extent that it bears on the credibility of the complainant. Of course there is a danger that, if this argument is accepted, a complainant who is not believed on one occasion will have this held up against him or her on a subsequent occasion where, for all that is known, both complaints may be genuine.

It is less clear how the new law applies to a contention that the complainant had consensual intercourse with a third party and lied about it afterwards. It is true that the making of a false complaint is not itself 'sexual behaviour', but the making of this particular false complaint can be established only if the defence adduce evidence which carries with it a necessary implication about the complainant's sexual behaviour. This would seem to be barred by the Act, as the reason for adducing such evidence is to impugn the credibility of the witness rather than to establish consent directly.

In some cases it may be arguable that the previous false complaint bears directly on consent, as where the circumstances of both cases are strikingly similar. This seems to have been the case in *Cox* (1987) 84 Cr App R 133, decided under s. 2 of the 1976 Act, where the complainant was said to have covered up her lapses from fidelity to her boyfriend by alleging that her other lovers were guilty of rape. Ultimately it might be said that, even in such a case, the evidence goes to credibility rather than directly to consent, but the line between the two purposes is so thin as to be almost imperceptible.

Issue raised by the prosecution: s. 41(5)

The alternative to reliance on s. 41(3) is for the defence to make its application under s. 41(5) on the ground that the evidence or question 'relates to any evidence adduced by the prosecution about any sexual behaviour of the complainant'. The effect of a successful application is to admit such evidence or questions as, in the opinion of the court, 'would go no further than is necessary to enable the evidence adduced by the prosecution to be rebutted or explained on behalf of the accused'. This is in addition to the requirement, in s. 41(2)(a) (see p. 96), that a refusal of leave may have the result of rendering unsafe a conclusion of the jury or court on any relevant issue in the case.

Section 41(5) appears to have in mind cases such as *Funderburk* [1990] 1 WLR 587. F was charged with unlawful sexual intercourse with a girl aged 13. When the child gave evidence it was in terms which strongly suggested that she had lost her virginity in consequence of the act of intercourse she claimed had occurred between herself and F. The defence was keen to supply evidence of the girl's sexual experience in order to show the jury how it was that the girl, if she was lying about F, could describe the act of intercourse in so detailed a fashion. It was held that the fact that the prosecution were 'putting her forward as a virgin' rendered relevant and admissible an admission she had made to the effect that she had previously had intercourse with two other men, and that furthermore the issue was sufficiently closely related to the subject-matter of the charge to be regarded as going to an issue in the case and not merely to the credit of the girl.

Section 41(5) provides a safety-valve for the defence to adduce evidence in a case where the prosecution (which, unlike the defence, is able to introduce any relevant evidence about the sexual behaviour of the complainant) brings evidence of sexual behaviour which shows the complainant in a misleading light. It does not appear to assist in the sort of case (in which s. 2 of the 1976 Act has frequently been invoked) in which the prosecution adduces no direct evidence, but the defence seek to forestall incorrect inferences about the complainant which they fear the jury may otherwise draw. The most obvious example is the case where, because a complainant is very young, the jury may assume she is sexually inexperienced. (See the discussion of the use of s. 2 of the 1976 Act in this regard in J. Temkin, 'Sexual History Evidence: The Ravishment of Section 2' [1993] Crim LR 3.) Another example is where the complainant is of a different colour to the accused, and the defence fear that the jury may infer that a consensual relationship is less likely to occur across a racial divide. It is this sort of 'reasoning' by defence counsel that has given rise to questions of a complainant of rape about the colour of her children. No doubt such questions are offensive but, if juries do harbour prejudices and make assumptions of this kind about complainants, the solution is not to require the accused to suffer the consequences but to confront the prejudice in some way.

Section 41(5) also fails to assist the defence in a case where the prosecution refrains from mentioning evidence which might be highly relevant but which is not otherwise admissible. In one case of which the author has been informed, a man in prison for a rape offence suggested that his sexual deviation was the fault of his sister, with whom he had played games of the 'doctor and patient' variety when they were children. The sister, a respectable matron in her thirties, was then prosecuted in respect of offences against her brother. Had s. 41 been in force, it would have been impossible for her to have questioned her accuser, or to have adduced evidence, about his subsequent sexual behaviour resulting in his conviction for rape. Unless the prosecution had chosen to adduce the evidence so as to put the jury in the picture, the matter would have been kept from them. If the sister's defence was that the evidence of the brother was a complete fabrication, the subsequent misconduct of the brother would seem a matter bearing ultimately on his credibility only. It could not therefore be adduced under s. 41(3)(a) because s. 41(4) prevents evidence emerging under any of the s. 41(3) exceptions if the main purpose of doing so is to impugn the complainant's credibility. Arguably it would have been admissible if she said he had forced her, as her lack of consent (as distinct from his) might be a matter on which the evidence goes beyond attacking his credibility and into the realms of a relevant propensity.

PROCEDURE

Section 43(1) requires the application for leave to adduce evidence under s. 41 to be heard 'in private and in the absence of the complainant'. Whether this suggests implicitly that the complainant must be a witness in the case is a moot point (see p. 94).

In the rare case where, for example, the complainant has died but it is intended to proceed using his written statement as evidence under the Criminal Justice Act 1988, s. 23, it could be argued that s. 41 was not intended to apply as the complainant's sensibilities are beyond protection. This would be to misunderstand the full thrust of the Government's strategy of reform, which was motivated not only by the desire to protect complainants and to encourage them to come forward but also by concern that the unnecessary admissibility of sexual history evidence prejudices the fairness of the trial.

Once the application has been determined, s. 43(2) obliges the court to state in open court its reasons for giving or refusing leave and, if leave is given, the extent to which evidence may be adduced or questions asked in pursuance of the leave. In jury trial, needless to say, the jury is not present when such a statement is made. A magistrates' court must enter the stated matters in the register of its proceedings. In giving and recording reasons, courts will be aware that it is only in cases in which the relevant decision goes against the accused and where a conviction is registered that there is any real risk of scrutiny by a higher court. It is to be hoped that, with this in mind, the courts will not be drawn into the habit of justifying their decision with an unconsidered recitation of a statutory formula.

Section 43(3) enables rules of court to be made for stipulating the particulars of the grounds for an application and to enable the court to 'request a party to the proceedings' to provide the court with information which would assist in determining leave. This should both improve the factual basis on which decisions are made and sharpen the arguments for and against admissibility. 'Party' is not defined but would not, on ordinary principles, include the complainant. Rules may also stipulate for the manner in which confidential information is to be treated and for its disclosure to, or its being withheld from, the parties.

DISCUSSION

Is s. 2 of the 1976 Act malfunctioning? The suggestion in *Speaking Up For Justice* that it is relies heavily on the number of applications allowed (75%) and on research evidence suggesting that the evidence is used to discredit the victim rather than to shed light on issues of direct relevance to the trial. Of this, the Lord Chief Justice Lord Bingham commented:

> That [the old section 2] strikes one as a good and well-designed provision. What more is needed? To answer that question, one must look at paragraph 9.64 of the consultation paper *Speaking Up For Justice*. That states that the working group reported overwhelming evidence that the present practice in the courts is unsatisfactory and that the existing law is not achieving its purpose.
> If there is such overwhelming evidence, the consultation paper is noticeably reticent in giving the details. It refers to some research carried out nearly 10 years ago which shows that 75 per cent of applications made under that section succeed. That may mean that applications are lightly made and lightly granted, but it may equally mean that applications are cautiously and prudently made and properly granted, in the main.
> There is a great deal of anecdote about this, but if one is to add to the mountain of it, I can tell your lordships that at a Judicial Studies Board seminar for judges who specialise in this field, the suggestion that this provision was disregarded provoked a vocal expression of strong disagreement. (2nd Reading, House of Lords, *Hansard*, 15 December 1998, col. 1272)

In promulgating the new sexual history provisions, the Government has clearly been influenced by feminist writing, most significantly the works of Zsuzsanna Adler (including *Rape on Trial* (London, 1989) and 'The Relevance of Sexual History Evidence in Rape: Problems of Subjective Interpretation [1985] Crim LR 769); Jennifer Temkin (including *Rape and the Legal Process* (London, 1983) and 'Regulating Sexual History Evidence — The Limits of Discretionary Legislation' (1984) 33 ICLQ 942) and Sue Lees (including *Carnal Knowledge: Rape on Trial* (London, 1996)). Even if the case against s. 2 is made out, however, there must be doubt about whether the best replacement is a provision which seeks to stipulate in advance of trial all of the situations in which sexual history evidence about the complainant may be relevant. The Government claimed that it had learned from the Canadian experience in *Seaboyer* [1991] 2 SCR 577, where a provision which admitted sexual history evidence only in limited and predetermined circumstances was held to violate the right of the accused to a fair trial. Nevertheless it is on this issue that the provisions are almost certain to be questioned, and quite possibly found wanting, in the light of the fair trial provisions of Article 6 of the European Convention on Human Rights. It is interesting that the Criminal Procedure (Scotland) Act 1995, ss. 274 and 275 regulates the introduction of sexual history evidence by means of stipulated categories of exception followed by a residual discretion to include evidence in the interests of justice. This was the model originally preferred by *Speaking Up For Justice* (Recommendation 63) but it has not prevailed, presumably because it is thought that any discretion would be given too wide a sphere of operation and become a device to resurrect the outdated notions of relevance which the Act seeks to lay to rest. On the other hand, a series of exceptions followed by a 'safety valve' might have served both to focus the thinking of judges and magistrates on what is really relevant (particularly if accompanied by a duty to give detailed reasons) and to prevent a miscarriage of justice in the event that relevant evidence comes to light which falls outside the categories. The making of previous false complaints by the complainant (see p. 101) is just one illustration of evidence which may fall foul of s. 41 but which could have been adduced had there been a safety-valve in the legislation. As things stand, the prosecutor will have to give careful consideration to adducing evidence which is considered to be highly relevant to the defence but which the defence is prevented from deploying by s. 41. The prosecutor must not, of course, betray the spirit of s. 41 by adducing such evidence where it has little relevance.

Recently published research not surprisingly suggests that the rape cases which are the most difficult to prove are those where there has been some prior relationship between the complainant and the accused. A Home Office Research Study by Jessica Harris and Sharon Grace, *A Question of Evidence? Investigating and Prosecuting Rape in the 1990's*, discovered that only 6% of a sample of nearly 500 complaints of rape resulted in conviction for rape or attempted rape. The authors state (p. 44):

... it is cause for concern that only 6 per cent of those initially accused of rape were convicted of rape or attempted rape. The figure rises to 9 per cent if no-crimed cases are removed and to 21 per cent if convictions for any offence are included, but these are still low. The problem is not primarily that cases are not cleared up — in the great majority of cases the identity of the alleged offender is known. But it is precisely because the victim so often knows the offender that difficulties often arise in pursuing cases to a successful conclusion.

The same study showed a great increase in the number of acquaintance and intimate rapes, with only 12% of reports concerning rape by strangers. Of those listed as acquaintance rapes, more than half were cases where the parties had met in the 24 hours preceding the incident. Consent was relied on in 62% of cases involving acquaintance and 50% of those involving intimates. Judges and barristers questioned for the survey tended to the view that the sexual history of a complainant was often relevant to the case and that blocking such evidence might present a false picture to the jury. (Significantly, however, many of those questioned were adamant that the complainant's sexual history was relevant only where it bore on the veracity of the complainant, which is a rather different perspective from that taken by s. 41.) The report was relied upon by the Government as evidence that there was a 'need to create a balance between the interests of the defendant and those of victims and witnesses' (P. Boateng, House of Commons Standing Committee E, *Hansard*, 17 June 1999). Whether the new balance is defensible remains to be seen. It may however be predicted with confidence that the new provisions will have a significant impact on the evidence which is admitted in many rape cases and that exclusion of sexual history evidence in some cases will be a critical factor in securing a conviction.

Chapter 8
Reporting Restrictions

OVERVIEW

The purposes of Part II, Chapter IV are to extend the scope of protective reporting restrictions relating to criminal proceedings, to assimilate the laws of England and Wales and Northern Ireland in this respect, and to extend the geographical area within which restrictions apply to include publications in Scotland.

Section 44 prohibits the publication of material which might lead to the public identification of a young person under 18 who is involved in a criminal investigation as suspect, victim or witness. A power to dispense with the restriction in the interests of justice is granted. Section 45 deals with reporting restrictions relating to juveniles in criminal courts and in this respect replaces the Children and Young Persons Act 1933, s. 39, which hereafter will apply only in relation to civil proceedings. The effect of s. 45 of the 1999 Act is to prohibit disclosure of the identities of defendants, victims and witnesses aged under 18. These restrictions may be dispensed with by the court either in the interests of justice, or in the interest of reporting criminal proceedings or on other public interest grounds. Section 46 permits courts to restrict the reporting of criminal proceedings in order to protect the identities of vulnerable adult witnesses in the interests of improving the quality of the evidence to be given or of enhancing the level of cooperation provided by such a witness in a criminal investigation. Section 47 creates a general restriction, for the duration of the relevant trial, on the reporting of applications in relation to, or the granting of, special measures directions under s. 19, and also applications for, or the granting of, directions prohibiting an accused person from personally cross-examining a particular witness under s. 36. Where an accused objects to the imposition of a reporting restriction, such restriction should be imposed only if the court is satisfied that it is in the interests of justice to do so.

Section 48 implements sch. 2 which amends various existing reporting restrictions in the interests of consistency. Section 49 creates offences of breaching reporting restrictions, which are subject to various defences set out in s. 50. Section 51 makes officers of corporate bodies and Scottish partnerships accomplices to offences committed by such bodies under s. 49. Section 52 sets out matters to which the court must have regard in determining issues of public interest in relation to the application of reporting restrictions. Transitional provisions are found in sch. 7, para. 6. Under these provisions, s. 44, once in force, will apply to all criminal investigations whenever started, but not to publications made before the section came into force. Sections 45 and 46 will apply only in relation to proceedings instituted on or after the relevant commencement date.

At the time of writing, the Government intend to bring these provisions into force at the end of 2000. Exceptionally, there are no current plans to implement s. 44 insofar as it relates to investigations involving juvenile victims or witnesses. This reflects concern about the extent to which this provision would restrict press freedom and hinder the vital assistance which the press can provide to police investigations. It appears that, for the time being, the Government are content to rely upon press self-regulation on this issue, with the legislative provision held in reserve should self-regulation fail to achieve an appropriate balance between the welfare of children, press freedom and publicity as an aid to investigation.

BACKGROUND

All criminal proceedings are subject to rules which suspend the reporting of certain matters until the conclusion of the case, in the interests of preventing prejudice to the accused. In relation to children, far more comprehensive reporting restrictions apply, both during proceedings and thereafter. These restrictions express the law's protective stance towards children and reflect their vulnerability and the social interest in steering children away from crime. The dominant principle is that children should not be harmed by involvement in the legal process. It is recognised that children who act as witnesses or victims may suffer stigma, embarrassment or reprisals if their involvement in a criminal case becomes widely known. In relation to child defendants, similar concerns apply but also it is recognised that publicity may lead to a child becoming 'labelled' as a criminal in the child's own mind or the minds of others and that this may tend to confirm the child in a pattern of criminal behaviour.

Accordingly, the Children and Young Persons Act 1933, s. 49 prohibits the publication of details relating to children who appear in the youth court as either defendants or witnesses. Generally, the prohibition applies both during the proceedings and after conviction; however, following amendment by the Crime (Sentences) Act 1997, s. 45, the court has a limited discretion to lift the ban publicising the identity of a child who has been convicted where it is in the public interest to do so.

Where children are involved in proceedings in other courts, s. 39 of the 1933 Act permits the court to prohibit the publication of details which might identify any child involved in the proceedings as defendant, complainant or witness. This provision applies where a child is tried with an adult in the magistrates' court or, for a serious offence, in the Crown Court under s. 53 of the 1933 Act. The courts have made clear that the imposition of restrictions under s. 39 should be considered the norm and that it 'will only be in rare and exceptional cases that directions under s. 39 will not be given' (*Leicester Crown Court, ex parte S (a minor)* [1993] 1 WLR 111, per Watkins LJ at p. 114). It is notable that, where restrictions were not imposed in a case involving two eleven-year-old children charged with murder, the publicity given to the identities of the children was the subject of severe criticism by the European Court of Human Rights (*T* v *UK and V* v *UK* [2000] Crim LR 187).

Restrictions on disclosing the identity of rape complainants after somebody had been charged with the offence were imposed by the Sexual Offences (Amendment) Act 1976, s. 4(1). This measure expressed the established principle (already applicable to children) that such restrictions might be applied to protect a witness from harm, but also reflected a new principle, that such restrictions might be applied in the interest of encouraging potentially reluctant victims to report crime against themselves, and to give evidence at any subsequent trial. The measure followed a recommendation of the Heilbron Committee (*Report of the Advisory Group on the Law of Rape*, Cmnd. 6352, 1975) who had recognised that, because of the social stigma which might be attached to a victim of an alleged rape, the harm or distress experienced by women victims might be increased by the publication of their identities and this in turn might lead to a significant under-reporting of rape offences.

The prohibition on publications which might disclose the identities of rape victims has since been extended to an earlier stage (after an allegation has been made), and also to a broad range of other sexual offences, by the Sexual Offences (Amendment) Act 1992. Male victims of rape are now also protected by virtue of the widening of the definition of rape to include offences against men in the Criminal Justice and Public Order Act 1994, s. 142.

The need to protect witnesses from harm is also the foundation of the common-law rule that, where a witness runs a risk of direct physical harm by giving evidence, the court may order that his identity need not be disclosed in court and that screens or other measures may be used so that he may not be visible (*X, Y and Z* (1990) 91 Cr App R 36). In less extreme cases a court may prohibit the publication of a witness's identity or other particulars under the Contempt of Court Act 1981, s. 11 for the purpose of preventing harm to the witness.

The provisions in the 1999 Act are largely inspired by proposals in *Speaking Up For Justice* (pp. 51 and 52). The primary proposal was that the courts should have powers to prohibit publication by the media of information which would be likely to lead to the identification of witnesses in cases where to do so might exacerbate witness intimidation. The power to make such restriction orders should not be limited to the period after arrest or during trial, but should be available at any stage after the initial complaint has been made. Any prohibition on reporting in relation to proceedings in England and Wales should also extend to publications in Scotland and Northern Ireland. Similarly, it was recommended that reporting restrictions applicable to rape and cognate sexual offences should be extended to publications in Scotland and Northern Ireland. *Speaking Up For Justice* also expressed concern that the protection given to juvenile participants in criminal trials was incomplete, because it came into operation only once formal proceedings had been initiated. Accordingly, it was recommended that restrictions should apply from the point of complaint. It was also recommended, in line with earlier proposals, that reporting restrictions relating to English and Welsh cases should be extended to publications in Northern Ireland.

As well as meeting the concerns expressed in *Speaking Up For Justice*, the Government took the opportunity presented by the Act to make needed minor amendments to provisions on reporting restrictions. Thus, to the list of sexual offences to which reporting restrictions apply are added two offences of abduction for sexual purposes which had been omitted in error from the list enacted in the Sexual Offences (Amendment) Act 1992.

In presenting these provisions, the Government acknowledged that it was seeking to achieve a compromise between a number of distinct interests:

(a) the defendant's right to a fair trial;
(b) the public interest in protecting children;
(c) the public interest in protecting victims and other witnesses;
(d) the public interest in encouraging witnesses to give evidence and in the quality of any evidence given;
(e) the public interest in the rapid dissemination of information about suspected offences as an aid to investigation; and
(f) the general public interest in being informed about matters of grave public concern.

Necessarily, these issues were discussed in the context of the European Convention on Human Rights, particularly Article 6 (the right to a fair trial), Article 8 (the right to respect for private and family life) and Article 10 (the right to freedom of expression, including the right to receive and impart information).

Although these provisions received broad support from all sides in Parliament, it was perhaps not surprising that the Bill was subject to constructive criticism, particularly from the press, that the proper balance had not been achieved. These arguments were considered carefully by the Government and led to a number of substantial amendments to the original Bill, including specific defences available to the press and what is effectively an undertaking by the Government not to implement reporting restrictions in relation to investigations involving young victims and witnesses while the press continue to act responsibly in this regard.

REPORTING RESTRICTIONS: COMMON ELEMENTS AND GENERAL ISSUES

Reporting restrictions under ss. 44, 45 and 46 and under amendments to earlier legislation have some common elements, which for convenience are considered here.

Identifying factors

Each of the reporting restrictions which is designed to prevent the identification of a person involved in an investigation or proceedings employs the phrase 'which is likely to lead members of the public to identify him as a person involved' in the offence or in the proceedings, as the case may be. Each provision lists a number of matters which would be likely to have this effect:

(a) the person's name;
(b) his address;
(c) the identity of any school or other educational establishment attended by him;
(d) the identity of any place of work; and
(e) any still or moving picture of him.

The list appears to be for guidance only since it is neither exhaustive, nor is it determinative. Thus, the publication of any other type of information could fall foul of the relevant prohibition if it would be likely to identify the relevant person, whereas the publication of matter falling within the list (such as a very blurred photograph) may be lawful if it would not be likely to do so.

Meaning of 'publication'

For the purposes of all reporting restrictions under the Act, 'publication' is defined by s. 63(1) to include 'any speech, writing, relevant programme or other communication in whatever form, which is addressed to the public at large or any section of the public (and for this purpose every relevant programme shall be taken to be so addressed), but [not] any indictment or other document prepared for use in legal proceedings'. The term 'relevant programme' is also defined by the same section, to mean 'a programme included in a programme service within the meaning of the Broadcasting Act 1990' (s. 201 of which lists the relevant television and radio broadcasting services).

Appeals

Where any reporting restrictions are imposed by the Crown Court in the course of a trial on indictment, an appeal will lie under the Criminal Justice Act 1988, s. 159(1)(c), which states:

(1) A person aggrieved may appeal to the Court of Appeal, if that court grants leave, against — ...
(c) any order restricting the publication of any report of the whole or any part of a trial on indictment or any such ancillary proceedings ...

This ground of appeal is limited to cases where a court has granted a restriction order. This power is not confined to parties and may be exercised by any person aggrieved, providing that the court gives leave. This might include a representative of the press. It appears that there is no remedy for a person aggrieved by the court's refusal to make such an order. However, where an appeal is taken against conviction or sentence, the Court of Appeal could exercise any of the powers in relation to reporting restrictions which could have been exercised at trial.

Where restrictions are imposed by a magistrates' court, appeal is to the Divisional Court by way of case stated. Since restrictions may, and in many cases should, be imposed by a court acting of its own motion, it is not clear who has standing to appeal. The better view is that either prosecution, defence or any other party with an interest in the matter, with leave of the court, has a right of appeal if aggrieved by a decision to impose or not to impose restrictions. It is also clear that the Court has a wide discretion to hear persons affected by the order, such as representatives of the press (*McKerry* v *Teesdale and Wear Valley Justices* [2000] *The Times*, 29 February 2000).

It should also be noted that under s. 44(11) and (12) there is a special power of appeal in relation to decisions by magistrates' courts whether or not to dispense with restrictions under s. 44. This is considered below.

RESTRICTION RELATING TO CRIMINAL INVESTIGATIONS: s. 44

Section 44 prohibits the publication of material which might lead to the public identification of a young person aged under 18 who is involved in a criminal investigation. As with other reporting restrictions, breach will amount to an offence for the editor, proprietor and publisher under s. 49.

The provision significantly extends the scope of reporting restrictions in two respects: first, by affording protection to witnesses and victims as well as defendants; secondly, by applying from the commencement of the investigation rather than to the formal proceedings. If fully implemented it would have a significant impact on the right of the press to report crime, on the right of the public to be informed or warned about it and on the extent to which prompt press reporting can assist in the investigation of crime and the apprehension of suspects. These issues were the subject of lobbying by press organisations and were discussed at each stage of the Parliamentary process, but particularly during the Commons Report Stage (*Hansard*, 8 July 1999, cols. 1235–1255). In the course of debates, it was pointed out that the breadth of the prohibition would prevent the media from publishing quite inoffensive material, such as a report that a 17-year-old pop singer had been the victim of theft, as well as news about major incidents such as the Dunblane tragedy. Also of concern was the fact that the press might be hampered in mobilising public support in finding child victims of kidnap or in alerting the public to risks from paedophiles or other offenders. Although the offence under s. 49 is subject to defences under s. 50 of public interest and consent, it was argued that these would not adequately protect responsible journalism. It was pointed out that local newspapers do not have well staffed legal departments to give advice on such matters at short notice and that an editor who believed that publication was in the public interest might be deterred by fear that a court might take a different view should he be prosecuted. As Mr Elfyn Llwyd MP put it:

> Do we really want editors to be constantly looking over their shoulders, having to second-guess whether a court would decide that a public interest defence will

succeed or fail? That is not healthy for any kind of press. It is not healthy for freedom of speech ... The measure is astonishing for a Government who are talking about freedom of information. (Commons, *Hansard*, 8 July 1999, col. 1248)

The consent defence was also considered inadequate in view of the difficulty which might be experienced in tracking down the person capable of giving consent, and the fact that it might be insensitive in some circumstances, for instance where a parent was traumatised by the kidnap of a child. In the light of these arguments, the Government undertook to suspend implementation of s. 44 to the extent that it protects young witnesses and victims.

The Minister's undertaking

At report stage in the Commons, John Greenway MP introduced an amendment for the purpose of forestalling any attempt by the Government to bring s. 44 into force to the extent that it protects victims and witnesses. Under the amendment, the Home Secretary would have been barred from making an order to implement the provision without first publishing a notice of intention to do so, giving reasons for deciding to do so, consulting with representatives of press organisations and allowing six months between giving notice of his intention and the making of the order (Commons, *Hansard*, 8 July 1999, col. 1236–1240). John Greenway's particular concern was that while it remained possible to implement the provision by order this might be done by the present or a future Home Secretary with little thought or consultation, and perhaps in response to a single notorious incident of irresponsible reporting which was unrepresentative of the general practice of the press. The amendment was lost following a division but, in the course of debate, the Home Office Minister, Paul Boateng, gave important undertakings concerning the provision.

In dismissing some of Mr Greenway's arguments, Mr Boateng pointed out that an order could not be made under s. 44(5) to implement the relevant restrictions without an affirmative resolution of each House. Parliamentary time would have to be found to debate the order and there would be ample opportunity for discussion, soundings and representations to be made (cols. 1253–1255). He indicated that the Government had received and heeded representations from bodies and individuals representing the press and also from the NSPCC and child protection organisations. He referred to the Code of Practice promulgated by the Press Complaints Commission and appeared to accept that 'best standards are already being applied by the press'. The Government's position on the issue was described in the following passages:

... our intentions are to proceed by recognising the potential of self-regulation to address the issue. The issue is a serious one — the welfare of children.

We are not giving the Executive powers to ban the publication of particular material; we are making sure that the best standards of self-regulation are applied.

... we are ensuring that [the best standards] will be upheld and become more firmly entrenched in the general approach of the media ...

It is important to make sure that standards are maintained and developed by all, and I cannot and will not fetter the discretion of future Ministers in that regard.

The conclusion must be that the Government recognise the delicate balance which must be achieved in this area and that it may be difficult to capture in legislation the fine distinctions which may need to be drawn between cases. In the light of this, the Government are content to leave the matter to self-regulation as policed by the Press Complaints Commission, but operating under the sword of Damocles — the threat that if the best standards and the right balance are not achieved, a future Home Secretary will act to implement the legislation. This suggests strongly that in developing best practice in this area the press should have regard to the scope of s. 44, whether or not it is ever fully brought into force.

The scope of the restriction

The restriction on reporting under s. 44 will apply in relation to offences against the law of England and Wales, and Northern Ireland (s. 44(1)(a)). This will include offences outside the relevant territories which fall within the jurisdiction of local courts, such as murder, offences under the Sex Offenders Act 1997 and offences on British ships and aircraft (see generally *Blackstone's Criminal Practice*, **D1.75** to **D1.88**). The restrictions will also apply to 'civil offences' committed in other jurisdictions by persons subject to service law (s. 44(1)(b) and (13)).

Section 44(4) defines the term 'person involved in the offence', i.e., those who receive protection. In relation to persons by whom the offence is alleged to have been committed, the provision is likely to be brought into force in the near future. As indicated above, the provision may also apply in relation to 'a person against or in respect of whom the offence is alleged to have been committed' and a 'person who is alleged to have been a witness to the commission of the offence', but will not do so unless and until an order is made under s. 44(5). It should be noted that the protection afforded by the provision is not limited to cases in which prosecutions are ultimately brought. Thus, persons 'by whom the offence is alleged to have been committed' will include those who have been suspects but who are never prosecuted and those who are dealt with by means of caution (while that disposal remains an option for young offenders) or reprimand or warning under the Crime and Disorder Act 1998, ss. 65 and 66.

Alleged perpetrators

It might be argued that the phrase 'persons by whom the offence is alleged to have been committed' might be understood to be confined to those alleged to have carried out the acts specified in the definition of the offence, i.e., principal offenders. The better view however is that the phrase would include both principals and accomplices on the basis that at common law being an accomplice is not a separate offence but rather simply an alternative mode of liability for the offence. Thus, it is perfectly accurate to describe both accomplices and principals as persons by whom the offence is committed.

Victims

A major concern of Government, as prompted by *Speaking Up For Justice*, is reporting in relation to victims. For the time being the press are trusted to act responsibly in this respect. However, it should be noted that the section abjures the term 'victim', employing instead the phrase 'person against or in respect of whom the offence is alleged to have been committed'. The phrase 'against whom' will clearly serve to include victims of offences against the person (including non-consensual sexual offences) and property offences, which are conceived in law as offences against a particular person's rights of ownership. The phrase 'in respect of whom the offence is alleged to have been committed' will avoid arguments about the concept of victim and will include offences which may be considered victimless (or which involve persons who would not consider themselves as victims). Thus, offences of unlawful sexual intercourse in respect of a consenting girl or offering drugs for sale to a willing potential customer will be included.

In order for a putative 'victim' to qualify for protection under s. 44 (if ever fully implemented), it would not be necessary that the charge is ultimately proven or even for proceedings to take place. In relation to victims the key question would be whether or not at some stage in the course of an investigation it has been *alleged* that an offence has been committed against or in respect of the young person in question. The operative allegation may be made by anybody, including the young person herself. Thus, a young person who claimed to have been the victim of a robbery which was subsequently investigated would be protected even if the police ultimately took no further action, believing the alleged offence to be a fabrication.

Witnesses

A definition of the term witness is provided by s. 63 (which provides definitions for the purposes of Part II 'except where the context otherwise requires') as follows: '"witness" in relation to any criminal proceedings, means any person called, or proposed to be called, to give evidence in the proceedings'. Two factors indicate that this, apparently general, definition should not apply in relation to s. 44. First, the definition in s. 63 applies in relation to criminal proceedings whereas s. 44 deals with 'investigations' (as compared to ss. 46 and 47 which explicitly deal with 'proceedings'). Secondly, the s. 63 definition can operate only once proceedings are contemplated and someone has made an initial decision about proposed witnesses. If this definition were applied, it would undermine the whole purpose of s. 44 which is to protect putative witnesses from the earliest stage of the investigation. It is submitted that the term 'witness' must be construed in the context of s. 44 and would include persons who claimed to have witnessed a crime, whether or not a prosecution was ever brought and whether or not that person gave evidence in court. In any event, decisions about whether or not details may be published will often necessarily be made at a time when the outcome of the investigation is a matter of speculation. Arguably, the safest course for editors and publishers will be to give the term 'witness' a wide rather than narrow interpretation.

In relation to witnesses, the provision offers protection only to those who allegedly witnessed the commission of the offence. (This may be compared with s. 49 of the 1933 Act which refers simply to a 'witness in the proceedings'.) The formula employed by s. 44 will exclude many witnesses who might be interviewed by the police in the course of an investigation and who would be able to give relevant evidence in court. Neither the child who sees the intending bank robber renting the lock-up garage in which stolen goods are later found nor the child to whom a murderer confesses could be said to witness the commission of the offence. Accordingly, neither child would be protected under s. 44. There is no reason in principle why such children should be any less in need of protection than other witnesses and it appears that their exclusion was the result of a drafting error. While this restriction remains unimplemented and reporting relating to witnesses falls to the discretion of the press, they might be wise to exercise circumspection in what they report concerning a child witness, whether or not the child would fall strictly within the scope of s. 44.

When s. 44 will not apply

In order to avoid overlap, alleged victims of sexual offences whose anonymity is protected by the Sexual Offences (Amendment) Act 1992, s. 1 are excluded from the ambit of s. 44 (s. 44(4)). For a similar reason, restrictions under s. 44 cease to apply once there are proceedings in court (s. 44(3)), at which time the court's power to impose restrictions under s. 45 will arise.

Criminal investigations

Reporting restrictions will begin to operate 'where a criminal investigation has begun' in respect of an alleged offence (s. 44(1)). It should be noted that in the transitional period reporting restrictions under s. 44 will apply, once that section is in force, to criminal investigations, whether begun before or after the section came into force (sch. 7, para. 6(1)).

'Criminal investigation' is defined by s. 44(13) as 'an investigation conducted by police officers, or other persons charged with the duty of investigating offences, with a view to it being ascertained whether a person should be charged with an offence'. This definition is effectively the same as that applicable to the Criminal Procedure and Investigations Act 1996, Part I by virtue of s. 1(4) of that Act, which itself borrows the phrase 'other persons charged with the duty of investigating offences' from the Police and Criminal Evidence Act 1984, s. 67(9). Under that Act the phrase has been held to apply to trading standards officers (*Dudley MBC* v *Debenhams* (1994) 154 JP 18; *Tiplady* (1995) 159 JP 548), electricity board officials who collect evidence with a view to prosecution (*Stewart* [1995] Crim LR 500), company security staff employed to investigate alleged offences (*Twaites* (1991) 92 Cr App R 106), and other private employees specifically engaged to investigate offences (*Halawa v Federation against Copyright Theft* [1995] 1 Cr App R 21). This list makes it clear that investigators whose duty stems from their contract of employment will be covered as well as those carrying out a statutory duty. This seems correct in principle, since whether or not the provision affords protection to a particular child should not depend upon who is conducting the investigation. However, rather oddly, it would seem that an investigation conducted by a private individual at his own discretion (e.g., a small shopkeeper) would not be covered.

Problems may arise as a result of restricting the scope of the provision to investigations which are carried out with a view to ascertaining whether a person should be charged with an offence. If 'charged' in this context refers to the formal accusation by which court proceedings are instituted, this would appear to exclude investigations relating to children where the only realistic disposals in contemplation would be reprimand or warning. This was surely not intended and suggests that 'charged' should be understood in the broader sense of an accusation of the commission of a crime, whatever formal response follows.

In the context of the Criminal Procedure and Investigations Act 1996, the courts have considered whether an investigation can begin prior to the alleged offence. When this was first considered by the Divisional Court in *Norfolk Stipendiary Magistrates, ex parte Keable* [1998] Crim LR 510, it was held that an investigation into an offence could not begin prior to the date of the alleged offence. This has now been disapproved in *Uxbridge Magistrates Court, ex parte Patel; R v City of London Magistrates' Court, ex parte Cropper* (2000) 164 JP 209, in which it was held that a criminal investigation into an offence may begin before it is committed, and in particular this may be so in a surveillance case or where the alleged offence forms part of a series of offences which were already under investigation at the relevant time. This will undoubtedly apply in relation to s. 44 but will have limited significance in practice since it would be very unusual for the press to be in a position to report on surveillance operations, nor would it normally be possible to identify suspects, witnesses, victims etc. prior to the commission of the relevant offence.

Dispensation in the interests of justice

Any criminal court has the discretionary power to dispense, or partly dispense, with the general restriction in relation to a young person where it is satisfied that it is necessary in the interests of justice to do so (s. 44(7)). This power may be exercised by a single justice (s. 44(10)). However, in deciding whether to make such an order, the court must have regard to the welfare of the young person in question (s. 44(8)). Where a magistrates' court (or a court of summary jurisdiction in Northern Ireland) makes, or refuses to make, an order under s. 44(7), any person who was a party to the proceedings on the application for the order and, with the leave of the court, any other person, may appeal against the making of such an order (s. 44(11)). Where such an appeal takes place, the same categories of persons have a right to be heard or represented at such an appeal. Crown Court rules will be made in relation to such appeals. In dealing with such appeals the Crown Court may make any order which is necessary to give effect to its determination of the appeal and any necessary incidental or consequential orders (s. 44(12)). No similar power of appeal is provided where the initial decision whether to make or refuse an order under s. 44(7) is made by the Crown Court itself.

The term 'the interests of justice' is not defined. It is clearly much narrower than the 'public interest' test which permits the court to dispense with reporting restrictions at trial. The interests of justice test would typically apply where the police wish to publicise a photofit or video footage as part of an appeal for help from the public. At Committee Stage in the Lords an amendment was debated which would have excepted the police and prosecuting authorities (and any publications emanating from them) from the scope of the general restriction. This would have been advantageous in terms of speed, flexibility and certainty for the police and would have avoided waste of resources on needless court hearings. This eminently practical measure was resisted by Lord Williams for the Government, partly on the ground that a dispensation could be granted very quickly by a single local magistrate (Lords, *Hansard*, 8 March 1999, col. 61). The assumption made appears to be that little time would be wasted because the magistrate would always accept the word of the police and grant the dispensation requested. If this is the case it might have been more sensible simply to leave the matter for the discretion of the police.

Dispensation depends upon the application of a two-stage test. First, the court must determine that it is necessary in the interest of justice to lift the restriction to some extent. Having done this, the court should then exercise its discretion and decide whether or not actually to lift the restriction, bearing in mind the welfare of the young person. This might, in theory, lead to a situation in which a court does not lift a restriction, having first determined that it is necessary in the interests of justice to do so. Thus, in theory, if a conflict between the welfare of a young person and the interests of justice arises in this context, the courts would be free to favour the former. This may go against the grain for some judges and whether they will actually balance competing interests in this way remains to be seen. If they do, it could lead to an increase in quashed convictions on appeal. This is for the simple reason that the Court of Appeal, in judging whether a conviction may stand, must apply the criterion of safety — a test which focuses solely on justice for the accused and permits no balancing against other interests, however worthy.

RESTRICTIONS ON REPORTING CRIMINAL PROCEEDINGS: s. 45

Section 45 empowers courts to impose reporting restrictions in relation to criminal proceedings involving juveniles. In this respect it replaces the Children and Young Persons Act 1933, s. 39, which will remain in force but will in future be applicable only to civil proceedings (sch. 2, para. 2). The new provision will apply in relation to criminal proceedings in the (adult) magistrates' court and the Crown Court in England, Wales or Northern Ireland, to criminal proceedings in a service court, whether in the UK or elsewhere (s. 45(1)) and also to appeals in criminal matters. The youth court is excluded because juveniles involved in proceedings in that court will be automatically protected by s. 49 of the 1933 Act (s. 45(2)), which remains in force, subject to amendments.

The court may direct that no matter relating to any juvenile (under 18) who is concerned in the proceedings should be included in any publication if it is likely to lead members of the public to identify him as being concerned in those proceedings (s. 45(3)). Orders under s. 45 may be made at any stage in the proceedings, including at a pre-trial hearing, or indeed after the proceedings have finished (*Harrow Crown Court, ex parte Perkins* (1998) 162 JP 527). It appears that, like the power under s. 39 of the 1933 Act which it replaces, an order under s. 45 may be made at the discretion of the court of its own motion. There is no application procedure; if the prosecution should mention the issue, this is by way of a reminder to the judge of his powers rather than as a formal application (*Ex parte Godwin* [1992] QB 190). As with the old s. 39 power, the judge will have complete discretion as to whom he permits to make representations, and this might include, for instance, journalists representing the public interest in disseminating information or a local authority standing *in loco parentis* to an affected child (*Central Criminal Court, ex parte Crook and Goodwin* [1995] 2 Cr App R 212). However, whatever representations are made, there is a duty on the court to have regard to the welfare of the affected juvenile when considering whether or not to make an order (s. 45(6)).

The persons who may be protected by an order under s. 45 are any person under 18 against or in respect of whom the proceedings are taken or any person under that age who is a witness in the proceedings (s. 45(7)). The phrase 'person ... in respect of whom the proceedings are taken' is taken from s. 39 of the 1933 Act and has been interpreted as meaning victims who are not called as witnesses. In view of the protective purpose of the provision, this should be limited to victims who are alive at the time of the proceedings. However, it would be no objection that an order effectively protected the identities of adult defendants or dead victims if this was necessarily incidental to protecting the identities of living juveniles involved in the case (*Crook and Goodwin*). Any order made will be automatically lifted when the person in respect of whom it is made becomes 18.

The meaning of 'publication' and the particularly relevant identifying factors (s. 45(8)) are the same as for other reporting restrictions (as discussed above). It was made clear in *Crook and Goodwin* that any order made by the court must be reduced to writing, must sufficiently identify the juveniles whose identities are to be protected, must be publicised by a notice with the daily court lists and must be made available in the court offices for inspection by members of the press or other affected parties.

Excepting directions

A court making an order under s. 45(3) has a further power to make an 'excepting direction' which has the effect of dispensing to a specified extent with the restrictions imposed by the order. An excepting direction may be made at the same time as the primary order under s. 45(3) or at any time subsequently (s. 45(10)(a)). The power may also be exercised by a court dealing with an appeal, including an appeal by way of case stated or a further appeal (s. 45(11)). Once made, an excepting direction may be varied or revoked by the court which made it or by any court dealing with an appeal (s. 45(10)). As with orders, the court may act of its own motion but may be prompted by a request, and will have a wide discretion as to whom to permit to make representations on the issue. It seems likely that excepting directions will permit the publication of specified material notwithstanding that it might lead to the identification of a party involved in the proceedings.

Excepting directions may be made under s. 45(4) and (5). Under s. 45(4), an excepting direction may be made if the court is satisfied that it is necessary to do so in the interests of justice. Under s. 45(5) an excepting direction may also be made if the court is satisfied that:

(a)   the effect of restrictions is to impose a substantial and unreasonable restriction on the reporting of the proceedings; and

(b)   that it is in the public interest to remove or relax that restriction.

When considering whether to make an excepting direction under either subsection, the court must have regard to the welfare of the juvenile for whose protection the order is made.

Public interest

In considering the issue of public interest, the court must consider the matters set out in s. 52(2) which are the interests in the open reporting of crime and matters relating to human health and safety and the interest in the exposure of miscarriages of justice. The welfare of the protected person and any views expressed by him or on his behalf must also be considered (s. 52(2)(b)&(c)).

The proper approach of the court to the public interest issue was recently considered by the Divisional Court in *McKerry* v *Teesdale and Wear Valley Justices* [2000] *The Times*, 29 February 2000. That case concerned an application on behalf of a 16-year-old who had been convicted of taking a vehicle without consent and was challenging an order made under s. 49 of the 1933 Act which partially lifted reporting restrictions relating to his case. Giving judgment, Lord Bingham LCJ endorsed the view expressed by Watkins LJ in *Leicester Crown Court, ex parte S (a minor)* (1992) 94 Cr App R 153; [1993] 1 WLR 111 (dealing with an application under s. 39) that: 'The mere fact that a person before the court is a child or young person will normally be a good reason for restricting reports of the proceedings . . .'. The Lord Chief Justice also stressed that the relevant provisions of domestic legislation must be read against the background of international law and practice, as drawn attention to by the European Court of Human Rights in *T* v *UK and V* v *UK* [2000] Crim LR 187. In particular he referred to the Beijing Rules adopted by the United Nations General Assembly on 29 November 1985, which provide in Rule 8:

8.1 The juvenile's right to privacy shall be respected at all stages in order to avoid harm being caused to her or him by undue publicity or by the process of labelling.

8.2 In principle, no information that may lead to the identification of a juvenile offender shall be published.

He also referred to the United Nations Convention on the Rights of the Child 1989:

Article 3.1 In all actions concerning children, whether undertaken by public or private social welfare institutions, courts of law, administrative authorities, or legislative bodies, the best interest of the child shall be the primary consideration.

Article 40.1 State Parties recognize the right of every child alleged as, accused of, or recognized as, having infringed the penal law to be treated in a manner consistent with the promotion of the child's sense of dignity and worth ... and which takes into account the child's age and the desirability of promoting the child's reintegration and the child's assuming a constructive role in society.

Article 40.2(b) Every child alleged as or accused of having infringed the penal law has at least the following guarantees: ...
(vii) To have his or her privacy fully respected at all stages of the proceedings.

Lord Bingham also referred to the rights guaranteed by the European Convention on Human Rights, notably Article 8 which provides that: 'Everyone has a right to respect for his private and family life ...' against which must be balanced the right to receive and impart information under Article 10.

In the instant case, Lord Bingham was satisfied that the magistrates had fully taken into account all relevant public interest and welfare factors in deciding partially to lift reporting restrictions. It was notable however that, having decided to release the boy's name, the magistrates sought to avoid excessive harassment of him by maintaining the ban in relation to photographs and details of his address and school. In this respect it was found that the magistrates had acted reasonably in view of the serious danger which the boy posed to the public. However, it was emphasised that it would be wholly wrong to invoke the power to publicise a child's identity as a form of additional punishment for a convicted juvenile.

The last point is reflected in s. 45(5) which provides that 'no excepting direction shall be given under this subsection by reason only of the fact that the proceedings have been determined in any way or abandoned'.

RESTRICTIONS ON REPORTING IN YOUTH COURTS: AMENDMENTS TO s. 49 OF THE CHILDREN AND YOUNG PERSONS ACT 1933

Section 49 of the Children and Young Persons Act 1933 (as amended) applies automatic reporting restrictions to proceedings in the youth court. This provision is amended by s. 48 of and sch. 2, para. 3 of the 1999 Act to make it consistent with other reporting restrictions considered here.

The main changes to s. 49 of the 1933 Act are as follows. References to subsections are to subsections of s. 49 as substituted or amended by the present Act.

The most important changes relate to the territorial application of the provision. The protection afforded to juveniles is extended to youth court proceedings in Northern Ireland. The restrictions on reporting are extended further to include publications in Northern Ireland and also Scotland (s. 49(12)).

The general restriction on reporting in s. 49(1) is redrafted to employ the same terms and concepts as the 1999 Act.

(1)   No matter relating to any child or young person concerned in proceedings to which this section applies shall while he is under the age of 18 be included in any publication if it is likely to lead members of the public to identify him as someone concerned in the proceedings.

'Publication', 'programme', 'programme service' and 'relevant programme' bear the same meanings as in relation to other reporting restrictions and the same particular identifying factors apply (s. 49(3), (3A) and (11)). The term 'person concerned in the proceedings' is defined as '(a) a person against or in respect of whom the proceedings are taken, or (b) a person called, or proposed to be called, to give evidence in the proceedings' (s. 49(4)). The offences which may be committed by breach of the restriction are also amended to bring them into line with similar offences under the 1999 Act (s. 49(9) to (9E)). The new offences are discussed below.

The extension of reporting restrictions to proceedings in youth courts in Northern Ireland has necessitated a number of minor modifications to the section applicable only to Northern Ireland and making reference to the appropriate Northern Irish legislation and institutions (s. 49(13)). The most significant modification is that for Northern Irish purposes s. 49 applies to young people under 17 (rather than 18) to reflect the jurisdictional age limit of youth courts in Northern Ireland.

RESTRICTIONS RELATING TO VULNERABLE ADULT WITNESSES: s. 46

Section 46 provides criminal courts in England, Wales and Northern Ireland, and service courts sitting anywhere, with a power to make reporting directions for the purpose of protecting the identities of vulnerable witnesses. Unlike the powers under ss. 44 and 45, which may be exercised of the court's own motion, the power under s. 46 may be exercised only on application by a party to the proceedings (s. 46(1)). Where an application is made, the court must apply a two-stage test and, where appropriate, exercise a discretion. The court must determine: first, that the witness is eligible for protection; secondly, that a reporting direction would be likely to improve the quality of the witness's evidence or the level of co-operation to a party. If these tests are satisfied then the court has a discretion whether or not to make an order. The stage in the proceedings at which a direction may be made is not specified. To be effective, such directions should be made at the earliest opportunity. Thus, for cases that are committed to the Crown Court, it may be necessary for a magistrates' court to make a direction which restricts reporting of the eventual trial on indictment.

Eligibility

A witness is eligible if the court is satisfied that the quality of evidence given by the witness, or the level of co-operation which the witness may give in relation to case preparation by one of the parties, is likely to be diminished by reason of fear or distress in connection with being identified by members of the public as a witness in the proceedings (s. 46(3)).

The 'quality of evidence' test refers to its completeness, coherence and accuracy (s. 46(12)(b)). In this context, 'coherence' refers to the witness's ability to give answers which address the questions put and which can be understood individually and collectively (s. 46(12)(b)).

Where the issue is the likely level of co-operation by the witness, this relates to 'case preparation' which is stated to include investigations carried out on behalf of the prosecution (s. 46(12)(c)). This however should not be understood to indicate that directions under s. 46 may be made during the investigative stage, prior to charge. The power to make a direction arises only in relation to criminal proceedings in court and thus pre-charge investigations are necessarily excluded. No doubt at the investigative stage the police may wish to comfort a vulnerable witness with the promise that a reporting direction will be sought. However, if part of the purpose of the provision is to ensure the availability of information at the investigative stage, the achievement of that purpose may be inhibited by the absence of a power to seek a direction from the court in advance of charge.

A number of factors are listed which the court must take into account in determining eligibility (s. 46(4)). These are the nature and circumstances of the alleged offence, the age of the witness and any behaviour towards the witness by the accused or by his associates or family or other potential witnesses in the proceedings. A further group of factors should also be taken into account if they appear to be relevant. These are the social and cultural background and ethnic origins of the witness, the domestic and employment circumstances of the witness and any religious beliefs or political opinions of the witness. The court must also consider any views expressed by the witness (s. 46(5)), although it appears that whether or not such views are solicited is a matter for the discretion of the parties or the court. These factors are the same as those applicable to the provision of assistance to witnesses under s. 17 (see pp. 42–43).

Notwithstanding the broad scope of the factors which must be considered in relation to eligibility, the test is closely focused on the effects of being identified by members of the public as a witness in the proceedings. Thus, the eligibility test might be satisfied in relation to an accountant or art dealer who had been the subject of fraud and was distressed by the potential damage to her reputation which publicity might bring. On the other hand, a witness who is simply in fear of reprisals from the defendant or his associates would not be eligible since his fear would not be linked to general publicity.

Improvement

The second test to be applied is whether making a reporting direction in relation to the witness is likely to improve the quality of evidence given by the witness or the level of co-operation given by the witness to any party to the proceedings in connection with that party's preparation of its case (s. 46(2)(b)). This test makes it clear that directions should be made only where they are likely to have some beneficial effect.

Discretion

Finally, even where the statutory criteria are satisfied, the court retains a discretion whether or not to make a reporting direction. In deciding whether to make a direction, the court must consider:

(a) whether it is in the interests of justice to do so; and
(b) the public interest in avoiding the imposition of a substantial and unreasonable restriction on the reporting of the proceedings (s. 46(8)).

As discussed above, recent case law on reporting restrictions under the Children and Young Persons Act 1933 suggests that the court has a wide discretion concerning who may be permitted to make representations to the court. In particular, members of the press, or representatives of such, should normally be permitted to make representations.

A reporting direction made under s. 46 will order that no matter relating to the relevant witness shall during the witness's lifetime be included in any publication if it is likely to lead members of the public to identify him as being a witness in the proceedings (s. 46(6)). The list of particular identifying factors, applicable generally to reporting restrictions, is applied to s. 46 by s. 46(7).

Reporting directions may be revoked (s. 46(10)) or partially dispensed with by an 'excepting direction', whether made at the same time as the reporting direction or subsequently (s. 46(9) and (11)). Both powers are stated to be exercisable either by 'the court or an appellate court'. The reference to 'the court' is ambiguous since it may refer either to the court which made the original reporting direction or to the court currently dealing with the case. It seems certain that 'the court' should be understood in the latter sense because otherwise a Crown Court would be bound by a direction made by a magistrates' court earlier in the proceedings. 'Appellate court' is defined as meaning a court dealing with an appeal (including an appeal by way of case stated) (s. 46(12)(a)).

Rather oddly, the section does not specify criteria for revocation although it does so for partial dispensation by excepting direction. Under s. 46(9), the court or appellate court may dispense, to an extent specified in the excepting direction, with reporting restrictions if it is satisfied either that it is necessary in the interests of justice to do so or both that the effect of the restrictions is to impose a substantial and unreasonable restriction on the reporting of the proceedings and that it is in the public interest to remove or relax that restriction.

RESTRICTIONS ON REPORTING SPECIAL MEASURES DIRECTIONS AND DIRECTIONS PROHIBITING PERSONAL CROSS-EXAMINATION: s. 47

Section 47 creates a general restriction, for the duration of the relevant trial, on the reporting of applications for, or the granting of, special measures directions under s. 19, and also in relation to applications for, or the granting of, directions prohibiting an accused person from personally cross-examining a particular witness under s. 36. Similar restrictions will apply in relation to the corresponding measures in Northern Ireland. The purpose of the section is to avoid prejudice to the accused which might arise if it became known that measures had been taken to protect the complainant or other witnesses in the proceedings.

Section 47(1) imposes a general ban on publishing reports of matters listed in s. 47(2) which are directions, or orders varying or discharging such directions, under ss. 19 and 36. The ban is automatically lifted after the relevant proceedings are either abandoned or determined by acquittal, conviction or otherwise (s. 47(6)). Where there is more than one accused, the ban will not be lifted until the proceedings are either abandoned or determined in relation to all of them.

The reference to the proceedings being 'abandoned' may be problematic. Presumably this refers to the Director of Public Prosecutions' power to discontinue proceedings under the Prosecution of Offences Act 1985, s 23(3). Under that provision the proceedings are discontinued from the date of notice but may be revived by the accused giving notice within 35 days under s. 23(7) of the 1985 Act. Even if this does not occur, the prosecution have the right to institute fresh proceedings at a later date (s. 23(9)), e.g., where new evidence is found. The contingent nature of discontinuance under this procedure makes it difficult to identify a point where abandonment has occurred. This is a matter of concern for the press, who need clear guidelines as to whether or not publication is lawful. It is also a matter of concern for the defendant who may be prejudiced by reports published during a period of temporary discontinuance. With these concerns in mind, it is tentatively suggested that, where a discontinuance notice has been issued, the proceeding should not be considered abandoned until the expiry of the 35-day period during which the accused may revive the proceedings. At this stage the proceeding should be considered abandoned notwithstanding the possibility of the new proceedings being instituted by the prosecution.

The court has a power to lift, in whole or in part, the general restriction on reporting under s. 47 of the 1999 Act (s. 47(3)). Since there is no application procedure in relation to this power, it appears that the court can act of its own motion and that any party to the proceedings or an interested third party (e.g., the press) may ask the court to exercise the power. It is implicit that, where the court is considering lifting a restriction, it must solicit the views of the accused. If one or more of the accused objects, the court must hear the representations of each of the accused and must not order the lifting of restrictions unless satisfied that it is in the interests of justice to do so (s. 47(4) and (5)).

It appears to be intended that, where a court acts under s. 47(4) or (5) to lift reporting restrictions, this will not permit the reporting of the accused's objections or representations to this procedure. This is the best interpretation which can be offered for the following passage in each of those subsections: '... and if the order [lifting reporting restrictions] is made it shall not apply to the extent that a report deals with any such objections or representations'. The suggestion seems to be that the general restriction on reporting proceedings under ss. 19 and 36 necessarily includes a restriction on reporting any consideration given by the court to the possible lifting of such reporting restrictions. Whereas an order under s. 47(4) or (5) may permit publication (to a specified extent) of information relating to directions or orders under ss. 19 and 36, it cannot permit publication of objections or representations made by the accused on this issue.

For the avoidance of doubt, s. 47(8) states that 'nothing in [s. 47] affects any prohibition or restriction by virtue of any other enactment on the inclusion of matter in a publication'. Thus, the lifting of reporting restrictions under s. 47(5) in relation to a youth court case would not override the general prohibition under s. 49 of the 1933 Act on publishing information identifying juvenile defendants.

Northern Ireland

Section 47 is applied to Northern Ireland by virtue of s. 47(2)(aa), which was inserted by the Criminal Evidence (Northern Ireland) Order 1999 (SI 1999/2789), art. 1(2). The restriction applies in relation proceedings under art. 7 of the Order which corresponds to s. 19, and to proceedings under art. 24 which corresponds to s. 36.

ANONYMITY OF VICTIMS OF SEXUAL OFFENCES: AMENDMENTS TO SEXUAL OFFENCES (AMENDMENT) ACTS 1976 AND 1992

The Sexual Offences (Amendment) Acts 1976 and 1992 prohibit the publication of any matter which might lead members of the public to identify the alleged victim of certain sexual offences. By virtue of the 1999 Act, s. 48 and sch. 2, these provisions are substantially reformed for three purposes:

(a)   to consolidate reporting restrictions relating to sexual offences in relation to England, Wales and Northern Ireland in a single Act;

(b)   to create consistency with reporting provisions under the 1999 Act;

(c)   to extend the area in which reporting restrictions apply to include Scotland.

Consolidating reporting restrictions in the Sexual Offences (Amendment) Act 1992

Formerly reporting restrictions specific to sexual offences were found in the Sexual Offences (Amendment) Acts 1976 and 1992 and in the Sexual Offences (Northern Ireland) Order 1978 and the Criminal Justice (Northern Ireland) Order 1994. These provisions are now consolidated in an amended Sexual Offences (Amendment) Act 1992 (SOAA 1992).

In detail the consolidation is achieved by amendments in sch. 2 to the 1999 Act as follows:

(a)   by omitting provisions relating to reporting restrictions from the other three pieces of legislation (paras. 4, 5 and 15);

(b)   by including rape and burglary with intent to rape within the list of offences to which the SOAA 1992 applies (para. 8(1) and (2));

(c)   by applying restrictions under the SOAA 1992 to Northern Irish proceedings and offences (paras 8(4) and 14);

(d)   by making various minor amendments to the SOAA 1992 to make it applicable to Northern Ireland (paras. 9 and 12(4));

(e)   in relation to the SOAA 1992, s. 4 (which removes the protection of reporting restrictions from consensual parties involved in offences of incest and buggery), various amendments are made in relation to its application to Northern Ireland to reflect the fact that the Sexual Offences Act 1956 does not apply in the province and to substitute references to corresponding offences under earlier legislation still applicable in Northern Ireland — notably references to the Punishment of Incest Act 1908 and the Offences Against the Person Act 1861 are substituted (sch. 2, para. 10);

(f)   by applying the 1992 Act to a list of offences contrary to Northern Irish law, corresponding to the English offences already covered (sch. 2, para. 6).

SOAA 1992: amendments in the interests of consistency

The amendments to make the SOAA 1992 consistent with the regime of reporting restrictions under the 1999 Act are as follows:

(a)   The SOAA 1992, s. 1(1) imposes reporting restrictions from the time when an allegation of sexual offence has been made. Formerly, the restriction applied to four specific facts relating to the alleged victim: name, address, and any still or moving picture of her. The specific list is now replaced by the general formula 'no matter relating to that person shall during that person's lifetime be included in any publication' (sch. 2, para. 7(2)) but, as before, the restriction will apply to the matter published only 'if it is likely to lead members of the public to identify that person as the person against whom the offence is alleged to have been committed'. The illustrative list of particular identifying factors which applies generally to reporting restrictions under the 1999 Act is now applied to the SOAA 1992 (sch. 2, para. 7(4) substituting a new s. 1(3A) in the SOAA 1992).

(b)   The former formula used by the SOAA 1992 to indicate the sorts of publications to which reporting restrictions applied is now replaced throughout that Act by the phrase 'included in a publication' with the general definition of 'publication' taken from s. 63(1) of the 1999 Act (see p. 207), which is now applied also to the 1992 Act by virtue of sch. 2, para. 12(1) and (2).

(c)   Section 1(3) is substituted (sch. 2, para. 7(4)). The effect of the new s. 1(3) is to distinguish between reporting restrictions which apply under s. 1(1) following an allegation of a relevant sexual offence, and those which apply under s. 1(2) after a person has been accused of the offence. Any restrictions under s. 1(2) are subject to the SOAA 1992, s. 3, under which the court has a power by direction to dispense with reporting restrictions relating to the identity of the complainant if this is required to induce witnesses to come forward or if the conduct of the accused's defence is likely to be prejudiced if a direction is not given.

(d)   The range of offences to which reporting restrictions under the SOAA 1992 apply is increased by the addition of aiding, abetting, counselling or procuring the commission of any of the offences already covered (sch. 2, para. 8(4)) and also abduction of a woman by force contrary to the Sexual Offences Act 1956, s. 17 (para. 8(5)). This change must be understood as being for the purpose of avoiding doubt since, under general principles, aiding, abetting, counselling and procuring are merely ways in which the substantive offence may be committed rather than separate offences. This amendment makes clear that reporting restrictions will apply to (doubly inchoate) charges of aiding, abetting, counselling or procuring another to incite a relevant sexual offence. By virtue of the 1999 Act, sch. 2, para. 3, which amends the SOAA 1992, s. 6(2A), it is made clear that, where a person is so charged as an accomplice to an incitement, the offence is deemed to be committed against the intended victim of the incited act and therefore reporting restrictions will apply in relation to such person.

(e)   The regime of reporting restrictions applicable to sexual offences dealt with at courts martial is amended by the substitution of a new SOAA 1992, s. 7 (sch. 2, para. 14).

Reporting restrictions to be extended to Scotland

Reporting restrictions relating to English, Welsh and Northern Irish proceedings will be extended to publications in Scotland (sch. 2, para. 14).

OFFENCES INVOLVING BREACH OF REPORTING RESTRICTIONS: s. 49

Section 49 creates new offences of breaching reporting restrictions. Offences will be committed by:

(a)   publishing matter likely to identify a juvenile involved in an offence, contrary to s. 44(2);

(b)   publishing matter likely to identify a juvenile involved in proceedings, where such publication has been prohibited under s. 45(3);

(c)   publishing matter which breaches a reporting direction given in relation to a witness under s. 46(2);

(d)   publishing a report relating to a special measures direction or in relation to a direction prohibiting the accused from conducting cross-examination in person, contrary to s. 47.

Exceptionally, prosecutions for breach of s. 47 may be instituted only with the consent of the Attorney General or the Attorney General for Northern Ireland, as appropriate (s. 49(6)).

Where the offending matter is published in a newspaper or periodical, the offence will be committed by the proprietor, editor and publisher (s. 49(2)). Where the publication is a programme, the offence is committed by any person having functions in relation to the programme corresponding to those of an editor of a newspaper, or by any body corporate or Scottish partnership engaged in providing the programme service in which the programme is included (s. 49(3)). Section 49(4) deals with other types of publication (e.g., on CD, DVD or via the Internet) and provides that: '[i]n the case of any other publication, any person publishing it is guilty of an offence'.

The terms 'publish' and 'publisher' are not defined by the Act. In other contexts the terms are given wide meanings. For instance, under the Obscene Publications Act 1959, s. 3, a person publishes an article who distributes, circulates, sells, lets on hire, gives or lends it or offers it for sale or, in relation to an article containing matter to be looked at or a record, shows, plays or projects it. This corresponds with the meaning given to the term at common law, for instance in relation to libel, and there seems to be no reason to believe that 'publish' will be given any narrower meaning under the 1999 Act.

It is envisaged that offences under s. 49 may be committed by companies (see s. 51(1)) acting as publisher, programme provider or proprietor of the medium of publication. This indicates that, as a matter of statutory interpretation, these are offences for which a company may be vicariously liable for the conduct of its employees. Where a limited company (or other corporation) commits a reporting restriction offence, s. 51 extends liability for the offence to any officer of the company where the offence is proved to have been either committed with the officer's consent or connivance or attributable to any neglect on the officer's part (s. 51(1)). An extension is also made for partners in a Scottish partnership who have consented to or connived in the offence, although oddly liability will not attach where there is mere neglect (s. 51(4)). 'Officer' for this purpose is rather loosely defined as director, manager, secretary or other similar officer of the corporate body, or a person purporting to act in any such capacity (s. 51(2)). If the affairs of a body corporate are managed by its members, 'director' is to be interpreted to mean a member of that body (s. 51(3)). The intention is clearly to include any senior figure with responsibility for the relevant publication. This intention may be frustrated by the vagueness of the definition employed. Whereas, director and secretary are offices recognised by law, manager is not. In *Tesco Supermarkets Ltd* v *Nattrass* [1972] AC 153 at p. 178, it was suggested that the term would apply to a manager of the company as a whole rather than of a separate unit, such as a shop within the company. Similar uncertainty attaches to the meaning of 'other similar officer'.

The offences are subject to the specific defences set out in s. 50 which are considered below. However, apart from this, the offence can be established without proof of *mens rea*. This underlines the duty of editors and publishers to be vigilant against the possibility of restrictions applying. The lack of a *mens rea* requirement will also avoid problems in deciding whether any particular individual's state of mind can be attributed to the company under the identification doctrine.

As indicated above, where a corporation commits an offence under s. 49, an officer may be liable but only if proven to be at fault by conniving in the offence, or where the offence is attributable to that officer's neglect. This is a standard formula applied to a number of statutory offences which appears to create a form of accomplice liability (see discussion in J.C. Smith, *Smith & Hogan, Criminal Law*, 1999, 9th ed., p. 187 and see commentary by J.C. Smith to *Wilson* [1997] Crim LR 53). In order to establish neglect, it would be necessary to demonstrate that the relevant officer had particular responsibility for the impugned publication. An oddity with this arrangement is that, if an individual (who may also be an 'officer' of a publishing company) is charged as a principal offender in his own right (whether or not the company is also charged), guilt will be determined on the basis of strict liability without the need to prove connivance or neglect.

Offences under s. 49 are triable summarily only and are subject to a maximum penalty of a level 5 fine (currently £5,000). Limiting the penalty to a fine proved controversial during the Parliamentary passage of the Act. It was pointed out that in relation to the most sensational cases, for the media, the incentive to breach reporting restrictions will be financial and, with a maximum fine of only £5,000, a newspaper or broadcasting channel might calculate that the financial benefit of publishing would outweigh the risk of being prosecuted and fined (per Lord Cope of Berkeley, Lords, *Hansard,* 8 March 1999, col. 73).

DEFENCES TO REPORTING RESTRICTION OFFENCES: s. 50

Section 50 establishes a number of defences applicable to offences of breaching reporting restrictions under s. 50. The defences are of three types:

(a)   proof that the defendant lacked awareness, suspicion or grounds for suspicion in relation to a relevant matter;

(b)   proof that publication was in the public interest;

(c)   proof that publication was made with the consent of the affected party.

These three categories of defence will be dealt with separately.

Lack of awareness, suspicion or grounds for suspicion

Section 50(1) creates a general defence, applicable to all offences under s. 49, where the defendant proves that at the time of the alleged offence he was not aware, and neither suspected nor had reason to suspect, that the publication included the matter or report in question. The burden of proving the defence is clearly placed on the defendant and under general principles the standard of proof will be on a balance of probabilities.

The application of the defence to corporate defendants will be problematic. Traditionally, where the criminal liability of a corporation depends upon proof of a state of mind, the state of mind of an individual who is the company's 'directing mind' or its 'embodiment', is attributed to the company under the doctrine of *Tesco Supermarkets Ltd* v *Nattrass* [1972] AC 153. Where material is published in breach of a reporting restriction it would be easy for a managing director who did not read every publication to claim lack of knowledge or actual suspicion. If the courts were to accept that the MD also lacked any reason for suspicion because he did not read the relevant publication, it would be made very difficult to gain a conviction against a corporate publisher. If corporations are to be made liable, it would be necessary to find that the mere fact that the publication contained the offending material was sufficient ground for suspicion.

A similar defence is provided by s. 50(2), which is applicable only to breaches of restrictions concerning juveniles involved in investigations contrary to s. 44(2). It is a defence to prove that at the time of the alleged offence (the defendant) was not aware, and neither suspected nor had reason to suspect, that the criminal investigation in question had begun.

The public interest defence

Section 50(3) provides a public interest defence relating to breaches of reporting restrictions relating to juveniles involved in investigations, contrary to s. 44(2). The defence is not available where the breach of the reporting restriction relates to either an alleged perpetrator of the relevant offence (s. 50(3)(b)(i)) or an alleged witness to a sexual offence which is subject to reporting restrictions under the SOAA 1992 (s. 50(3)(b)(ii)). The effect of this is to distinguish between, on the one hand, alleged defendants and victims of sexual offences for whom reporting restrictions are absolute and, on the other hand, victims and witnesses whose interest in privacy may bend to the public interest. This was justified by the Home Office Minister, Lord Williams of Mostyn, on the grounds of the need to allow greater scope for reporting news stories of national importance which may be fast-breaking (Lords, *Hansard,* 8 March 1999, cols. 71–72). Until s. 44 is fully implemented by order, the defence will serve no practical purpose except to indicate the standards to which the press must operate if the threat of full implementation is to be averted.

If and when s. 44 is fully implemented, a person charged with its breach would need to establish two things in order to escape liability on public interest grounds. These would be:

(a)   that the restriction under s. 44(2) amounted to a substantial and unreasonable restriction on reporting matters connected with the offence; and accordingly

(b)   that it was in the public interest to publish the relevant matter in breach of the restriction.

The matters to which the court must have regard, if relevant, when determining public interest are set out in s. 52(2). These are the interests in each of the following:

(a)   the open reporting of crime;

(b)   the open reporting of matters relating to human health or safety and the prevention and exposure of miscarriage of justice;

(c)   the welfare of the person protected by the reporting restriction; and

(d)   any views expressed by either the protected person or, if that person is under 16, their parent or guardian (or any other person who is the 'appropriate person' for the purpose of s. 50(9) to (12)).

The provision of a public interest defence is initially attractive in view of the acknowledged competing interests which must be balanced in this area. Whether relying upon an *ex post facto* defence is the most sensible means of achieving the necessary balance may be open to question. It will be recalled that s. 44(3) contains a procedure for dispensing with reporting restrictions where this is in the interests of justice. If a procedure for dispensing with restrictions in the public interest had been provided, in appropriate cases it would be possible to put the argument before a court in advance of publication, thereby avoiding the risk of prosecution. It is also perhaps strange in view of the public interest issues involved that the opportunity was not taken to make decisions to prosecute for breach of s. 44 subject to consent of the relevant Attorney-General as is required for breach of s. 47.

The procedure in court where a public interest defence is raised may also be problematic. The court is required to consider any views expressed by the protected juvenile, if over 16, but alternatively the views of the 'appropriate person' (normally her parent or guardian) on her behalf if she is under that age (s. 52(2)(c)). This approach runs against the modern trend to hear children on issues affecting their welfare. It also generates a practical problem. By constituting the child and her carer as alternative voices, the possibility arises of a court heeding the view of a parent whilst never hearing the very different view of an articulate 15-year-old victim. This difficulty might have been avoided if both parent and child had the right to have their views heard, or if the courts were to extend the law and adopt this as a matter of practice. It is also not made clear how the views of the protected person are to be obtained. There is no duty on any party or the court to seek such views, but unless this is done it seems unlikely that the relevant view will be put before the court. A problem with the procedure is that, for the protected person, contemplating the lifting of the restriction and expressing a view about it may be a source of considerable stress.

Defences based on consent

Section 50 provides for two defences which are established where the protected person, or an appropriate person on behalf of a protected person under 16, consents to the publishing of the matter in breach of reporting restrictions. The definition of 'appropriate person' is considered below.

Section 50(5) provides a consent defence relating to publications in breach of restrictions on reporting investigations concerning juveniles under s. 44(2). The defence does not apply if the protected person is either the alleged offender or a witness aged under 16 to an alleged sexual offence to which the SOAA 1992, s. 1 applies (s. 50(4)(b)). The rationales for these two exceptions are as follows. Where the protected person is the alleged offender, the long standing policy that juvenile offenders should not be named applies, making it inappropriate to permit the lifting of reporting restrictions by consent. Where the protected person is an alleged witness to a sexual offence, who may of course be the victim, there is a special need to protect the youngster from the stigma which may attach to children involved in such offences.

The provision for surrogate consent by an appropriate person in relation to children under 16 is problematic. First, the denial of competence to those aged under 16 is inconsistent with modern law in relation to consent to medical treatment under which decision-making competence is determined according to the maturity and under-standing of the child rather than according to age (*Gillick* v *West Norfolk* [1986] AC 112). Although it should be noted that, where consent is given by an adult on behalf of the child, the child is given a power of veto under s. 50(6) (see below). Secondly, there is a risk that appropriate persons may not act in the best interests of the child. Thirdly, since more than one person may fulfil the definition of appropriate person, there is a risk that appropriate persons may disagree as to the best course (e.g., where two parents have separated).

The Act addresses the second problem by requiring that before consent by an appropriate person can be effective that person must have been given a written notice drawing his attention to the need to consider the welfare of the protected person when deciding whether to give consent (s. 50(5)). This assumes that consent by a parent or guardian will have been given in response to a request rather than spontaneously. The requester is thus placed under a duty to give the required written notice. This seems a very weak mechanism to counter possible manipulation of parents by the media, particulary since there is no bar on offering financial inducements.

The third problem is addressed in s. 50(6), which provides that the effect of a consent by an appropriate person may be negatived by a written notice withdrawing consent given by any other appropriate person or by the protected person herself. The notice must be given to a person described as 'the appropriate recipient', defined as the person to whom the notice of consent was given, the person by whom the matter in question was published or any other person with responsibility for that publication (s. 50(14)). The effect of the provision is that any appropriate person or the protected child may veto consent. This seems right in principle but may not work in practice. Where one appropriate person has given consent it may be that the protected child or other appropriate persons discover this when they see the case reported in a newspaper.

The second consent defence is found in s. 50(7) and relates to reporting restrictions to protect vulnerable adults under s. 46(2). It will be a defence to a charge under s. 49 if the person protected by such a restriction gave written consent to the inclusion of the relevant matter in the publication. The provision of this defence is rather incongruous in view of the purpose of s. 46 which is to employ the mechanism of witness protection in aid of the public interest in enhancing the availability and quality of evidence. It seems wrong in principle that a public benefit can be dispensed with by private arrangement. It also seems unlikely that the defence will be much relied upon during the currency of the proceedings since a reporting direction under s. 46 will be given only where the court is satisfied that the adult in question would suffer fear or distress if publicly identified. Perhaps the most likely situation in which this defence would be relied upon, is where it is intended to publish a report of a case sometime after its conclusion at a stage when emotions associated with the case have abated.

A defence raised under either s. 50(5) or (7) will fail if it is proved that any person, intending to gain consent, interfered with the peace or comfort of either or both of the protected person and any appropriate person who gave consent on behalf of the protected person (s. 50(8)). The phrase 'peace or comfort' is borrowed from the offence of harassment contrary to the Protection from Eviction Act 1977, s. 1(3). In the leading case on the meaning of the phrase, *Burke* [1991] 1 AC 135, the House of Lords held that interference with peace or comfort might be committed without an actionable civil wrong or behaviour which would otherwise amount to an offence. Arguably, the term could cover conduct such as persistent requests by telephone as well as threats and intimidation. The interference does not have to emanate from the person who obtains consent. Thus, a consent defence would be defeated if a newspaper reporter enlisted a relative of a protected person to pester them to give consent.

The appropriate person in relation to children under 16

For the purpose of defences under s. 50, consents and expressions of view may be given on behalf of protected persons who are children under 16 by an 'appropriate person'. The definitions of 'appropriate person' set out below which relate to the different jurisdictions within the UK are all subject to a standard exception relating to any person who is alleged to have committed the offence in relation to which the reporting restriction applies (s. 50(13)).

In England and Wales, appropriate person means a parent or guardian of the protected person, with 'guardian' meaning a person who has parental responsibility under the Children Act 1989 (s. 50(9)). Where a child is looked after by a local authority under the Children Act 1989, the appropriate person is either a representative of that authority or a parent or guardian with whom the child is allowed to live (s. 50(10)).

In Northern Ireland, an appropriate person means a parent or guardian of the protected person, with 'guardian' meaning a person who has parental responsibility under the Children (Northern Ireland) Order 1995 (s. 50(9)). Where a child is looked after by an authority under the Children (Northern Ireland) Order 1995, the appropriate person is either an officer of that authority or a parent or guardian with whom the child is allowed to live (s. 50(11)).

In Scotland, an appropriate person is someone with parental responsibilities for the protected person under the Children (Scotland) Act 1995, s. 1(3) (s. 50(9)). Where a child is looked after by a local authority under the Children (Scotland) Act 1995, s. 17(6), the appropriate person is either a representative of that authority or a person with parental responsibilities under that Act with whom the child is allowed to live (s. 50(12)).

OFFENCES OF BREACHING REPORTING RESTRICTIONS UNDER THE CHILDREN AND YOUNG PERSONS ACT 1933

Paragraph 3 of sch. 2 to the Act substitutes a new provision for the Children and Young Persons Act 1933, s. 49(9). This subsection makes it an offence to publish matter in breach of s. 49 which identifies children involved in proceedings in the youth court. The purpose of the substitution is to make the offence under that section consistent with the offences involving breach of reporting restrictions under s. 49 of the 1999 Act and defences thereto under s. 50 (see pp. 130–35). The substituted provisions are a new s. 49(9), followed by further new subsections numbered (9A) to (9E).

Section 49(9) of the 1933 Act creates the offence of publishing any matter in contravention of s. 49(1) of that Act and makes it punishable on summary conviction by fine not exceeding level 5 on the standard scale. The persons who may commit the offence are the same as for s. 49 of the 1999 Act. Section 49(9A) of the 1933 Act provides for a defence where the publisher was not aware and neither suspected nor had grounds for suspecting that the publication contained the offending matter. Section 49(9B) to (9E) extends liability to officers of a company or a Scottish partnership as under s. 51(1) to (4) of the 1999 Act.

OFFENCES OF BREACHING REPORTING RESTRICTIONS UNDER THE SEXUAL OFFENCES (AMENDMENT) ACT 1992

Paragraph 11 of sch. 2 to the 1999 Act amends the SOAA 1992, s. 5 (which created the offence of breaching reporting restrictions under that Act) so as to make it consistent with similar offences under the 1999 Act. In summary, the amendments to SOAA 1992, s. 5 are as follows. The substituted s. 5(1) creates an offence of breaching restrictions under the 1992 Act; it is in similar terms to the original but the offence may be committed by the same persons and subject to the same penalties as the offence under s. 49(2) to (5) of the 1999 Act (see pp. 129–30). In view of the extension of publishing restrictions, a new s. 5(8) extends liability of Scottish partnerships to their members who have connived or consented in a publication in breach of the SOAA 1992. By virtue of an amendment to s. 5(3), the protected person's consent to publication will not operate as a defence where the protected person was under 16 at the relevant time. By amendment to s. 5(4) (which requires Attorney-General's consent for prosecution), similar consent of the Attorney-General for Northern Ireland will be required for prosecutions under s. 5 in that province. By virtue of a new s. 5(5A), a new defence will apply where a person has published matter identifying a complainant or witness after an allegation of a sexual offence has been made contrary to the SOAA 1992, s. 1(1). The new defence will be established if the person in question proves that he was not aware and neither suspected nor had reason to suspect that the relevant allegation had been made.

Chapter 9
Competence of Witnesses, Sworn and Unsworn Evidence, and Compellability

OVERVIEW

Sections 53 to 57 reform the rules relating to competence and the giving of sworn evidence. Section 53 lays down a clear presumption of competence for all witnesses, exempting only those incapable of making themselves understood. Section 54 contains the procedure for determining competence. Section 55 makes provision for witnesses over the age of 14 who understand the significance of giving evidence on oath to do so. Witnesses who are competent under the general test but who lack the understanding required by s. 55 give their evidence unsworn by virtue of s. 56. Section 57 makes it an offence wilfully to give false unsworn testimony. These provisions are due to come into force by the end of 2000, according to *Action For Justice: Implementing the Speaking Up For Justice Report in England and Wales* (Home Office, 1999). The transitional arrangements in sch. 7, para. 7 provide that none of the new provisions apply to proceedings instituted before the commencement date.

Paragraph 4 of sch. 4 to the Act reformulates the provisions of the Criminal Evidence Act 1898, s. 1, by virtue of which the accused is a competent witness in his own defence. Paragraphs 12 and 13 of sch. 4 amend the provisions in the Police and Criminal Evidence Act 1984, s. 80 relating to the competence and compellability of the spouse of the accused. It is anticipated that these provisions will come into effect at the same time as the new rules on competence.

BACKGROUND

At common law, there was a general requirement that witnesses give evidence on oath. An oath is normally in the form dictated by the witness's religious beliefs, although the Oaths Act 1978, s. 5 permits a witness who objects to being sworn to make a solemn affirmation instead. (The term 'sworn' covers evidence given on oath and affirmation.) The giving of evidence on oath or affirmation necessarily requires of the witness a certain level of understanding and the onus at common law fell on the party tendering the witness to establish that he had:

> a sufficient appreciation of the solemnity of the occasion, and the added responsibility to tell the truth, which is involved in taking an oath, over and above the duty to tell the truth which is an ordinary duty of normal social conduct. (*Hayes* [1977] 1 WLR 234)

Witnesses with a mental illness or learning disability were not necessarily incompetent to testify applying this test, and many were able to give evidence either on oath or on affirmation (*Bellamy* (1985) 82 Cr App R 222). Where a witness failed to display the required degree of understanding of a witness's obligations, however, he was incompetent to testify even if he was perfectly able to give a coherent account of relevant events. This was a particular problem where the putative witness claimed that he had been the victim of crime, but the allegation could not be pursued to conviction without the evidence of the victim.

The evidence of children had for some time been governed by a statutory exception to the common-law rule, so that it was possible for the evidence of a child of limited understanding to be received unsworn. At one time it was a requirement that the child had to be of sufficient intelligence to justify the reception of his evidence and that he understood the duty of speaking the truth. Even this reduced threshold was lowered in the Criminal Justice Act 1988, s. 33A(1) of which provided that no child aged under 14 should give sworn evidence, but the court was bound to receive such a child's unsworn evidence unless it appeared to the court that he was incapable of giving intelligible testimony (s. 33A(2A)). This provision had the potential to admit the evidence of some very young witnesses, including some whose understanding of the duty to tell the truth was likely to be limited or non-existent. In *Director of Public Prosecutions* v *M* [1997] 2 All ER 749, the Divisional Court affirmed that the statutory words meant what they said. The issue was whether the Crown Court was right to decline to hear a five-year-old by reason of her age alone. It was held that under s. 33A(2A) the only consideration was whether the child satisfied the intelligibility test. If she did, the mandatory language of the section provided no ground for refusing to hear her evidence. So far as the meaning of intelligibility was concerned, the proper inquiry was whether the child '... is able to understand questions and to answer them in a manner which is coherent and comprehensible' (see also *G* v *Director of Public Prosecutions* [1998] QB 919).

The policy behind the development in the law relating to children is that magistrates and juries are capable of deciding for themselves what weight to attach to the word of a very young witness of limited understanding. Furthermore, in an increasingly secular society, the guarantee of truthfulness which an oath supplies is of diminishing importance. *Speaking Up For Justice* suggested that the same considerations should apply to the evidence of an adult witness whose evidence is intelligible (or is capable of being rendered intelligible with appropriate aids). The unsworn evidence of a witness of limited understanding might be difficult to assess, but the presumption should be that it should be called to be evaluated by the jury as best it can (para. 11.26). It is on this principle, which represents a considerable departure from the common-law approach to adult witnesses, that the 1999 Act is built.

COMPETENCE: THE NEW RULES

Section 53(1) lays down a general presumption of competence for all witnesses. Only where it appears to the court that an individual is unable to understand questions put to him as a witness and to give answers to them which can be understood is he incompetent (s. 53(2) and (3)). This is effectively the same limitation as that which applied to children under the Criminal Justice Act 1988 (as interpreted in *Director of Public Prosecutions* v *M* [1997] 2 All ER 749 and *G* v *Director of Public Prosecutions* [1998] QB 919). The provisions of the 1988 Act are repealed by sch. 6 to the 1999 Act, thus marking the end of a separate threshold of competence for children.

The onus of proving competence is on the party calling the witness (s. 54(2)) wherever the issue is raised, either by a party to the proceedings or by the court (s. 54(1)). In conformity with the preference expressed at common law (*Hampshire* [1995] 3 WLR 260), the hearing to determine competence takes place in the absence of the jury (s. 54(4)), expert evidence is receivable (s. 54(5)), and any necessary questioning of the witness is conducted by the court in the presence of the parties (s. 54(6)). If a special measures direction has been given to assist the witness in testifying (see Chapters 4 and 5), or the court proposes to give one, then the witness is treated as having the benefit of that direction for the purposes of assessing his competence. So, for example, a witness who could cope with questions in the less formal setting which prevails when testimony is pre-recorded under s. 27 (see p. 62), but not with the same questions in a court setting, is competent under s. 53 provided that the court is prepared to direct in favour of pre-recording. Similarly, a witness who can be understood only with the aid of an intermediary is competent provided that the court is prepared to give a direction allowing evidence to be given through such a person (s. 29: see p. 75). In the light of the importance of special measures in the determination of competence, it is envisaged that competence should be assessed at the same time as an application for a special measures direction (Lord Williams of Mostyn, House of Lords, *Hansard*, 8 February 1999, col. 79).

SWORN AND UNSWORN EVIDENCE

Who may give sworn evidence

Section 55 provides that a witness may not give sworn evidence unless:

(a)   he has attained the age of 14 (preserving the present rule); and

(b)   he has a sufficient appreciation of the solemnity of the occasion and of the particular responsibility to tell the truth which is involved in taking an oath (again, this reflects the current law on oath-taking).

Giving Unsworn Evidence

There is an evidential burden on any party asserting that a witness competent within the meaning of s. 53 should not be sworn (s. 55(4)), alternatively the court may of its own motion raise the issue (s. 55(1)(b)) and put the party calling the witness to proof. Section 56 provides that any competent person who is not permitted to give sworn evidence shall give evidence unsworn.

It is not a ground for allowing an appeal that a witness who has given evidence unsworn should have given evidence on oath (s. 56(5)). This provision will be useful in cases where there has been an oversight resulting in the failure to administer the oath. In *Simmonds* [1996] Crim LR 816, S was convicted of indecent assault on the evidence of the complainant, a girl who had turned 14 at the time of the trial. Her evidence in chief was quite properly given by means of a video recorded interview. However she was not, as she should have been, sworn before being cross-examined. As her unsworn answers were not admissible evidence, S's conviction was quashed. The effect of the 1999 Act is to remove the objection to the admissibility of the girl's unsworn evidence, so that a failure to administer the oath at the appropriate point no longer affords a valid reason for disturbing a conviction. Whether the same weight can attach to the unsworn as to the sworn evidence of such a witness is a question for the jury or magistrates to decide.

If a witness gives unsworn evidence it is generally desirable to remind him of the need to tell the truth. In court a procedure has developed in relation to child witnesses where the judge 'admonishes' the child in the following way: 'Tell us all you can remember of what happened. Don't make anything up or leave anything out. This is very important'. This form of words, which was originally suggested by the Pigot Committee (*Report of the Advisory Group on Video Evidence* (Home Office, 1989)) was endorsed by Auld J in *Hampshire* [1995] 3 WLR 260. It is also a suitable formula for an interviewer to adopt when participating in the video recording of a witness's evidence in chief, and it is referred to with approval in the *Memorandum of Good Practice on Video Recorded Interviews with Child Witnesses for Criminal Proceedings* (Home Office and Department of Health, 1992, para. 3.10–11). The Memorandum also explains that, if an admonition is to be given at a recorded interview, it needs to be in the context of a discussion with the witness in which the interviewer can convey the need to speak the truth and the acceptability of saying 'I don't know', or 'I don't understand'. Although it is undoubtedly helpful for the court, when the tape is played, to know that the witness was made aware of the need to speak the truth, interviewers also have to be conscious that a young witness may misinterpret the admonition and may fear that his truthful account will not be believed. The interviewer therefore needs to approach the matter sensitively. The Memorandum is being rewritten to reflect the inclusion in the 1999 Act of a wider range of vulnerable witnesses who may benefit from such measures as pre-recorded evidence and the giving of evidence unsworn in court. It is, however, likely that the guidance with regard to admonishing interviewees and witnesses in court will continue to be part of the process of taking unsworn evidence.

Corroboration

Under the Criminal Justice Act 1988, s. 34(3), a change to the corroboration rules was effected by the provision that the evidence of an unsworn child could corroborate evidence (sworn or unsworn) given by any other person. Paragraph 17 of sch. 4 to the 1999 Act amends s. 34(3) of the 1988 Act so that any unsworn evidence admitted by virtue of s. 56 of the 1999 Act may in future be corroborative. At the time of the 1988 legislation, there were various technical mandatory requirements for corroboration, or for a corroboration warning to be given to a jury, and s. 34(3) of the 1988 Act was designed to ensure that unsworn evidence was capable of having corroborative effect under these rules.

Corroboration in its technical sense could be provided only by evidence which was independent of the evidence to be corroborated and which confirmed that evidence in a material particular (*Baskerville* [1916] KB 658). This formula, which engendered a large body of case law and was at the root of many appeals, is rarely invoked nowadays, because the technical corroboration rules were drastically curtailed by the Criminal Justice and Public Order Act 1994, ss. 32 and 33. These reforms removed the largest and most important categories of sexual cases and cases involving the evidence of accomplices from the ambit of the corroboration rules.

Corroboration also has a less technical meaning, namely evidence which provides some degree of support for the word of a witness. In this sense it may still feature in criminal trials, either because the judge directs that the jury ought to look for such support (*Makanjuola* [1995] 1 WLR 1348) or because the jury or magistrates decide that it would be advisable to do so.

The amendments to s. 34(3) of the 1988 Act ensure that unsworn evidence can provide corroboration in either its technical or non-technical meaning.

IMPACT OF ss. 53 to 56

Taken as a whole, the new provisions, though they should have little impact on the evidence of children, represent a significant and long overdue reform for vulnerable adults (see A. Sanders, J. Creaton, S. Bird and L. Weber, *Victims with Learning Disabilities: Negotiating the Criminal Justice System* (Oxford, 1997)). *Speaking Up For Justice* noted that a police officer investigating a complaint involving an adult of questionable competence was likely to form a judgment that the case was not worth proceeding with, so that such cases were likely to be filtered out of the system long before the trial stage (para. 11.2). The new measures mean that such complaints will now be able to proceed. Their chances of success, however, may not be greatly improved, as there remains the question of the weight to be accorded to the vulnerable witness's testimony. A witness may be competent to give unsworn evidence without knowing the difference between truth and a lie and the importance of speaking the truth in the proceedings (Auld LJ in *Hampshire* [1995] 3 WLR 260). It does not follow that such a witness would carry any conviction.

The assessment of the credibility of a witness at trial is a matter for the jury. It has traditionally been held that the prosecution cannot lead expert evidence to bolster the credibility of its own witness in the eyes of the jury, although such evidence may be adduced to counter a challenge by the defence (*Robinson* (1994) 3 All ER 346). If the jury have no help in assessing the weight to be given to the testimony of, say, a prosecution witness with a learning disability, they may err on the side of caution and acquit. It may be that a relaxation of the traditional rule is called for if such witnesses are to have a fair hearing. Two important research studies have called for a broadening of the terms on which expert evidence is received before the jury: the study by Sanders *et al.* (above) at p. 77, and G. Davis, L. Hoyano, C. Keenan, L. Maitland and R. Morgan, *An Assessment of the Admissibility and Sufficiency of Evidence in Child Abuse Prosecutions* (Home Office, 1999) at p. 67. However, the 1999 Act provides only for the reception of expertise on issues to which the jury will not be privy, such as competence (s. 54(5)), oath-taking (s. 55(6)) and the desirability of special measures (s. 20(6)(c)). Whether this is an indication that no wider change was considered desirable, or whether it was considered better to leave it to the courts to develop the common-law principles, is not apparent.

WILFULLY GIVING FALSE UNSWORN EVIDENCE

Section 57 makes it an offence wilfully to give false unsworn evidence. It is couched in terms similar to the Children and Young Persons Act 1933, s. 38(2) (which is repealed by sch. 6) except that the earlier provision is confined to child witnesses. The issue on a prosecution for the s. 57 offence is whether the accused has wilfully given false evidence 'in such circumstances that, had the evidence been given on oath, he would have been guilty of perjury'.

Where a witness who ought not to have been sworn gives evidence on oath, he cannot be guilty of perjury (*Clegg* (1868) 19 LT 14). Perjury applies only to a witness 'lawfully sworn' (Perjury Act 1911, s. 1(1)). A witness unlawfully sworn who wilfully gives false evidence appears to commit the s. 57 offence.

The 1999 Act does not amend the Perjury Act 1911. Section 16(2) of the 1911 Act provides that the Perjury Act does not apply to the unsworn evidence of a child. The provisions in the 1999 Act for the giving of unsworn evidence are not confined to child witnesses, but there does not in any case appear to be overlap with the offences under the 1911 Act, the relevant provisions of which apply only to sworn evidence.

A person cannot be convicted of perjury under the 1911 Act 'solely upon the evidence of one witness as to the falsity of the statement alleged to be false' — one of the last vestiges of the corroboration rule in English law. It is doubtful whether the new offence in s. 57 of the 1999 Act is intended to be read as though it included this procedural limitation: the question whether the accused 'would have been guilty of perjury' had the evidence been given on oath seems to raise only an issue relating to the substance of his conduct and not to the method of its proof. If this is wrong, however, it may be that s. 16(2) of the 1911 Act prevents the application of the corroboration rule in relation to a child witness but not an adult, which is incongruous.

COMPETENCE OF AN ACCUSED

The common-law rule is that a person charged in criminal proceedings is not competent to give evidence for the prosecution (*Rhodes* [1899] 1 QB 77). Thus one co-accused may not give evidence as a prosecution witness against the other at any stage of the proceedings (*Grant* [1944] 2 All ER 311). To give evidence for the prosecution, the co-accused must cease to be a person who is charged in the proceedings, which may occur on his plea of guilty, or his acquittal, or by the dropping of the charges against him. Section 53(4) and (5) of the 1999 Act restate these rules in statutory form, by way of an exception to the new general rule on competence in s. 53(1) which states that 'all persons are ... competent to give evidence'. Without the exception the accused would become competent for the prosecution, even though his 'incompetence' at common law is incompetence through interest, not through lack of capacity.

The competence of the accused as a witness in his own defence, and for any co-accused, was governed by the Criminal Evidence Act 1898, s. 1, which rendered him a competent, but not a compellable, witness for the defence. The general rule on competence in s. 53(1) now subsumes this old provision to the extent that the 1999 Act becomes the authority on competence, but the 1898 Act remains the source of the rule on compellability. The old s. 1(a), which is to be renamed s. 1(1), now provides (by virtue of sch. 4, para. 1):

A person charged in criminal proceedings shall not be called as a witness in the proceedings except upon his own application.

The words 'upon his own application' continue to ensure that the accused cannot be compelled to testify for a co-accused.

UNSWORN EVIDENCE BY AN ACCUSED

Paragraph 10 of sch. 4 to the Act amends the Criminal Justice Act 1982, s. 72(1), which abolished the historic right of the accused to make an unsworn statement from the dock. Such statements, which originated at a time when the accused could not give sworn evidence, could not be challenged by cross-examination and were of uncertain evidential status, although juries were directed that they could give them 'such weight as they thought fit' (*Frost & Hale* (1964) 48 Cr App R 284). The Criminal Law Revision Committee (Eleventh Report, *Evidence (General)*, Cmnd. 4991 (1972)) commented that it might have been expected that the right to make an unsworn statement would have been abolished in 1898, when the Criminal Evidence Act of that year allowed the accused to give evidence on oath. Not only was there a possible advantage to the accused if the jury or magistrates did not appreciate the distinction between sworn and unsworn testimony, but the unsworn statement also provided a possible vehicle for the accused to make imputations on prosecution witnesses which, had he been on oath, would have cost him his shield under the 1898

Act, s. 1(f). The CLRC concluded that it was not in the interests of justice that these advantages should accrue to the accused, but it was not until 1982 that their recommendation was implemented.

The effect of s. 72(1) of the 1982 Act was to leave the accused with two options: to give evidence on oath subject to cross-examination or to remain silent. The problems that this might have posed for an adult accused who was unable to understand an oath appear never to have been put to the test, perhaps because such a person might have been unfit to plead (cf. *Friend* [1997] 1 WLR 1433). Alternatively it is possible that in some cases the rules were relaxed and the oath administered whether or not it was fully understood. The amendment makes the provision in s. 72(1) that the accused shall give evidence on oath subject to the provisions of ss. 55 and 56 of the 1999 Act. It follows that an accused who is competent within the meaning of s. 53 may give evidence sworn if he understands the nature of the oath (s. 55) and unsworn if he does not.

Unsworn evidence under the 1999 Act is an entirely different creature from the evidence of which the CLRC so roundly disapproved in 1972. It will be subject to cross-examination and, because it ranks as 'evidence', may trigger the provisions of the 1898 Act by which the accused's shield against evidence of bad character may be lost.

CRIMINAL EVIDENCE ACT 1898, s. 1(e) and (f)

The renumbering of the provisions of s. 1 of the 1898 Act effected by para. 1(7) of sch. 4 to the 1999 Act means that s. 1(e) (which requires the accused to answer questions in cross-examination notwithstanding that they incriminate him as to the offence charged) becomes s. 1(2). Section 1(f), which provides (subject to exceptions), a shield against questions relating to other offences and to aspects of the accused's bad character, becomes s. 1(3). This appears simply to be an exercise in tidying up the face of a much-amended statute, but it is doubtful whether any thought was given to the convenience of practitioners who will have to remember which of the former provisos translates into which of the new subsections. The Law Commission has this area of law under review and is currently preparing a report on evidence of misconduct of the accused (see the Consultation Paper No.141, *Evidence in Criminal Proceedings: Previous Misconduct of a Defendant* (1996)). If the recommendations in the Consultation Paper are followed, s. 1 (e) and (f) will be extensively revised. It might have been better to retain the traditional designation of the provisos in the meanwhile. The minor textual amendments contained in para. 1(4) and (5) of sch. 4, on the other hand, are necessary to achieve consistency with ss. 53 to 57 of the 1999 Act.

COMPELLABILITY OF SPOUSES

Under the provisions of the Police and Criminal Evidence Act 1984, s. 80(1) to (3), the wife or husband of an accused person was compellable to give evidence on behalf of the accused and competent (but only in exceptional cases compellable) on behalf of the prosecution or any co-accused. All of these rules were subject to s. 80(4), which provided that where a husband and wife were 'jointly charged with an offence' neither spouse attracted the provisions of s. 80(1) to (3). The result was that the common-law rules regarding co-defendants (see p. 143) applied, so that H was competent but not compellable for W and vice versa and neither was competent for the prosecution. Unfortunately, s. 80(4) was badly drafted in that it applied only where there was a joint charge rather than (as it should have done) in every case of a joint trial. If H was charged with theft and W with handling, for example, H was unintentionally rendered competent for the prosecution. The section does not seem to have given rise to difficulty in practice, perhaps because the error was not noted, but the 1999 Act provides the opportunity for a revised draft.

Under the 1999 Act the competence of both spouses and accused persons derives from the provision in s. 53(1) that 'all persons are ... competent to give evidence', but this is now clearly subject in all cases to s. 53(4) which ensures that no accused person is ever competent for the prosecution (see p. 143).

Section 80 of the 1984 Act continues in force, but its significance is now limited to compellability. Paragraph 13 of sch. 4 substitutes new sub-sections 80(2) to (4), which have the following effect:

(a)   the wife or husband of a person charged in the proceedings is compellable as a witness on behalf of that person (s. 80(2)) except where the wife or husband is also charged in the proceedings (s. 80(4));

(b)   the wife or husband of a person charged in the proceedings is compellable to give evidence for the prosecution or a co-accused, but only in respect of a specified offence (s. 80(2A)) — again, this does not apply where the wife or husband is also charged in the proceedings (s. 80(4));

(c)   the specified offences are offences involving assault, injury or a threat of injury to the wife or husband or a person who was at the material time under 16, sexual offences alleged to have been committed in respect of a person who was under 16, and offences of attempting, inciting or of conspiring to commit any such offence or of being a party to it (s. 80(3)).

The new version of s. 80 is an improvement in that it removes the original drafting error, and also makes it clear (as the old s. 80 did not) that compellability in respect of the specified offence is, in a case where more than one offence is charged, limited to the specified offence. Unfortunately it perpetuates the anomaly that a spouse is compellable in a case involving a technical indecent assault on a willing 15-year-old, but not in a case involving the rape and murder of a 17-year-old (the example given in C. Tapper, *Cross & Tapper on Evidence* (9th ed.) at p. 222, where the learned author also points out that 'if the potential availability of evidence is an important consideration, cases of homicide might seem eligible for addition to the category where the spouse is compellable'). Section 80 was formulated at a time when children and complainants were subjected to strict technical requirements in respect of corroboration, the need for which might have provided a more secure foundation for compellability in relation to offences against minors. These requirements were removed by the Criminal Justice and Public Order Act 1994, ss. 32 and 33, so that in modern times the line drawn appears far more arbitrary.

Another question left unresolved by the redrafted s. 80 is whether sexual offences such as rape which are committed by one spouse on another are specified offences by virtue of the reference to assault. The Law Commission considered the matter and recommended that the wife should be unequivocally stated to be a compellable witness where her husband is charged with a sexual offence against her (Report No. 215, *Criminal Law: Rape Within Marriage* (1992)). Although it was acknowledged that rape is arguably covered by the reference to assault, the fact that the 1984 Act dealt separately with assaults and sexual offences in relation to victims under the age of 16 was seen as providing an argument to the contrary. The 1999 Act is similarly open to both interpretations and some clarification would have been desirable.

The old s. 80(8) provided that the failure of the wife or husband of the accused to give evidence was not to be the subject of any comment by the prosecution. This is repealed and replaced by s. 80A, which provides a more carefully limited rule that the failure of the wife or husband of any person charged *in any proceedings* to give evidence *in the proceedings* shall not be made the subject of any comment by the prosecution. It would be futile to assert that this provision in any way modifies the effect of the Criminal Justice and Public Order Act 1994, s. 35 (inferences from the accused's failure to give evidence at trial) in a case where the said 'wife or husband' is also on trial in the proceedings, as the section is obviously not intended to have this effect.

Schedule 6 repeals that part of the Theft Act 1968, s. 30(2) which renders the spouse who brings proceedings against the other spouse competent for the prosecution throughout the proceedings. The provision is unnecessary in the light of the generality of s. 53.

Chapter 10
Silence as Evidence

OVERVIEW

Section 58 of the 1999 Act amends the provisions of the Criminal Justice and Public Order Act 1994 under which adverse inferences can be drawn from silence when a suspect is questioned. The effect of the amendment, which was necessitated by the judgment of the European Court of Human Rights in the case of *Murray* v *UK* (1996) 22 EHRR 29, is to prohibit the drawing of inferences where the suspect has not been allowed an opportunity to consult a solicitor. Section 58 cannot be brought into force until provision has been made for amending the Code of Practice for the Detention, Treatment and Questioning of Persons by Police Officers (PACE Code C). The procedure for review of the Codes is subject to statutory consultation periods and it is unlikely that the amendments will be made before Autumn 2000.

THE PROVISIONS

Section 59 introduces sch. 3, which amends a range of statutory provisions in the light of the decision of the European Court of Human Rights in *Saunders* v *UK* (1996) 23 EHRR 313. The Court ruled that it was a breach of Article 6 of the European Convention on Human Rights to admit in evidence statements made by S to inspectors appointed under the Companies Act 1985. The effect of the amendment is to restrict the use that can be made at trial of information that has been obtained under compulsory powers, including the power in issue in *Saunders* v *UK*. Section 59 and sch. 3 came into force on 14 April 2000 (Youth Justice and Criminal Evidence Act 1999 (Commencement No. 2) Order 2000 (SI 2000 No. 1034)).

Prohibition on inferences from silence: s. 58

The provisions amended by s. 58 are the Criminal Justice and Public Order Act 1994, ss. 34 and 36 to 38. The equivalent provisions in the Criminal Evidence (Northern Ireland) Order 1988, which were the actual subject of the decision of the European Court of Human Rights in *Murray* v *UK*, are also amended by the Criminal Evidence (Northern Ireland) Order 1999, art. 36.

The amended provisions deal with three of the four situations in which adverse inferences may be drawn. The fourth (adverse inferences from failure to testify at trial under s. 35 of the 1994 Act and art. 4 of the 1988 Order) is unaffected. Section 34 of the 1988 Act (art. 3 of the 1988 Order) permits an inference to be drawn from an accused person's failure to mention, when charged or questioned under caution, a fact which he could reasonably have been expected to mention at that time and on which he subsequently relies in his defence. Section 36 (art. 5 of the 1988 Order) permits an inference to be drawn where a person, having been arrested by a constable, fails when required to do so to account for some object, substance or mark which is reasonably believed to be relevant to the commission of an offence. Section 37 (art. 6 of the 1988 Order) is in similar form to s. 36 and permits an inference to be drawn where the arrested person fails or refuses to account to a constable for his presence in a location at the time when the offence is alleged to have been committed.

The effect of the amendments in s. 58 of the 1999 Act and art. 36 of the 1999 Order is that the part of the original provision under which an adverse inference may be drawn does not apply in any case where the accused was at an authorised place of detention at the time of the relevant failure or refusal and had not been allowed an opportunity to consult a solicitor prior to the questioning or charge (in s. 34/art. 3) or prior to the request to account for the relevant facts (in s. 36/art. 5 and s. 37/art. 6). The amendments appear as new provisions ss. 34(2A), 36(4A) and 37(3A) in the 1994 Act, and as new paragraphs (2A), (4A) and (3A) in the 1988 Order. Section 38 of the 1994 Act (art. 2 of the 1988 Order), which is the interpretation provision, is also amended so as to provide a definition of 'authorised place of detention' for each of these new provisions. Such a place is either (a) a police station or (b) another place prescribed for the purpose by the Secretary of State. According to the Explanatory Notes which accompany the 1999 Act, (b) is to take account of detention by other investigators such as Customs and Excise.

The prohibition on inferences contained in the new provisions operates whether or not the accused was *lawfully* denied an opportunity to consult with a solicitor. A suspect normally enjoys a right of access to legal advice, but the exercise of the right may be delayed in a range of circumstances, one example being where it is feared that a suspect in detention for a serious arrestable offence will use it to alert other suspects or interfere with evidence or with witnesses. (The key provision in England and Wales is the Police and Criminal Evidence Act 1984, s. 58.) Where a suspect's right of access is properly delayed but he is nevertheless questioned, charged or required to account for relevant facts, the prospect of drawing any adverse inferences from his silence or refusal is lost in consequence of the amendments.

The new provisions apply only where the suspect is not allowed an 'opportunity' to consult with a solicitor. If the suspect declines the opportunity when it is offered, he cannot hide behind the provisions, nor do they appear to apply after there has been a consultation at the relevant stage of the process, even if the solicitor then leaves the place of detention and is not present at the time when the relevant questioning or charge takes place or the request to account for relevant facts is put. If the accused contends that it would be unfair to rely on his failure or refusal in such circumstances, he may seek to invoke the court's general power under s. 78 of the 1984 Act to exclude evidence which it is adverse to the fairness of the proceedings to admit.

Murray and access to legal advice

In *Murray* v *UK* (1996) 22 EHRR 29, M was convicted of aiding and abetting the unlawful imprisonment of a man, L, who was an informer against the IRA. M was discovered in highly incriminating circumstances in the house in which L was being held in captivity and was denied legal advice for 48 hours following his arrest under the Northern Ireland (Emergency Provisions) Act 1987, s. 15. During that time M was asked to account for his presence at the scene of the crime under art. 6 of the 1988 order and declined to do so. The European Court of Human Rights held by a majority that there had been a violation of Article 6(1) of the Convention in conjunction with paragraph 3(c). Article 6(1) guarantees the right to a fair trial, one aspect of which, in paragraph 3(c), is the right to defend oneself through legal assistance. The Court noted that there had been a lawful exercise of the power to deny access, but considered that even the lawful exercise of such a power might, depending on the circumstances, be sufficient to deprive the accused of a fair procedure under art. 6. In *Murray*, the circumstance which had to be considered was the scheme of the 1988 Order:

> The Court is of the opinion that the scheme contained in the Order is such that it is of paramount importance for the rights of the defence that an accused has access to a lawyer at the initial stages of police interrogation. It observes in this context that, under the Order, at the beginning of police interrogation, an accused is confronted with a fundamental dilemma relating to his defence. If he chooses to remain silent, adverse inferences may be drawn against him in accordance with the provisions of the Order. On the other hand, if the accused opts to break his silence during the course of an interrogation, he runs the risk of prejudicing his defence without necessarily removing the possibility of inferences being drawn against him.
>
> Under such conditions the concept of fairness enshrined in Article 6 requires that the accused has the benefit of the assistance of a lawyer already at the initial stages of police interrogation. To deny access to a lawyer for the first 48 hours of police questioning, in a situation where the rights of the defence may well be irretrievably prejudiced, is — whatever the justification for such a denial — incompatible with the rights of the accused under Article 6. (p. 67)

It will be seen that the effect of the amendments to the statutory scheme for drawing inferences is to relieve the suspect of his 'fundamental dilemma' by removing the situation where his rights may be 'irretrievably prejudiced' by his silence without benefit of the assistance of a lawyer. Under the amended scheme, the opportunity for drawing adverse inferences from silence or refusal is postponed until the accused has had to option to consult with a legal adviser. It may be, of course, that during interrogation where access is delayed the suspect is not silent, but acts to his detriment by making statements which a lawyer might have advised him not to make or to present in a different manner. The 1999 Act and 1999 Order do nothing to improve the position of a suspect in such a case.

Murray and the right to silence

The Court in *Murray* was also asked whether the scheme for the drawing of inferences had itself led to a breach of Article 6(1) and (2) of the Convention (the presumption of innocence) in relation to M and concluded that it had not. However, the Court stopped short of a wholesale endorsement of the scheme. In its favour, the Court accepted that the right of silence and the privilege against self-incrimination, though 'generally recognised international standards which lie at the heart of the notion of a fair procedure under Article 6', were not absolute rights, in that the decision to remain silent at the various stages of criminal proceedings might have implications when the trial court weighs up the evidence against an accused person. Whether the drawing of adverse inferences from silence infringes Article 6 was said to be:

> . . . a matter to be determined in the light of all the circumstances of the case, having particular regard to the situations where inferences may be drawn, the weight attached to them by the national courts in their assessment of the evidence, and the degree of compulsion inherent in the situation. (p. 61)

This test was passed, in the circumstances prevailing in *Murray*, in relation to the strong inferences drawn by the trial judge from M's failure to account for his presence in the house (art. 6 of the 1988 Order) and his failure to testify at trial (art. 4). However, the Court emphasised that Murray was tried by 'an experienced judge' rather than by a jury, one consequence of which was that the reasoning of the trial court was open to scrutiny and it could be seen that the inferences drawn were no more than common sense inferences which were proper in the light of the formidable case against M.

There is a very strong statement in *Murray* that it would be incompatible with the accused's rights to base a conviction 'solely or mainly on the accused's silence or on a refusal to answer questions or to give evidence himself'. The scheme contains safeguards to prevent a conviction solely on the silence of the accused, but it does not expressly prevent a conviction founded 'mainly' on silence. Trial by judge alone, which may occur in Northern Ireland, generates a written judgment which renders explicit the extent to which silence figures in a conviction, but this is not a feature of criminal trials in England and Wales. It is unclear, therefore, what the Court in *Murray* would have made of the provisions of the 1994 Act, designed as they are to be operated by a jury or magistrates without the giving of reasons.

Condron and the Criminal Justice and Public Order Act 1994

The most recent pronouncement of the European Court of Human Rights regarding the scheme for drawing inferences under the 1994 Act is *Condron* (2000) *The Times*, 9 May 2000. WC and KC were interviewed about supply and possession of heroin at a time when their solicitor considered that they were unfit to be questioned because they were suffering from heroin withdrawal symptoms. They remained silent when questioned under caution by police, on the advice of their solicitor, but relied at trial upon exculpatory facts that the prosecution contended could have been mentioned at the interview. The trial judge left it to the jury to decide whether the accused could reasonably have been expected to mention the facts when questioned. The Court of Appeal (*Condron* [1997] 1 WLR 827) upheld the resultant convictions, in the light of the 'almost overwhelming' evidence of drug supply found at the accused's house. However, the court considered that it would have been 'desirable' for the jury to have been explicitly directed to draw no adverse inference from the failure of the accused at interview to mention the facts unless satisfied that the silence of the accused could only sensibly be attributed to their having no tenable explanation to give at that stage. The European Court of Human Rights unanimously held that there had been a violation of the right to a fair trial guaranteed by Article 6(1) of the Convention. The safeguards noted in *Murray* (above) were absent in a case where the discretion over whether to draw adverse inferences was delegated to a jury. It was thus even more compelling to ensure that the jury were properly advised on how to address the issue of silence, and in particular it was essential, and not merely 'desirable', that they were directed in the terms outlined by the Court of Appeal. The omission to so direct them was incompatible with the exercise of the accused's right to silence in the police station, and the defect was not cured by the Court of Appeal's conclusion that the conviction was safe because that court 'had no means of ascertaining whether or not the applicants' silence played a significant role in the jury's decision to convict'.

It appears that the rights guaranteed by Article 6 of the Convention are not necessarily infringed by the drawing of inferences from silence, but that the approach required by the Convention involves looking beyond the safeguards provided on the face of the statutory scheme for drawing inferences in order to see whether the right balance has been struck between on the one hand the right to silence and on the other the drawing of appropriate inferences. It must follow that the amendments to the statutory scheme in s. 58 of the 1999 Act and art. 36 of the 1999 Order do not of themselves guarantee that adverse inferences drawn under the amended provisions are proof against a challenge under the Convention (whether in Strasbourg or under the Human Rights Act 1998).

Evidence obtained under compulsion: s. 59 and sch. 3

The right to silence and the privilege against self-incrimination were also considered by the European Court of Human Rights in *Saunders* v *UK* (1996) 23 EHRR 313.

The case arose out of a takeover battle involving the company of which S was director and chief executive, in the course of which it was alleged that criminal misconduct had occurred. Inspectors were appointed under the Companies Act 1985 to investigate the affairs of S's company and S was later convicted of offences arising out of the takeover. The European Court held that there had been a violation of S's right to a fair trial under art. 6(1) of the Convention because of the use at his trial of evidence obtained in the course of the inspectors' inquiries. S had been obliged by the Companies Act 1985, ss. 434 and 436 to answer the questions put to him by the inspectors and much of what he had said was admitted in evidence at his trial. The effect of the legislation was that a refusal to answer would have rendered S liable to a fine or committal to prison for up to two years, and there was no defence in such proceedings that the questions were of an incriminating nature. The view of the Court, echoing what was said in *Murray* v *UK* (see p. 149), was that the right to silence and the right not to incriminate oneself, though not specifically mentioned in art. 6, were generally recognised international standards lying at the heart of the notion of a fair procedure. Furthermore the right not to incriminate oneself 'presupposes that the prosecution in a criminal case should seek to prove their case against the accused without resort to evidence obtained through methods of coercion or oppression in defiance of the will of the accused'. In response to a Government argument that the right was infringed only where the evidence obtained was self-incriminating, the court stated that even evidence which appeared to be of a non-incriminating nature (and some of S's answers fell in this category) might be deployed in criminal proceedings in support of the prosecution's case, for example to contradict or cast doubt on statements made by the maker when giving evidence. S's answers were used to incriminate him and that was sufficient to establish a breach of the Convention.

Schedule 3 to the 1999 Act, which is given effect by s. 59, restricts the use which can be made of evidence obtained under compulsion under a variety of statutory provisions regulating commercial or financial activities, including the Companies Act 1995, s. 434, the provision in issue in *Saunders* v *UK*. The powers of investigation themselves are not affected, only the use of evidence obtained under them. The effect of the amendments to s. 434 is that in criminal proceedings the prosecution will not be able to adduce evidence, or put questions, about the accused's answers to inspectors conducting an investigation using their powers of compulsion unless the evidence is first adduced, or a question asked, by or on behalf of the accused in the proceedings. Thus, if the accused seeks to raise an issue which involves a consideration of his answers, the prosecution may adduce evidence in rebuttal or put questions which relate to those answers, but not otherwise. The other provisions which are amended to similar effect are the Insurance Companies Act 1982, ss. 43A and 44; the Companies Act 1985, s. 447; the Insolvency Act 1986, s. 433; the Company Directors Disqualification Act 1986, s. 20; the Building Societies Act 1986, s. 57; the Financial Services Act 1986, ss. 105 and 177; the Companies (Northern Ireland) Order 1986, arts 427 and 440; the Banking Act 1987, ss. 39, 41 and 42; the Criminal Justice Act 1987, s. 2; the Companies Act 1989, s. 83; the Companies (Northern Ireland) Order 1989, art. 23; the Insolvency (Northern Ireland) Order 1989, art. 375; the Friendly Societies Act 1992, s. 67; the Criminal Law (Consolidation) (Scotland) Act 1995, s. 28 and the Proceeds of Crime (Northern Ireland) Order 1996, sch. 2, para. 6.

The new restrictions do not apply in a case where the charge against the accused relates to his failure or refusal to answer a question or to disclose a material fact or relates to the provision of false information. Thus, for example, the amendment to the Companies Act 1985, s. 447 is expressed not to apply to a charge under s. 447(6) (non-compliance with, *inter alia*, a requirement to provide an explanation or make a statement).

Chapter 11
Evidence from Computers

Section 60 of the 1999 Act provides that the Police and Criminal Evidence Act 1984, s. 69 shall cease to have effect. The repeal took effect on 14 April 2000 (Youth Justice And Criminal Evidence Act 1999 (Commencement No. 2) Order 2000 (SI 2000 No. 1034)).

SECTION 69 AND EVIDENCE FROM COMPUTERS

Section 69 of the Police and Criminal Evidence Act 1984 governed the admissibility of evidence from computer records. It imposed stringent conditions on a party seeking to tender such evidence, for no better reason than that the evidence was produced by a computer. The underlying rationale was that computers are 'imperfect devices' (per Steyn J in *Minors & Harper* [1989] 1 WLR 441) and that the evidence they produce should be received only where there was clear proof of reliability. There were two aspects to this concern: the risk that the computer itself might be malfunctioning, for example because of 'bugs' in its software, and the possibility that the operation of the computer might have been affected by some person tampering with it. Section 69 therefore erected two high hurdles in the way of the party putting the evidence forward. A statement in a document produced by a computer was inadmissible unless it was proved (a) that there were no reasonable grounds for believing that improper use of the computer had rendered the statement inaccurate and (b) that the computer was operating properly at all material times or, failing that, that any respect in which it was not so operating was not such as to affect the production of the document or the reliability of its contents.

REPORT OF THE LAW COMMISSION

The Law Commission recommended the repeal of s. 69 (Report No. 245, *Evidence in Criminal Proceedings: Hearsay and Related Topics*, Cm 3670 (1997) Part XIII). Computer evidence is not necessarily hearsay evidence, but much hearsay evidence is held in the form of computer records, so s. 69 represented a considerable impediment to the use of the sort of evidence with which the Commission was primarily concerned. The aim of the Law Commission was to devise a regime to facilitate the use of computer evidence, while at the same time recognising that computers might be fallible. The Law Commission identified four main objections to s. 69.

(a)   Most computer error is either easily detectable or results from error in the data entered into the machine. Section 69 failed to address the second issue, which was in fact the most worrying cause of inaccuracy in computer evidence.

(b)   Advances in computer technology made it increasingly difficult for a party to certify that a computer was working properly, particularly where more than one computer was involved in the production of the document (for example, where systems are networked).

(c)   The *recipient* of a computer-produced document who wished to rely on it in evidence might be in no position to satisfy the court about the operation of the computer. His opponent might be in a far better position to do so, but did not bear the onus of proof.

(d)   It had been held that s. 69 did not apply to a computer-produced document used by an expert to reach his conclusions or by a witness to refresh memory. If such documents were too unreliable to be received as evidence on their own account unless s. 69 was complied with, it seemed illogical to sanction their use in this alternative manner.

The Law Commission pointed out that, were s. 69 to be repealed, a common-law presumption would come into play. Where evidence is provided by a mechanical instrument, it is presumed that the instrument was working properly in the absence of evidence to the contrary (*Castle* v *Cross* [1984] 1 WLR 1372). If such evidence is adduced, the onus is on the party tendering the evidence to show (in the case of the prosecution, beyond reasonable doubt; in the case of the defence, on a balance of probabilities) that the device was working properly. This presumption applies to devices such as traffic lights and speedometers and was applied to computer evidence before the advent of s. 69. The view of the Law Commission, which was endorsed by the vast majority of those who responded to the Consultation Paper that preceded the 1997 Report, was that the common-law rule was a sufficient safeguard against unreliable computer evidence (para. 13.23).

PROBLEMS WITH THE COMMON LAW

The effect of the implementation of the Law Commission's recommendation to repeal s. 69 is that the common-law presumption has come into play and the courts will presume that computers are working properly unless evidence is adduced to the contrary. This may create a set of problems which are in essence the converse of some of those which were generated by s. 69. The party against whom a computer-produced document is tendered may believe that it is inaccurate, but may not be in a position to produce direct evidence to that effect. This may arise, for example, because the computer is under the exclusive control of his opponent or because the computer system which generated the document is so complex that it is not possible to produce evidence about the manner in which it was working at the relevant time. The party thus affected could, of course, produce any evidence in his possession which *indirectly* challenges the computer evidence: a motorist charged with drink-driving who contests the computerised reading which shows him to be over the limit could testify, or call witnesses to prove, that he has not been drinking (*Cracknell* v *Willis* [1988] AC 450).

The Law Commission were aware of the difficulty which might face a party, particularly a defendant, in scraping together evidence to make a direct challenge to the reliability of computer evidence. The Report correctly notes that the evidential burden imposed by the common-law presumption is flexible, in that a party cannot be expected to produce more by way of evidence than one in his or her position could be expected to produce. It might take very little for the presumption to be rebutted if the party could not, in the circumstances, be expected to produce more (para. 13.18). A cryptic suggestion is also made that, as the presumption was the creature of the common law, it was 'unlikely that it would be permitted to work injustice' (para. 13.22).

Although the repeal of s. 69 is not without its difficulties, the stringent conditions of proof which the section imposed were not shown to have been justified. The common-law presumption will in most cases provide a fair and workable alternative, though the courts will need to be alert to the possibility that, in some instances, the evidential burden it generates may be impossible for an accused person to shoulder.

HEARSAY EVIDENCE: FURTHER REFORMS

The repeal of s. 69 is the only one of the recommendations of the Law Commission's Report No. 245 (*Evidence in Criminal Proeedings: Hearsay and Related Topics*, Cm 3670 (1997)) to have been enacted. The Report contains a plethora of other recommendations and a Draft Bill, the aim of which is to reform the rules regarding the reception of hearsay evidence in criminal cases. The Home Office timetable for implementing Part II of the 1999 Act (*Action for Justice: Implementing the Speaking Up For Justice Report in England and Wales*, Home Office, 1999) notes that the Government has accepted all of the other recommendations in the Report and is committed to bringing forward legislation to implement the remaining recommendations when Parliamentary time allows.

Chapter 12
Youth Justice: Pre-Consolidation Amendments

Schedule 5 contains a group of amendments to earlier legislation dealing with the sentencing of juveniles. The provisions, described as 'pre-consolidation amendments', are the third batch of such amendments, designed to expunge minor problems, ambiguities or omissions in the legislation prior to full-scale consolidation of the sentencing powers of the criminal courts. Earlier batches of such amendments were found in schedules to the Crime (Sentences) Act 1997 and the Crime and Disorder Act 1998. In fact sch. 5 has proved to be remarkably short-lived, coming into force on 1 January 2000 (by SI 1999 No. 3427) and repealed by sch. 12 to the Powers of Criminal Courts (Sentencing) Act 2000, which received Royal Assent on 25 May and came into force three months later (25 August 2000). The individual amendments will of course survive the repeal of sch. 5 in the newly consolidated sentencing provisions in that Act. An outline of the changes made by these amendments is given below. In each case two references are given: the first relates to the relevant paragraph of sch. 5 to the 1999 Act and the second relates to the corresponding provision of the PCC(S)A 2000.

SUPERVISION ORDERS

A number of minor changes are made to the supervision order regime, applicable to offenders aged under 18, and now found in the PCC(S)A 2000, part V. It is now made clear that, where a young offender is ordered to 'make reparation' as a condition of a supervision order, this must be done otherwise than by paying compensation (para. 2; sch. 6, para. 2). For supervision orders that are made on appeal, it is made clear that for procedural purposes the order is deemed to have been made by the magistrates' court or Crown Court from which the appeal was taken (para. 3(3); sch. 7, para. 8). Where a person who is subject to a supervision order has attained the age of 18 during the period of the order and is brought before the magistrates for breach, the court is given power (as befits the offender's newly acquired adult status) to remand the offender to a remand centre, if available, and otherwise to a prison (para. 4(5); sch. 7, para. 7(7)).

DETENTION AND TRAINING ORDERS

Greater flexibility is provided to courts in making detention and training orders and, in particular, where successive orders are made, the courts' powers will no longer be shackled by a cumulative maximum sentence of 24 months. The court is now given power to impose on a young offender a further detention and training order to commence on the expiration of the term of any earlier such detention and training order (para. 6(2); s. 101(3)). This ensures that a young offender will not receive the benefit which might accrue to him where two such orders run in parallel thereby reducing the total time served under the order. The most likely circumstance in which a second detention and training order will be imposed during the term of an earlier order would be where the offender commits a further offence whilst under supervision following the completion of the custodial element of the sentence. When this occurs, the custody element of the new order will commence immediately and it will not be necessary to wait until the period of supervision under the original order has expired. Where a subsequent order is imposed, the total period to be served may exceed 24 months (para. 6; s. 101(6) and (7)). A court imposing a detention and training order will now be required to take into account any period during which the offender was remanded in custody, but such period should not be taken into account again if the offender is subject to a subsequent detention and training order (para. 6(4); s. 101(8) and (9)). The rules relating to the interaction between detention and training orders and other periods of detention are clarified. Where a young offender is, on a separate occasion, made subject to either an order that he should be detained in secure accommodation or an order that he should be returned to prison, the court is given an absolute discretion to determine whether the period during which he is kept in secure accommodation or returned to prison is served before, after or concurrently with the relevant detention and training order (para. 9; s. 106(3)).

A new power of appeal is provided to the Crown Court against an order made by a magistrates' courts relating to breach of any requirement of the supervision element of a detention and training order (para. 8; s. 104(6)).

REPARATION AND ACTION PLAN ORDERS

As with supervision orders, for procedural reasons, a reparation or action plan order which is made on appeal will now be deemed to have been made by the magistrates' court or Crown Court from which the appeal originally emanated (para. 10; sch. 8, para. 2(8)). Again, as with supervision orders, where a young offender has turned 18 during the continuance of the order, where such offender is brought before the court for breach of the relevant order, the court is given power to remand him either to a remand centre (if available) or to prison (para. 11; sch. 8, para. 6(7)).

Appendix 1
Text of the Youth Justice and Criminal Evidence Act 1999

YOUTH JUSTICE AND CRIMINAL EVIDENCE ACT 1999

CHAPTER 23
ARRANGEMENT OF SECTIONS
PART I
REFERRALS TO YOUTH OFFENDER PANELS

Referral orders

PART II
GIVING OF EVIDENCE OR INFORMATION FOR PURPOSES OF CRIMINAL PROCEEDINGS

CHAPTER I
SPECIAL MEASURES DIRECTIONS IN CASE OF VULNERABLE AND INTIMIDATED WITNESSES

Preliminary

Special measures directions

Special measures

Supplementary

CHAPTER II
PROTECTION OF WITNESSES FROM CROSS-EXAMINATION BY ACCUSED IN PERSON

General prohibitions

Prohibition imposed by court

YOUTH JUSTICE AND CRIMINAL EVIDENCE ACT 1999
(1999 c. 23)

An Act to provide for the referral of offenders under 18 to youth offender panels; to make provision in connection with the giving of evidence or information for the purposes of criminal proceedings; to amend section 51 of the Criminal Justice and Public Order Act 1994; to make pre-consolidation amendments relating to youth justice; and for connected purposes.   [27th July 1999]

BE IT ENACTED by the Queen's most Excellent Majesty, by and with the advice and consent of the Lords Spiritual and Temporal, and Commons, in this present Parliament assembled, and by the authority of the same, as follows:—

PART I
REFERRALS TO YOUTH OFFENDER PANELS

Referral orders

1. Referral of young offenders to youth offenders panels

(1)   This section applies where a youth court or other magistrates' court is dealing with a person under the age of 18 for an offence and—

(a)   neither the offence nor any associated offence is one for which the sentence is fixed by law;

(b)   the court is not, in respect of the offence or any associated offence, proposing to impose a custodial sentence on the offender or make a hospital order in his case; and

(c)   the court is not proposing to discharge him absolutely in respect of the offence.

(2)   If—

(a)   the compulsory referral conditions are satisfied in accordance with section 2, and

(b)   referral is available to the court,

the court shall sentence the offender for the offence by ordering him to be referred to a youth offender panel.

(3)   If—

(a)   the discretionary referral conditions are satisfied in accordance with section 2, and

(b)   referral is available to the court,

the court may sentence the offender for the offence by ordering him to be referred to a youth offender panel.

(4)   For the purposes of this section referral is available to a court if—

(a)   the court has been notified by the Secretary of State that arrangements for the implementation of referral orders are available in the area in which it appears to the court that the offender resides or will reside; and

(b)   the notice has not been withdrawn.

(5)   In this Part 'referral order' means an order under subsection (2) or (3).

2. The referral conditions

(1)   For the purposes of section 1(2) the compulsory referral conditions are satisfied in relation to an offence if the offender—

(a)   pleaded guilty to the offence and to any associated offence;

(b)   has never been convicted by or before a court in the United Kingdom of any offence other than the offence and any associated offence; and

(c)   has never been bound over in criminal proceedings in England and Wales or Northern Ireland to keep the peace or to be of good behaviour.

(2)   For the purposes of section 1(3) the discretionary referral conditions are satisfied in relation to an offence if—

(a)   the offender is being dealt with by the court for the offence and one or more associated offences;

(b)   although he pleaded guilty to at least one of the offences mentioned in paragraph (a), he also pleaded not guilty to at least one of them;

(c)   he has never been convicted by or before a court in the United Kingdom of any offence other than the offences mentioned in paragraph (a); and

(d)   he has never been bound over in criminal proceedings in England and Wales or Northern Ireland to keep the peace or to be of good behaviour.

(3)   The Secretary of State may by regulations make such amendments of this section as he considers appropriate for altering in any way the descriptions of offenders in the case of which the compulsory referral conditions or the discretionary referral conditions fall to be satisfied for the purposes of section 1(2) or (3) (as the case may be).

(4)   Any description of offender having effect for those purposes by virtue of such regulations may be framed by reference to such matters as the Secretary of State considers appropriate, including (in particular) one or more of the following—

(a)   the offender's age;

(b)   how the offender has pleaded;

(c)   the offence (or offences) of which the offender has been convicted;

(d)   the offender's previous convictions (if any);

(e)   how (if at all) the offender has been previously punished or otherwise dealt with by any court; and

(f)   any characteristics or behaviour of, or circumstances relating to, any person who has at any time been charged in the same proceedings as the offender (whether or not in respect of the same offence).

(5)   For the purposes of this section an offender who has been convicted of an offence in respect of which he was conditionally discharged (whether by a court in England and Wales or in Northern Ireland) shall be treated, despite—

(a)   section 1C(1) of the Powers of Criminal Courts Act 1973 (conviction of offence for which offender so discharged deemed not a conviction), or

(b)   Article 6(1) of the Criminal Justice (Northern Ireland) Order 1996 (corresponding provision for Northern Ireland),
as having been convicted of that offence.

3.   Making of referral orders: general

(1)   A referral order shall—

(a)   specify the youth offending team responsible for implementing the order;

(b)   require the offender to attend each of the meetings of a youth offender panel to be established by the team for the offender; and

(c) specify the period for which any youth offender contract taking effect between the offender and the panel under section 8 is to have effect (which must not be less than 3 nor more than 12 months).

(2) The youth offending team specified under subsection (1)(a) shall be the team having the function of implementing referral orders in the area in which it appears to the court that the offender resides or will reside.

(3) On making a referral order the court shall explain to the offender in ordinary language—

(a) the effect of the order; and

(b) the consequences which may follow—

(i) if no youth offender contract takes effect between the offender and the panel under section 8, or

(ii) if the offender breaches any of the terms of any such contract.

(4) Subsections (5) to (7) apply where, in dealing with an offender for two or more associated offences, a court makes a referral order in respect of each, or each of two or more, of the offences.

(5) The orders shall have the effect of referring the offender to a single youth offender panel; and the provision made by them under subsection (1) shall accordingly be the same in each case, except that the periods specified under subsection (1)(c) may be different.

(6) The court may direct that the period so specified in either or any of the orders is to run concurrently with or be additional to that specified in the other or any of the others; but in exercising its power under this subsection the court must ensure that the total period for which such a contract as is mentioned in subsection (1)(c) is to have effect does not exceed 12 months.

(7) Each of the orders mentioned in subsection (4) shall, for the purposes of this Part, be treated as associated with the other or each of the others.

4.   Making of referral orders: effect on court's other sentencing powers

(1) Subsections (2) to (5) apply where a court makes a referral order in respect of an offence.

(2) The court may not deal with the offender for the offence in any of the prohibited ways.

(3) The court—

(a) shall, in respect of any associated offence, either sentence the offender by making a referral order or make an order discharging him absolutely; and

(b) may not deal with the offender for any such offence in any of the prohibited ways.

(4) For the purposes of subsections (2) and (3) the prohibited ways are—

(a) imposing a community sentence (within the meaning of Part I of the Criminal Justice Act 1991) on the offender;

(b) ordering him to pay a fine;

(c) making a reparation order under section 67 of the Crime and Disorder Act 1998 in respect of him; and (d)　making an order discharging him conditionally.

(5)　The court may not make, in connection with the conviction of the offender for the offence or any associated offence—

(a)　an order binding him over to keep the peace or to be of good behaviour;

(b)　an order under section 58 of the Criminal Justice Act 1991 (binding over of parent or guardian); or

(c)　a parenting order under section 8 of the Crime and Disorder Act 1998.

(6)　Subsections (2), (3) and (5) do not affect the exercise of any power to deal with the offender conferred by paragraph 5 (offender referred back to court by panel) or paragraph 14 (powers of a court where offender convicted while subject to referral) of Schedule 1.

(7)　Where section 1(2) above requires a court to make a referral order, the court may not under section 1 of the Powers of Criminal Courts Act 1973 defer passing sentence on him, but section 1(2) and subsection (3)(a) above do not affect any power or duty of a magistrates' court under—

(a)　section 56 of the Children and Young Persons Act 1933 (remission to youth court, or another such court, for sentence),

(b)　section 7(8) of the Children and Young Persons Act 1969 (remission to youth court for sentence),

(c)　section 10(3) of the Magistrates' Courts Act 1980 (adjournment for inquiries),

(d)　section 37 of that Act (committal to Crown Court for sentence), or

(e)　section 35, 38, 43 or 44 of the Mental Health Act 1983 (remand for reports, interim hospital orders and committal to Crown Court for restriction order).

5.　Making of referral orders: attendance of parents etc.

(1)　A court making a referral order may make an order requiring—

(a)　the appropriate person, or

(b)　in a case where there are two or more appropriate persons, any one or more of them,

to attend the meetings of the youth offender panel.

(2)　Where an offender is under the age of 16 when a court makes a referral order in his case—

(a)　the court shall exercise its power under subsection (1) so as to require at least one appropriate person to attend meetings of the youth offender panel; and

(b)　if the offender falls within subsection (6), the person or persons so required to attend those meetings shall be or include a representative of the local authority mentioned in that subsection.

(3)　The court shall not under this section make an order requiring a person to attend meetings of the youth offender panel—

(a)　if the court is satisfied that it would be unreasonable to do so, or

(b)　to an extent which the court is satisfied would be unreasonable.

(4)　Except where the offender falls within subsection (6), each person who is a parent or guardian of the offender is an 'appropriate person' for the purposes of this section.

(5)   Where the offender falls within subsection (6), each of the following is an 'appropriate person' for the purposes of this section—

(a)   a representative of the local authority mentioned in that subsection, and

(b)   each person who is a parent or guardian of the offender with whom the offender is allowed to live.

(6)   An offender falls within this subsection if he is (within the meaning of the Children Act 1989) a child who is looked after by a local authority.

(7)   If, at the time when a court makes an order under this section—

(a)   a person who is required by the order to attend meetings of a youth offender panel is not present in court, or

(b)   a local authority whose representative is so required to attend such meetings is not represented in court,

the court must send him or (as the case may be) the authority a copy of the order forthwith.

(8)   In this section 'guardian' has the same meaning as in the Children and Young Persons Act 1933.

Youth offender panels

6.   Establishment of panels

(1)   Where a referral order has been made in respect of an offender (or two or more associated referral orders have been so made), it is the duty of the youth offending team specified in the order (or orders)—

(a)   to establish a youth offender panel for the offender;

(b)   to arrange for the first meeting of the panel to be held for the purposes of section 8; and

(c)   subsequently to arrange for the holding of any further meetings of the panel required by virtue of section 10 (in addition to those required by virtue of any other provision of this Part).

(2)   A youth offender panel shall—

(a)   be constituted,

(b)   conduct its proceedings, and

(c)   discharge its functions under this Part (and in particular those arising under section 8),

in accordance with guidance given from time to time by the Secretary of State.

(3)   At each of its meetings a panel shall, however, consist of at least—

(a)   one member appointed by the youth offending team from among its members; and

(b)   two members so appointed who are not members of the team.

(4)   The Secretary of State may by regulations make provision requiring persons appointed as members of a youth offender panel to have such qualifications, or satisfy such other criteria, as are specified in the regulations.

(5)   Where it appears to the court which made a referral order that, by reason of either a change or a prospective change in the offender's place or intended place of residence, the youth offending team for the time being specified in the order ('the

current team') either does not or will not have the function of implementing referral orders in the area in which the offender resides or will reside, the court may vary the order so that it instead specifies the team which has the function of implementing such orders in that area ('the new team').

(6)   Where a court so varies a referral order—

(a)   subsection (1)(a) shall apply to the new team in any event;

(b)   subsection (1)(b) shall apply to the new team if no youth offender contract has (or has under paragraph (c) below been treated as having) taken effect under section 8 between the offender and a youth offender panel established by the current team;

(c)   if such a contract has (or has previously under this paragraph been treated as having) so taken effect, it shall (after the variation) be treated as if it were a contract which had taken effect under section 8 between the offender and the panel being established for the offender by the new team.

(7)   References in this Part to the meetings of a youth offender panel (or any such meeting) are to the following meetings of the panel (or any of them)—

(a)   the first meeting held in pursuance of subsection (1)(b);

(b)   any further meetings held in pursuance of section 10;

(c)   any progress meeting held under section 11; and

(d)   the final meeting held under section 12.

7.   Attendance at panel meetings

(1)   The specified team shall, in the case of each meeting of the panel established for the offender, notify—

(a)   the offender, and

(b)   any person to whom an order under section 5 applies,

of the time and place at which he is required to attend that meeting.

(2)   If the offender fails to attend any part of such a meeting the panel may—

(a)   adjourn the meeting to such time and place as it may specify; or

(b)   end the meeting and refer the offender back to the appropriate court;

and subsection (1) shall apply in relation to any such adjourned meeting.

(3)   One person aged 18 or over chosen by the offender, with the agreement of the panel, shall be entitled to accompany the offender to any meeting of the panel (and it need not be the same person who accompanies him to every meeting).

(4)   The panel may allow to attend any such meeting—

(a)   any person who appears to the panel to be a victim of, or otherwise affected by, the offence, or any of the offences, in respect of which the offender was referred to the panel;

(b)   any person who appears to the panel to be someone capable of having a good influence on the offender.

(5)   Where the panel allows any such person as is mentioned in subsection (4)(a) ('the victim') to attend a meeting of the panel, the panel may allow the victim to be accompanied to the meeting by one person chosen by the victim with the agreement of the panel.

Youth offender contracts

8. First meeting: agreement of contract with offender

(1)   At the first meeting of the youth offender panel established for an offender the panel shall seek to reach agreement with the offender on a programme of behaviour the aim (or principal aim) of which is the prevention of re-offending by the offender.

(2)   The terms of the programme may, in particular, include provision for any of the following—

(a)   the offender to make financial or other reparation to any person who appears to the panel to be a victim of, or otherwise affected by, the offence, or any of the offences, for which the offender was referred to the panel;

(b)   the offender to attend mediation sessions with any such victim or other person;

(c)   the offender to carry out unpaid work or service in or for the community;

(d)   the offender to be at home at times specified in or determined under the programme;

(e)   attendance by the offender at a school or other educational establishment or at a place of work;

(f)   the offender to participate in specified activities (such as those designed to address offending behaviour, those offering education or training or those assisting with the rehabilitation of persons dependent on, or having a propensity to misuse, alcohol or drugs);

(g)   the offender to present himself to specified persons at times and places specified in or determined under the programme;

(h)   the offender to stay away from specified places or persons (or both);

(i)   enabling the offender's compliance with the programme to be supervised and recorded.

(3)   The programme may not, however, provide—

(a)   for the electronic monitoring of the offender's whereabouts; or

(b)   for the offender to have imposed on him any physical restriction on his movements.

(4)   No term which provides for anything to be done to or with any such victim or other affected person as is mentioned in subsection (2)(a) may be included in the programme without the consent of that person.

(5)   Where a programme is agreed between the offender and the panel, the panel shall cause a written record of the programme to be produced forthwith—

(a)   in language capable of being readily understood by, or explained to, the offender, and

(b)   for signature by him.

(6)   Once the record has been signed—

(a)   by the offender, and

(b)   by a member of the panel on behalf of the panel,

the terms of the programme, as set out in the record, take effect as the terms of a 'youth offender contract' between the offender and the panel; and the panel shall cause a copy of the record to be given or sent to the offender.

9. First meeting: duration of contract

(1)   This section applies where a youth offender contract has taken effect under section 8 between an offender and a youth offender panel.

(2)   The day on which the contract so takes effect shall be the first day of the period for which it has effect.

(3)   Where the panel was established in pursuance of a single referral order, the length of the period for which the contract has effect shall be that of the period specified under section 3(1)(c) in the referral order.

(4)   Where the panel was established in pursuance of two or more associated referral orders, the length of the period for which the contract has effect shall be that resulting from the court's directions under section 3(6).

(5)   Subsections (3) and (4) have effect subject to—

(a)   any order under paragraph 11 or 12 of Schedule 1 extending the length of the period for which the contract has effect; and

(b)   subsection (6).

(6)   If the referral order, or each of the associated referral orders, is revoked (whether under paragraph 5(2) of Schedule 1 or by virtue of paragraph 14(2) of that Schedule), the period for which the contract has effect expires at the time when the order or orders is or are revoked unless it has already expired.

10.   First meeting: failure to agree contract

(1)   Where it appears to a youth offender panel to be appropriate to do so, the panel may—

(a)   end the first meeting (or any further meeting held in pursuance of paragraph (b)) without having reached agreement with the offender on a programme of behaviour of the kind mentioned in section 8(1), and

(b)   resume consideration of the offender's case at a further meeting of the panel.

(2)   If, however, it appears to the panel at the first meeting or any such further meeting that there is no prospect of agreement being reached with the offender within a reasonable period after the making of the referral order (or orders)—

(a)   subsection (1)(b) shall not apply; and

(b)   instead the panel shall refer the offender back to the appropriate court.

(3)   If at a meeting of the panel—

(a)   agreement is reached with the offender but he does not sign the record produced in pursuance of section 8(5), and

(b)   his failure to do so appears to the panel to be unreasonable,

the panel shall end the meeting and refer the offender back to the appropriate court.

11.   Progress meetings

(1)   At any time—

(a)   after a youth offender contract has taken effect under section 8, but

(b)   before the end of the period for which the contract has effect,

the specified team shall, if so requested by the panel, arrange for the holding of a meeting of the panel under this section ('a progress meeting').

(2)   The panel may make a request under subsection (1) if it appears to the panel to be expedient to review—

(a)   the offender's progress in implementing the programme of behaviour contained in the contract, or

(b)   any other matter arising in connection with the contract.

(3)   The panel shall make such a request if—

(a)   the offender has notified the panel that—

(i)   he wishes to seek the panel's agreement to a variation in the terms of the contract, or

(ii)   he wishes the panel to refer him back to the appropriate court with a view to the referral order (or orders) being revoked on account of a significant change in his circumstances (such as his being taken to live abroad) making compliance with any youth offender contract impractical; or

(b)   it appears to the panel that the offender is in breach of any of the terms of the contract.

(4)   At a progress meeting the panel shall do such one or more of the following things as it considers appropriate in the circumstances, namely—

(a)   review the offender's progress or any such other matter as is mentioned in subsection (2);

(b)   discuss with the offender any breach of the terms of the contract which it appears to the panel that he has committed;

(c)   consider any variation in the terms of the contract sought by the offender or which it appears to the panel to be expedient to make in the light of any such review or discussion;

(d)   consider whether to accede to any request by the offender that he be referred back to the appropriate court.

(5)   Where the panel has discussed with the offender such a breach as is mentioned in subsection (4)(b)—

(a)   the panel and the offender may agree that the offender is to continue to be required to comply with the contract (either in its original form or with any agreed variation in its terms) without being referred back to the appropriate court; or

(b)   the panel may decide to end the meeting and refer the offender back to that court.

(6)   Where a variation in the terms of the contract is agreed between the offender and the panel, the panel shall cause a written record of the variation to be produced forthwith—

(a)   in language capable of being readily understood by, or explained to, the offender; and

(b)   for signature by him.

(7)   Any such variation shall take effect once the record has been signed—

(a)   by the offender, and

(b)   by a member of the panel on behalf of the panel;

and the panel shall cause a copy of the record to be given or sent to the offender.

(8)   If at a progress meeting—

(a)   any such variation is agreed but the offender does not sign the record produced in pursuance of subsection (6), and

(b)   his failure to do so appears to the panel to be unreasonable,
the panel may end the meeting and refer the offender back to the appropriate court.

(9)   Section 8(2) to (4) shall apply in connection with what may be provided for by the terms of the contract as varied under this section as they apply in connection with what may be provided for by the terms of a programme of behaviour of the kind mentioned in section 8(1).

(10)   Where the panel has discussed with the offender such a request as is mentioned in subsection (4)(d), the panel may, if it is satisfied that there is (or is soon to be) such a change in circumstances as is mentioned in subsection (3)(a)(ii), decide to end the meeting and refer the offender back to the appropriate court.

12.   Final meeting

(1)   Where the compliance period in the case of a youth offender contract is due to expire, the specified team shall arrange for the holding, before the end of that period, of a meeting of the panel under this section ('the final meeting').

(2)   At the final meeting the panel shall—

(a)   review the extent of the offender's compliance to date with the terms of the contract; and

(b)   decide, in the light of that review, whether his compliance with those terms has been such as to justify the conclusion that, by the time the compliance period expires, he will have satisfactorily completed the contract;
and the panel shall give the offender written confirmation of its decision.

(3)   Where the panel decides that the offender's compliance with the terms of the contract has been such as to justify that conclusion, the panel's decision shall have the effect of discharging the referral order (or orders) as from the end of the compliance period.

(4)   Otherwise the panel shall refer the offender back to the appropriate court.

(5)   Nothing in section 7(2) prevents the panel from making the decision mentioned in subsection (3) in the offender's absence if it appears to the panel to be appropriate to do that instead of exercising either of its powers under section 7(2).

(6)   Section 7(2)(a) does not permit the final meeting to be adjourned (or re-adjourned) to a time falling after the end of the compliance period.

(7)   In this section 'the compliance period' in relation to a youth offender contract means the period for which the contract has effect in accordance with section 9.

Further court proceedings

13.   Offender referred back to court or convicted while subject to referral order

Schedule 1, which—

(a)   in Part I makes provision for what is to happen when a youth offender panel refers an offender back to the appropriate court, and

(b)   in Part II makes provision for what is to happen when an offender is convicted of further offences while for the time being subject to a referral order,
shall have effect.

Supplementary

14. Functions of youth offending teams

(1)   The functions of a youth offending team responsible for implementing a referral order include, in particular, arranging for the provision of such administrative staff, accommodation or other facilities as are required by the youth offender panel established in pursuance of the order.

(2)   During the period for which a youth offender contract between a youth offender panel and an offender has effect—

(a)   the specified team shall make arrangements for supervising the offender's compliance with the terms of the contract; and

(b)   the person who is the member of the panel referred to in section 6(3)(a) shall ensure that records are kept of the offender's compliance (or non-compliance) with those terms.

(3)   In implementing referral orders a youth offending team shall have regard to any guidance given from time to time by the Secretary of State.

15. Interpretation of Part I

(1)   In this Part—

'the appropriate court' shall be construed in accordance with paragraph 1(2) of Schedule 1;

'custodial sentence' means a sentence of detention in a young offender institution, a secure training order under section 1 of the Criminal Justice and Public Order Act 1994, a detention and training order within the meaning given by section 73(3) of the Crime and Disorder Act 1998 or a sentence of detention under section 53(3) of the Children and Young Persons Act 1933;

'hospital order' has the meaning given in section 37 of the Mental Health Act 1983;

'meeting', in relation to a youth offender panel, shall be construed in accordance with section 6(7);

'referral order' means (in accordance with section 1(5)) an order under section 1(2) or (3);

'the specified team', in relation to an offender to whom a referral order applies (or two or more associated referral orders apply), means the youth offending team for the time being specified in the order (or orders);

'youth offending team' means a team established under section 39 of the Crime and Disorder Act 1998.

(2)   For the purposes of this Part an offence is associated with another if the offender falls to be dealt with for it at the same time as he is dealt with for the other offence (whether or not he is convicted of the offences at the same time or by or before the same court).

(3)   References in this Part to a referral order being associated with another shall be construed in accordance with section 3(7).

PART II
GIVING OF EVIDENCE OR INFORMATION FOR PURPOSES OF
CRIMINAL PROCEEDINGS

CHAPTER I
SPECIAL MEASURES DIRECTIONS IN CASE OF VULNERABLE AND
INTIMIDATED WITNESSES

Preliminary

16.   Witnesses eligible for assistance on grounds of age or incapacity

(1)   For the purposes of this Chapter a witness in criminal proceedings (other than the accused) is eligible for assistance by virtue of this section—

(a)   if under the age of 17 at the time of the hearing; or

(b)   if the court considers that the quality of evidence given by the witness is likely to be diminished by reason of any circumstances falling within subsection (2).

(2)   The circumstances falling within this subsection are—

(a)   that the witness—

(i)   suffers from mental disorder within the meaning of the Mental Health Act 1983, or

(ii)   otherwise has a significant impairment of intelligence and social functioning;

(b)   that the witness has a physical disability or is suffering from a physical disorder.

(3)   In subsection (1)(a) 'the time of the hearing', in relation to a witness, means the time when it falls to the court to make a determination for the purposes of section 19(2) in relation to the witness.

(4)   In determining whether a witness falls within subsection (1)(b) the court must consider any views expressed by the witness.

(5)   In this Chapter references to the quality of a witness's evidence are to its quality in terms of completeness, coherence and accuracy; and for this purpose 'coherence' refers to a witness's ability in giving evidence to give answers which address the questions put to the witness and can be understood both individually and collectively.

17.   Witnesses eligible for assistance on grounds of fear or distress about testifying

(1)   For the purposes of this Chapter a witness in criminal proceedings (other than the accused) is eligible for assistance by virtue of this subsection if the court is satisfied that the quality of evidence given by the witness is likely to be diminished by reason of fear or distress on the part of the witness in connection with testifying in the proceedings.

(2)   In determining whether a witness falls within subsection (1) the court must take into account, in particular—

(a)   the nature and alleged circumstances of the offence to which the proceedings relate;

   (b)   the age of the witness;
   (c)   such of the following matters as appear to the court to be relevant, namely—
      (i)   the social and cultural background and ethnic origins of the witness,
      (ii)   the domestic and employment circumstances of the witness, and
      (iii) any religious beliefs or political opinions of the witness;
   (d)   any behaviour towards the witness on the part of—
      (i)   the accused,
      (ii)   members of the family or associates of the accused, or
      (iii) any other person who is likely to be an accused or a witness in the proceedings.

(3)   In determining that question the court must in addition consider any views expressed by the witness.

(4)   Where the complainant in respect of a sexual offence is a witness in proceedings relating to that offence (or to that offence and any other offences), the witness is eligible for assistance in relation to those proceedings by virtue of this subsection unless the witness has informed the court of the witness' wish not to be so eligible by virtue of this subsection.

18.   Special measures available to eligible witnesses

(1)   For the purposes of this Chapter—
   (a)   the provision which may be made by a special measures direction by virtue of each of sections 23 to 30 is a special measure available in relation to a witness eligible for assistance by virtue of section 16; and
   (b)   the provision which may be made by such a direction by virtue of each of sections 23 to 28 is a special measure available in relation to a witness eligible for assistance by virtue of section 17;
but this subsection has effect subject to subsection (2).

(2)   Where (apart from this subsection) a special measure would, in accordance with subsection (1)(a) or (b), be available in relation to a witness in any proceedings, it shall not be taken by a court to be available in relation to the witness unless—
   (a)   the court has been notified by the Secretary of State that relevant arrangements may be made available in the area in which it appears to the court that the proceedings will take place, and
   (b)   the notice has not been withdrawn.

(3)   In subsection (2) 'relevant arrangements' means arrangements for implementing the measure in question which cover the witness and the proceedings in question.

(4)   The withdrawal of a notice under that subsection relating to a special measure shall not affect the availability of that measure in relation to a witness if a special measures direction providing for that measure to apply to the witness's evidence has been made by the court before the notice is withdrawn.

(5)   The Secretary of State may by order make such amendments of this Chapter as he considers appropriate for altering the special measures which, in accordance with subsection (1)(a) or (b), are available in relation to a witness eligible for assistance by virtue of section 16 or (as the case may be) section 17, whether—

(a)   by modifying the provisions relating to any measure for the time being available in relation to such a witness,

(b)   by the addition—

(i)   (with or without modifications) of any measure which is for the time being available in relation to a witness eligible for assistance by virtue of the other of those sections, or

(ii)   of any new measure, or

(c)   by the removal of any measure.

Special measures directions

19.   Special measures direction relating to eligible witness

(1)   This section applies where in any criminal proceedings—

(a)   a party to the proceedings makes an application for the court to give a direction under this section in relation to a witness in the proceedings other than the accused, or

(b)   the court of its own motion raises the issue whether such a direction should be given.

(2)   Where the court determines that the witness is eligible for assistance by virtue of section 16 or 17, the court must then—

(a)   determine whether any of the special measures available in relation to the witness (or any combination of them) would, in its opinion, be likely to improve the quality of evidence given by the witness; and

(b)   if so—

(i)   determine which of those measures (or combination of them) would, in its opinion, be likely to maximise so far as practicable the quality of such evidence; and

(ii)   give a direction under this section providing for the measure or measures so determined to apply to evidence given by the witness.

(3)   In determining for the purposes of this Chapter whether any special measure or measures would or would not be likely to improve, or to maximise so far as practicable, the quality of evidence given by the witness, the court must consider all the circumstances of the case, including in particular—

(a)   any views expressed by the witness; and

(b)   whether the measure or measures might tend to inhibit such evidence being effectively tested by a party to the proceedings.

(4)   A special measures direction must specify particulars of the provision made by the direction in respect of each special measure which is to apply to the witness's evidence.

(5)   In this Chapter 'special measures direction' means a direction under this section.

(6)   Nothing in this Chapter is to be regarded as affecting any power of a court to make an order or give leave of any description (in the exercise of its inherent jurisdiction or otherwise)—

(a)   in relation to a witness who is not an eligible witness, or

(b)   in relation to an eligible witness where (as, for example, in a case where a foreign language interpreter is to be provided) the order is made or the leave is given otherwise than by reason of the fact that the witness is an eligible witness.

20.   Further provisions about directions: general
(1)   Subject to subsection (2) and section 21(8), a special measures direction has binding effect from the time it is made until the proceedings for the purposes of which it is made are either—

(a)   determined (by acquittal, conviction or otherwise), or

(b)   abandoned,

in relation to the accused or (if there is more than one) in relation to each of the accused.

(2)   The court may discharge or vary (or further vary) a special measures direction if it appears to the court to be in the interests of justice to do so, and may do so either—

(a)   on an application made by a party to the proceedings, if there has been a material change of circumstances since the relevant time, or

(b)   of its own motion.

(3)   In subsection (2) 'the relevant time' means—

(a)   the time when the direction was given, or

(b)   if a previous application has been made under that subsection, the time when the application (or last application) was made.

(4)   Nothing in section 24(2) and (3), 27(4) to (7) or 28(4) to (6) is to be regarded as affecting the power of the court to vary or discharge a special measures direction under subsection (2).

(5)   The court must state in open court its reasons for—

(a)   giving or varying,

(b)   refusing an application for, or for the variation or discharge of, or

(c)   discharging,

a special measures direction and, if it is a magistrates' court, must cause them to be entered in the register of its proceedings.

(6)   Rules of court may make provision—

(a)   for uncontested applications to be determined by the court without a hearing;

(b)   for preventing the renewal of an unsuccessful application for a special measures direction except where there has been a material change of circumstances;

(c)   for expert evidence to be given in connection with an application for, or for varying or discharging, such a direction;

(d)   for the manner in which confidential or sensitive information is to be treated in connection with such an application and in particular as to its being disclosed to, or withheld from, a party to the proceedings.

21.   Special provisions relating to child witnesses
(1)   For the purposes of this section—

(a)   a witness in criminal proceedings is a 'child witness' if he is an eligible witness by reason of section 16(1)(a) (whether or not he is an eligible witness by reason of any other provision of section 16 or 17);

(b)   a child witness is 'in need of special protection' if the offence (or any of the offences) to which the proceedings relate is—

(i)   an offence falling within section 35(3)(a) (sexual offences etc.), or

(ii)   an offence falling within section 35(3)(b), (c) or (d) (kidnapping, assaults etc.); and

(c)   a 'relevant recording', in relation to a child witness, is a video recording of an interview of the witness made with a view to its admission as evidence in chief of the witness.

(2)   Where the court, in making a determination for the purposes of section 19(2), determines that a witness in criminal proceedings is a child witness, the court must—

(a)   first have regard to subsections (3) to (7) below; and

(b)   then have regard to section 19(2);

and for the purposes of section 19(2), as it then applies to the witness, any special measures required to be applied in relation to him by virtue of this section shall be treated as if they were measures determined by the court, pursuant to section 19(2)(a) and (b)(i), to be ones that (whether on their own or with any other special measures) would be likely to maximise, so far as practicable, the quality of his evidence.

(3)   The primary rule in the case of a child witness is that the court must give a special measures direction in relation to the witness which complies with the following requirements—

(a)   it must provide for any relevant recording to be admitted under section 27 (video recorded evidence in chief); and

(b)   it must provide for any evidence given by the witness in the proceedings which is not given by means of a video recording (whether in chief or otherwise) to be given by means of a live link in accordance with section 24.

(4)   The primary rule is subject to the following limitations—

(a)   the requirement contained in subsection (3)(a) or (b) has effect subject to the availability (within the meaning of section 18(2)) of the special measure in question in relation to the witness;

(b)   the requirement contained in subsection (3)(a) also has effect subject to section 27(2); and

(c)   the rule does not apply to the extent that the court is satisfied that compliance with it would not be likely to maximise the quality of the witness's evidence so far as practicable (whether because the application to that evidence of one or more other special measures available in relation to the witness would have that result or for any other reason).

(5)   However, subsection (4)(c) does not apply in relation to a child witness in need of special protection.

(6)   Where a child witness is in need of special protection by virtue of subsection (1)(b)(i), any special measures direction given by the court which complies with the requirement contained in subsection (3)(a) must in addition provide for the special measure available under section 28 (video recorded cross-examination or re-examination) to apply in relation to—

(a)   any cross-examination of the witness otherwise than by the accused in person, and

(b)   any subsequent re-examination.

(7)   The requirement contained in subsection (6) has effect subject to the following limitations—

(a)   it has effect subject to the availability (within the meaning of section 18(2)) of that special measure in relation to the witness; and

(b)   it does not apply if the witness has informed the court that he does not want that special measure to apply in relation to him.

(8)   Where a special measures direction is given in relation to a child witness who is an eligible witness by reason only of section 16(1)(a), then—

(a)   subject to subsection (9) below, and

(b)   except where the witness has already begun to give evidence in the proceedings,

the direction shall cease to have effect at the time when the witness attains the age of 17.

(9)   Where a special measures direction is given in relation to a child witness who is an eligible witness by reason only of section 16(1)(a) and—

(a)   the direction provides—

(i)   for any relevant recording to be admitted under section 27 as evidence in chief of the witness, or

(ii)   for the special measure available under section 28 to apply in relation to the witness, and

(b)   if it provides for that special measure to so apply, the witness is still under the age of 17 when the video recording is made for the purposes of section 28,

then, so far as it provides as mentioned in paragraph (a)(i) or (ii) above, the direction shall continue to have effect in accordance with section 20(1) even though the witness subsequently attains that age.

22.   Extension of provisions of section 21 to certain witnesses over 17

(1)   For the purposes of this section—

(a)   a witness in criminal proceedings (other than the accused) is a 'qualifying witness' if he—

(i)   is not an eligible witness at the time of the hearing (as defined by section 16(3)), but

(ii)   was under the age of 17 when a relevant recording was made;

(b)   a qualifying witness is 'in need of special protection' if the offence (or any of the offences) to which the proceedings relate is—

(i)   an offence falling within section 35(3)(a) (sexual offences etc.), or

(ii)   an offence falling within section 35(3)(b), (c) or (d) (kidnapping, assaults etc.); and

(c)   a 'relevant recording', in relation to a witness, is a video recording of an interview of the witness made with a view to its admission as evidence in chief of the witness.

(2)   Subsections (2) to (7) of section 21 shall apply as follows in relation to a qualifying witness—

(a)   subsections (2) to (4), so far as relating to the giving of a direction complying with the requirement contained in subsection (3)(a), shall apply to a qualifying witness in respect of the relevant recording as they apply to a child witness (within the meaning of that section);

(b)   subsection (5), so far as relating to the giving of such a direction, shall apply to a qualifying witness in need of special protection as it applies to a child witness in need of special protection (within the meaning of that section); and

(c)   subsections (6) and (7) shall apply to a qualifying witness in need of special protection by virtue of subsection (1)(b)(i) above as they apply to such a child witness as is mentioned in subsection (6).

Special measures

23.   Screening witness from accused

(1)   A special measures direction may provide for the witness, while giving testimony or being sworn in court, to be prevented by means of a screen or other arrangement from seeing the accused.

(2)   But the screen or other arrangement must not prevent the witness from being able to see, and to be seen by—

(a)   the judge or justices (or both) and the jury (if there is one);

(b)   legal representatives acting in the proceedings; and

(c)   any interpreter or other person appointed (in pursuance of the direction or otherwise) to assist the witness.

(3)   Where two or more legal representatives are acting for a party to the proceedings, subsection (2)(b) is to be regarded as satisfied in relation to those representatives if the witness is able at all material times to see and be seen by at least one of them.

24.   Evidence by live link

(1)   A special measures direction may provide for the witness to give evidence by means of a live link.

(2)   Where a direction provides for the witness to give evidence by means of a live link, the witness may not give evidence in any other way without the permission of the court.

(3)   The court may give permission for the purposes of subsection (2) if it appears to the court to be in the interests of justice to do so, and may do so either—

(a)   on an application by a party to the proceedings, if there has been a material change of circumstances since the relevant time, or

(b)   of its own motion.

(4)   In subsection (3) 'the relevant time' means—

(a)   the time when the direction was given, or

(b)   if a previous application has been made under that subsection, the time when the application (or last application) was made.

(5)   Where in proceedings before a magistrates' court—

(a)   evidence is to be given by means of a live link in accordance with a special measures direction, but

(b)   suitable facilities for receiving such evidence are not available at any petty-sessional court-house in which that court can (apart from this subsection) lawfully sit,

the court may sit for the purposes of the whole or any part of those proceedings at a place where such facilities are available and which has been appointed for the purposes of this subsection by the justices acting for the petty sessions area for which the court acts.

(6)   A place appointed under subsection (5) may be outside the petty sessions area for which it is appointed; but (if so) it is to be regarded as being in that area for the purpose of the jurisdiction of the justices acting for that area.

(7)   In this section 'petty-sessional court-house' has the same meaning as in the Magistrates' Courts Act 1980 and 'petty sessions area' has the same meaning as in the Justices of the Peace Act 1997.

(8)   In this Chapter 'live link' means a live television link or other arrangement whereby a witness, while absent from the courtroom or other place where the proceedings are being held, is able to see and hear a person there and to be seen and heard by the persons specified in section 23(2)(a) to (c).

25.   Evidence given in private

(1)   A special measures direction may provide for the exclusion from the court, during the giving of the witness's evidence, of persons of any description specified in the direction.

(2)   The persons who may be so excluded do not include—

(a)   the accused,

(b)   legal representatives acting in the proceedings, or

(c)   any interpreter or other person appointed (in pursuance of the direction or otherwise) to assist the witness.

(3)   A special measures direction providing for representatives of news gathering or reporting organisations to be so excluded shall be expressed not to apply to one named person who—

(a)   is a representative of such an organisation, and

(b)   has been nominated for the purpose by one or more such organisations,

unless it appears to the court that no such nomination has been made.

(4)   A special measures direction may only provide for the exclusion of persons under this section where—

(a)   the proceedings relate to a sexual offence; or

(b)   it appears to the court that there are reasonable grounds for believing that any person other than the accused has sought, or will seek, to intimidate the witness in connection with testifying in the proceedings.

(5)   Any proceedings from which persons are excluded under this section (whether or not those persons include representatives of news gathering or reporting

organisations) shall nevertheless be taken to be held in public for the purposes of any privilege or exemption from liability available in respect of fair, accurate and contemporaneous reports of legal proceedings held in public.

26. Removal of wigs and gowns

A special measures direction may provide for the wearing of wigs or gowns to be dispensed with during the giving of the witness's evidence.

27. Video recorded evidence in chief

(1)   A special measures direction may provide for a video recording of an interview of the witness to be admitted as evidence in chief of the witness.

(2)   A special measures direction may, however, not provide for a video recording, or a part of such a recording, to be admitted under this section if the court is of the opinion, having regard to all the circumstances of the case, that in the interests of justice the recording, or that part of it, should not be so admitted.

(3)   In considering for the purposes of subsection (2) whether any part of a recording should not be admitted under this section, the court must consider whether any prejudice to the accused which might result from that part being so admitted is outweighed by the desirability of showing the whole, or substantially the whole, of the recorded interview.

(4)   Where a special measures direction provides for a recording to be admitted under this section, the court may nevertheless subsequently direct that it is not to be so admitted if—

(a)   it appears to the court that—

(i)   the witness will not be available for cross-examination (whether conducted in the ordinary way or in accordance with any such direction), and

(ii)   the parties to the proceedings have not agreed that there is no need for the witness to be so available; or

(b)   any rules of court requiring disclosure of the circumstances in which the recording was made have not been complied with to the satisfaction of the court.

(5)   Where a recording is admitted under this section—

(a)   the witness must be called by the party tendering it in evidence, unless—

(i)   a special measures direction provides for the witness's evidence on cross-examination to be given otherwise than by testimony in court, or

(ii)   the parties to the proceedings have agreed as mentioned in subsection (4)(a)(ii); and

(b)   the witness may not give evidence in chief otherwise than by means of the recording—

(i)   as to any matter which, in the opinion of the court, has been dealt with adequately in the witness's recorded testimony, or

(ii)   without the permission of the court, as to any other matter which, in the opinion of the court, is dealt with in that testimony.

(6)   Where in accordance with subsection (2) a special measures direction provides for part only of a recording to be admitted under this section, references in subsections (4) and (5) to the recording or to the witness's recorded testimony are references to the part of the recording or testimony which is to be so admitted.

(7)   The court may give permission for the purposes of subsection (5)(b)(ii) if it appears to the court to be in the interests of justice to do so, and may do so either—

(a)   on an application by a party to the proceedings, if there has been a material change of circumstances since the relevant time, or

(b)   of its own motion.

(8)   In subsection (7) 'the relevant time' means—

(a)   the time when the direction was given, or

(b)   if a previous application has been made under that subsection, the time when the application (or last application) was made.

(9)   The court may, in giving permission for the purposes of subsection (5)(b)(ii), direct that the evidence in question is to be given by the witness by means of a live link; and, if the court so directs, subsections (5) to (7) of section 24 shall apply in relation to that evidence as they apply in relation to evidence which is to be given in accordance with a special measures direction.

(10)   A magistrates' court inquiring into an offence as examining justices under section 6 of the Magistrates' Courts Act 1980 may consider any video recording in relation to which it is proposed to apply for a special measures direction providing for it to be admitted at the trial in accordance with this section.

(11)   Nothing in this section affects the admissibility of any video recording which would be admissible apart from this section.

28.   Video recorded cross-examination or re-examination

(1)   Where a special measures direction provides for a video recording to be admitted under section 27 as evidence in chief of the witness, the direction may also provide—

(a)   for any cross-examination of the witness, and any re-examination, to be recorded by means of a video recording; and

(b)   for such a recording to be admitted, so far as it relates to any such cross-examination or re-examination, as evidence of the witness under cross-examination or on re-examination, as the case may be.

(2)   Such a recording must be made in the presence of such persons as rules of court or the direction may provide and in the absence of the accused, but in circumstances in which—

(a)   the judge or justices (or both) and legal representatives acting in the proceedings are able to see and hear the examination of the witness and to communicate with the persons in whose presence the recording is being made, and

(b)   the accused is able to see and hear any such examination and to communicate with any legal representative acting for him.

(3)   Where two or more legal representatives are acting for a party to the proceedings, subsection (2)(a) and (b) are to be regarded as satisfied in relation to those representatives if at all material times they are satisfied in relation to at least one of them.

(4)   Where a special measures direction provides for a recording to be admitted under this section, the court may nevertheless subsequently direct that it is not to be

so admitted if any requirement of subsection (2) or rules of court or the direction has not been complied with to the satisfaction of the court.

(5)   Where in pursuance of subsection (1) a recording has been made of any examination of the witness, the witness may not be subsequently cross-examined or re-examined in respect of any evidence given by the witness in the proceedings (whether in any recording admissible under section 27 or this section or otherwise than in such a recording) unless the court gives a further special measures direction making such provision as is mentioned in subsection (1)(a) and (b) in relation to any subsequent cross-examination, and re-examination, of the witness.

(6)   The court may only give such a further direction if it appears to the court—

(a)   that the proposed cross-examination is sought by a party to the proceedings as a result of that party having become aware, since the time when the original recording was made in pursuance of subsection (1), of a matter which that party could not with reasonable diligence have ascertained by then, or

(b)   that for any other reason it is in the interests of justice to give the further direction.

(7)   Nothing in this section shall be read as applying in relation to any cross-examination of the witness by the accused in person (in a case where the accused is to be able to conduct any such cross-examination).

29.   Examination of witness through intermediary

(1)   A special measures direction may provide for any examination of the witness (however and wherever conducted) to be conducted through an interpreter or other person approved by the court for the purposes of this section ('an intermediary').

(2)   The function of an intermediary is to communicate—

(a)   to the witness, questions put to the witness, and

(b)   to any person asking such questions, the answers given by the witness in reply to them,

and to explain such questions or answers so far as necessary to enable them to be understood by the witness or person in question.

(3)   Any examination of the witness in pursuance of subsection (1) must take place in the presence of such persons as rules of court or the direction may provide, but in circumstances in which—

(a)   the judge or justices (or both) and legal representatives acting in the proceedings are able to see and hear the examination of the witness and to communicate with the intermediary, and

(b)   (except in the case of a video recorded examination) the jury (if there is one) are able to see and hear the examination of the witness.

(4)   Where two or more legal representatives are acting for a party to the proceedings, subsection (3)(a) is to be regarded as satisfied in relation to those representatives if at all material times it is satisfied in relation to at least one of them.

(5)   A person may not act as an intermediary in a particular case except after making a declaration, in such form as may be prescribed by rules of court, that he will faithfully perform his function as intermediary.

(6)   Subsection (1) does not apply to an interview of the witness which is recorded by means of a video recording with a view to its admission as evidence in chief of the witness; but a special measures direction may provide for such a recording to be admitted under section 27 if the interview was conducted through an intermediary and—

(a)   that person complied with subsection (5) before the interview began, and

(b)   the court's approval for the purposes of this section is given before the direction is given.

(7)   Section 1 of the Perjury Act 1911 (perjury) shall apply in relation to a person acting as an intermediary as it applies in relation to a person lawfully sworn as an interpreter in a judicial proceeding; and for this purpose, where a person acts as an intermediary in any proceeding which is not a judicial proceeding for the purposes of that section, that proceeding shall be taken to be part of the judicial proceeding in which the witness's evidence is given.

30.   Aids to communication

A special measures direction may provide for the witness, while giving evidence (whether by testimony in court or otherwise), to be provided with such device as the court considers appropriate with a view to enabling questions or answers to be communicated to or by the witness despite any disability or disorder or other impairment which the witness has or suffers from.

Supplementary

31.   Status of evidence given under Chapter I

(1)   Subsections (2) to (4) apply to a statement made by a witness in criminal proceedings which, in accordance with a special measures direction, is not made by the witness in direct oral testimony in court but forms part of the witness's evidence in those proceedings.

(2)   The statement shall be treated as if made by the witness in direct oral testimony in court; and accordingly—

(a)   it is admissible evidence of any fact of which such testimony from the witness would be admissible;

(b)   it is not capable of corroborating any other evidence given by the witness.

(3)   Subsection (2) applies to a statement admitted under section 27 or 28 which is not made by the witness on oath even though it would have been required to be made on oath if made by the witness in direct oral testimony in court.

(4)   In estimating the weight (if any) to be attached to the statement, the court must have regard to all the circumstances from which an inference can reasonably be drawn (as to the accuracy of the statement or otherwise).

(5)   Nothing in this Chapter (apart from subsection (3)) affects the operation of any rule of law relating to evidence in criminal proceedings.

(6)   Where any statement made by a person on oath in any proceeding which is not a judicial proceeding for the purposes of section 1 of the Perjury Act 1911 (perjury) is received in evidence in pursuance of a special measures direction, that proceeding shall be taken for the purposes of that section to be part of the judicial proceeding in which the statement is so received in evidence.

(7)   Where in any proceeding which is not a judicial proceeding for the purposes of that Act—

(a)   a person wilfully makes a false statement otherwise than on oath which is subsequently received in evidence in pursuance of a special measures direction, and

(b)   the statement is made in such circumstances that had it been given on oath in any such judicial proceeding that person would have been guilty of perjury,

he shall be guilty of an offence and liable to any punishment which might be imposed on conviction of an offence under section 57(2) (giving of false unsworn evidence in criminal proceedings).

(8)   In this section 'statement' includes any representation of fact, whether made in words or otherwise.

32.   Warning to jury

Where on a trial on indictment evidence has been given in accordance with a special measures direction, the judge must give the jury such warning (if any) as the judge considers necessary to ensure that the fact that the direction was given in relation to the witness does not prejudice the accused.

33.   Interpretation etc. of Chapter I

(1)   In this Chapter—

'eligible witness' means a witness eligible for assistance by virtue of section 16 or 17;

'live link' has the meaning given by section 24(8);

'quality', in relation to the evidence of a witness, shall be construed in accordance with section 16(5);

'special measures direction' means (in accordance with section 19(5)) a direction under section 19.

(2)   In this Chapter references to the special measures available in relation to a witness shall be construed in accordance with section 18.

(3)   In this Chapter references to a person being able to see or hear, or be seen or heard by, another person are to be read as not applying to the extent that either of them is unable to see or hear by reason of any impairment of eyesight or hearing.

(4)   In the case of any proceedings in which there is more than one accused—

(a)   any reference to the accused in sections 23 to 28 may be taken by a court, in connection with the giving of a special measures direction, as a reference to all or any of the accused, as the court may determine, and

(b)   any such direction may be given on the basis of any such determination.

CHAPTER II
PROTECTION OF WITNESSES FROM CROSS-EXAMINATION BY
ACCUSED IN PERSON

General prohibitions

34.   Complainants in proceedings for sexual offences

No person charged with a sexual offence may in any criminal proceedings cross-examine in person a witness who is the complainant, either—

    (a)   in connection with that offence, or

    (b)   in connection with any other offence (of whatever nature) with which that person is charged in the proceedings.

35.   Child complainants and other child witnesses

    (1)   No person charged with an offence to which this section applies may in any criminal proceedings cross-examine in person a protected witness, either—

    (a)   in connection with that offence, or

    (b)   in connection with any other offence (of whatever nature) with which that person is charged in the proceedings.

    (2)   For the purposes of subsection (1) a 'protected witness' is a witness who—

    (a)   either is the complainant or is alleged to have been a witness to the commission of the offence to which this section applies, and

    (b)   either is a child or falls to be cross-examined after giving evidence in chief (whether wholly or in part)—

        (i)   by means of a video recording made (for the purposes of section 27) at a time when the witness was a child, or

        (ii)   in any other way at any such time.

    (3)   The offences to which this section applies are—

    (a)   any offence under—

        (i)   the Sexual Offences Act 1956,

        (ii)   the Indecency with Children Act 1960,

        (iii)   the Sexual Offences Act 1967,

        (iv)   section 54 of the Criminal Law Act 1977, or

        (v)   the Protection of Children Act 1978;

    (b)   kidnapping, false imprisonment or an offence under section 1 or 2 of the Child Abduction Act 1984;

    (c)   any offence under section 1 of the Children and Young Persons Act 1933;

    (d)   any offence (not within any of the preceding paragraphs) which involves an assault on, or injury or a threat of injury to, any person.

    (4)   In this section 'child' means—

    (a)   where the offence falls within subsection (3)(a), a person under the age of 17; or

    (b)   where the offence falls within subsection (3)(b), (c) or (d), a person under the age of 14.

    (5)   For the purposes of this section 'witness' includes a witness who is charged with an offence in the proceedings.

Prohibition imposed by court

36.   Direction prohibiting accused from cross-examining particular witness

    (1)   This section applies where, in a case where neither of sections 34 and 35 operates to prevent an accused in any criminal proceedings from cross-examining a witness in person—

    (a)   the prosecutor makes an application for the court to give a direction under this section in relation to the witness, or

(b)   the court of its own motion raises the issue whether such a direction should be given.

(2)   If it appears to the court—

(a)   that the quality of evidence given by the witness on cross-examination—

(i)   is likely to be diminished if the cross-examination (or further cross-examination) is conducted by the accused in person, and

(ii)   would be likely to be improved if a direction were given under this section, and

(b)   that it would not be contrary to the interests of justice to give such a direction,

the court may give a direction prohibiting the accused from cross-examining (or further cross-examining) the witness in person.

(3)   In determining whether subsection (2)(a) applies in the case of a witness the court must have regard, in particular, to—

(a)   any views expressed by the witness as to whether or not the witness is content to be cross-examined by the accused in person;

(b)   the nature of the questions likely to be asked, having regard to the issues in the proceedings and the defence case advanced so far (if any);

(c)   any behaviour on the part of the accused at any stage of the proceedings, both generally and in relation to the witness;

(d)   any relationship (of whatever nature) between the witness and the accused;

(e)   whether any person (other than the accused) is or has at any time been charged in the proceedings with a sexual offence or an offence to which section 35 applies, and (if so) whether section 34 or 35 operates or would have operated to prevent that person from cross-examining the witness in person;

(f)   any direction under section 19 which the court has given, or proposes to give, in relation to the witness.

(4)   For the purposes of this section—

(a)   'witness', in relation to an accused, does not include any other person who is charged with an offence in the proceedings; and

(b)   any reference to the quality of a witness's evidence shall be construed in accordance with section 16(5).

37.   Further provisions about directions under section 36

(1)   Subject to subsection (2), a direction has binding effect from the time it is made until the witness to whom it applies is discharged.

In this section 'direction' means a direction under section 36.

(2)   The court may discharge a direction if it appears to the court to be in the interests of justice to do so, and may do so either—

(a)   on an application made by a party to the proceedings, if there has been a material change of circumstances since the relevant time, or

(b)   of its own motion.

(3)   In subsection (2) 'the relevant time' means—

(a)   the time when the direction was given, or

(b)   if a previous application has been made under that subsection, the time when the application (or last application) was made.

(4)   The court must state in open court its reasons for—

(a)   giving, or

(b)   refusing an application for, or for the discharge of, or

(c)   discharging,

a direction and, if it is a magistrates' court, must cause them to be entered in the register of its proceedings.

(5)   Rules of court may make provision—

(a)   for uncontested applications to be determined by the court without a hearing;

(b)   for preventing the renewal of an unsuccessful application for a direction except where there has been a material change of circumstances;

(c)   for expert evidence to be given in connection with an application for, or for discharging, a direction;

(d)   for the manner in which confidential or sensitive information is to be treated in connection with such an application and in particular as to its being disclosed to, or withheld from, a party to the proceedings.

Cross-examination on behalf of accused

38.   Defence representation for purposes of cross-examination

(1)   This section applies where an accused is prevented from cross-examining a witness in person by virtue of section 34, 35 or 36.

(2)   Where it appears to the court that this section applies, it must—

(a)   invite the accused to arrange for a legal representative to act for him for the purpose of cross-examining the witness; and

(b)   require the accused to notify the court, by the end of such period as it may specify, whether a legal representative is to act for him for that purpose.

(3)   If by the end of the period mentioned in subsection (2)(b) either—

(a)   the accused has notified the court that no legal representative is to act for him for the purpose of cross-examining the witness, or

(b)   no notification has been received by the court and it appears to the court that no legal representative is to so act,

the court must consider whether it is necessary in the interests of justice for the witness to be cross-examined by a legal representative appointed to represent the interests of the accused.

(4)   If the court decides that it is necessary in the interests of justice for the witness to be so cross-examined, the court must appoint a qualified legal representative (chosen by the court) to cross-examine the witness in the interests of the accused.

(5)   A person so appointed shall not be responsible to the accused.

(6)   Rules of court may make provision—

(a)   as to the time when, and the manner in which, subsection (2) is to be complied with;

(b)   in connection with the appointment of a legal representative under subsection (4), and in particular for securing that a person so appointed is provided with evidence or other material relating to the proceedings.

(7)   Rules of court made in pursuance of subsection (6)(b) may make provision for the application, with such modifications as are specified in the rules, of any of the provisions of—

(a)   Part I of the Criminal Procedure and Investigations Act 1996 (disclosure of material in connection with criminal proceedings), or

(b)   the Sexual Offences (Protected Material) Act 1997.

(8)   For the purposes of this section—

(a)   any reference to cross-examination includes (in a case where a direction is given under section 36 after the accused has begun cross-examining the witness) a reference to further cross-examination; and

(b)   'qualified legal representative' means a legal representative who has a right of audience (within the meaning of the Courts and Legal Services Act 1990) in relation to the proceedings before the court.

39.   Warning to jury

(1)   Where on a trial on indictment an accused is prevented from cross-examining a witness in person by virtue of section 34, 35 or 36, the judge must give the jury such warning (if any) as the judge considers necessary to ensure that the accused is not prejudiced—

(a)   by any inferences that might be drawn from the fact that the accused has been prevented from cross-examining the witness in person;

(b)   where the witness has been cross-examined by a legal representative appointed under section 38(4), by the fact that the cross-examination was carried out by such a legal representative and not by a person acting as the accused's own legal representative.

(2)   Subsection (8)(a) of section 38 applies for the purposes of this section as it applies for the purposes of section 38.

40.   Funding of defence representation

(1)   In section 19(3) of the Prosecution of Offences Act 1985 (regulations authorising payments out of central funds), after paragraph (d) there shall be inserted—

'(e)   to cover the proper fee or costs of a legal representative appointed under section 38(4) of the Youth Justice and Criminal Evidence Act 1999 (defence representation for purposes of cross-examination) and any expenses properly incurred in providing such a person with evidence or other material in connection with his appointment.'

(2)   In section 21(3) of the Legal Aid Act 1988 (cases where, subject to means, representation must be granted), after paragraph (d) there shall be inserted—

'(e)   where a person is prevented from conducting any cross-examination as mentioned in section 38(1) of the Youth Justice and Criminal Evidence Act 1999 (defence representation for purposes of cross-examination), for conducting the cross-examination on behalf of that person (otherwise than as a person appointed under section 38(4) of that Act).'

CHAPTER III
PROTECTION OF COMPLAINANTS IN PROCEEDINGS FOR SEXUAL OFFENCES

41.   Restriction on evidence or questions about complainant's sexual history

(1)   If at a trial a person is charged with a sexual offence, then, except with the leave of the court—

(a)   no evidence may be adduced, and

(b)   no question may be asked in cross-examination,

by or on behalf of any accused at the trial, about any sexual behaviour of the complainant.

(2)   The court may give leave in relation to any evidence or question only on an application made by or on behalf of an accused, and may not give such leave unless it is satisfied—

(a)   that subsection (3) or (5) applies, and

(b)   that a refusal of leave might have the result of rendering unsafe a conclusion of the jury or (as the case may be) the court on any relevant issue in the case.

(3)   This subsection applies if the evidence or question relates to a relevant issue in the case and either—

(a)   that issue is not an issue of consent; or

(b)   it is an issue of consent and the sexual behaviour of the complainant to which the evidence or question relates is alleged to have taken place at or about the same time as the event which is the subject matter of the charge against the accused; or

(c)   it is an issue of consent and the sexual behaviour of the complainant to which the evidence or question relates is alleged to have been, in any respect, so similar—

(i)   to any sexual behaviour of the complainant which (according to evidence adduced or to be adduced by or on behalf of the accused) took place as part of the event which is the subject matter of the charge against the accused, or

(ii)   to any other sexual behaviour of the complainant which (according to such evidence) took place at or about the same time as that event,

that the similarity cannot reasonably be explained as a coincidence.

(4)   For the purposes of subsection (3) no evidence or question shall be regarded as relating to a relevant issue in the case if it appears to the court to be reasonable to assume that the purpose (or main purpose) for which it would be adduced or asked is to establish or elicit material for impugning the credibility of the complainant as a witness.

(5)   This subsection applies if the evidence or question—

(a)   relates to any evidence adduced by the prosecution about any sexual behaviour of the complainant; and

(b)   in the opinion of the court, would go no further than is necessary to enable the evidence adduced by the prosecution to be rebutted or explained by or on behalf of the accused.

(6)   For the purposes of subsections (3) and (5) the evidence or question must relate to a specific instance (or specific instances) of alleged sexual behaviour on the part of the complainant (and accordingly nothing in those subsections is capable of applying in relation to the evidence or question to the extent that it does not so relate).

(7)   Where this section applies in relation to a trial by virtue of the fact that one or more of a number of persons charged in the proceedings is or are charged with a sexual offence—

(a)   it shall cease to apply in relation to the trial if the prosecutor decides not to proceed with the case against that person or those persons in respect of that charge; but

(b)   it shall not cease to do so in the event of that person or those persons pleading guilty to, or being convicted of, that charge.

(8)   Nothing in this section authorises any evidence to be adduced or any question to be asked which cannot be adduced or asked apart from this section.

42.   Interpretation and application of section 41

(1)   In section 41—

(a)   'relevant issue in the case' means any issue falling to be proved by the prosecution or defence in the trial of the accused;

(b)   'issue of consent' means any issue whether the complainant in fact consented to the conduct constituting the offence with which the accused is charged (and accordingly does not include any issue as to the belief of the accused that the complainant so consented);

(c)   'sexual behaviour' means any sexual behaviour or other sexual experience, whether or not involving any accused or other person, but excluding (except in section 41(3)(c)(i) and (5)(a)) anything alleged to have taken place as part of the event which is the subject matter of the charge against the accused; and

(d)   subject to any order made under subsection (2), 'sexual offence' shall be construed in accordance with section 62.

(2)   The Secretary of State may by order make such provision as he considers appropriate for adding or removing, for the purposes of section 41, any offence to or from the offences which are sexual offences for the purposes of this Act by virtue of section 62.

(3)   Section 41 applies in relation to the following proceedings as it applies to a trial, namely—

(a)   proceedings before a magistrates' court inquiring into an offence as examining justices,

(b)   the hearing of an application under paragraph 5(1) of Schedule 6 to the Criminal Justice Act 1991 (application to dismiss charge following notice of transfer of case to Crown Court),

(c)   the hearing of an application under paragraph 2(1) of Schedule 3 to the Crime and Disorder Act 1998 (application to dismiss charge by person sent for trial under section 51 of that Act),

(d)   any hearing held, between conviction and sentencing, for the purpose of determining matters relevant to the court's decision as to how the accused is to be dealt with, and

(e)   the hearing of an appeal,

and references (in section 41 or this section) to a person charged with an offence accordingly include a person convicted of an offence.

43.   Procedure on applications under section 41

(1)   An application for leave shall be heard in private and in the absence of the complainant.

In this section 'leave' means leave under section 41.

(2)   Where such an application has been determined, the court must state in open court (but in the absence of the jury, if there is one)—

(a)   its reasons for giving, or refusing, leave, and

(b)   if it gives leave, the extent to which evidence may be adduced or questions asked in pursuance of the leave,

and, if it is a magistrates' court, must cause those matters to be entered in the register of its proceedings.

(3)   Rules of court may make provision—

(a)   requiring applications for leave to specify, in relation to each item of evidence or question to which they relate, particulars of the grounds on which it is asserted that leave should be given by virtue of subsection (3) or (5) of section 41;

(b)   enabling the court to request a party to the proceedings to provide the court with information which it considers would assist it in determining an application for leave;

(c)   for the manner in which confidential or sensitive information is to be treated in connection with such an application, and in particular as to its being disclosed to, or withheld from, parties to the proceedings.

CHAPTER IV
REPORTING RESTRICTIONS

Reports relating to persons under 18

44.   Restrictions on reporting alleged offences involving persons under 18

(1)   This section applies (subject to subsection (3)) where a criminal investigation has begun in respect of—

(a)   an alleged offence against the law of—

(i)   England and Wales, or

(ii)   Northern Ireland; or

(b)   an alleged civil offence (other than an offence falling within paragraph (a)) committed (whether or not in the United Kingdom) by a person subject to service law.

(2)   No matter relating to any person involved in the offence shall while he is under the age of 18 be included in any publication if it is likely to lead members of the public to identify him as a person involved in the offence.

(3)   The restrictions imposed by subsection (2) cease to apply once there are proceedings in a court (whether a court in England and Wales, a service court or a court in Northern Ireland) in respect of the offence.

(4)   For the purposes of subsection (2) any reference to a person involved in the offence is to—

(a)   a person by whom the offence is alleged to have been committed; or

(b)   if this paragraph applies to the publication in question by virtue of subsection (5)—

(i)   a person against or in respect of whom the offence is alleged to have been committed, or

(ii)   a person who is alleged to have been a witness to the commission of the offence;

except that paragraph (b)(i) does not include a person in relation to whom section 1 of the Sexual Offences (Amendment) Act 1992 (anonymity of victims of certain sexual offences) applies in connection with the offence.

(5)   Subsection (4)(b) applies to a publication if—

(a)   where it is a relevant programme, it is transmitted, or

(b)   in the case of any other publication, it is published,

on or after such date as may be specified in an order made by the Secretary of State.

(6)   The matters relating to a person in relation to which the restrictions imposed by subsection (2) apply (if their inclusion in any publication is likely to have the result mentioned in that subsection) include in particular—

(a)   his name,

(b)   his address,

(c)   the identity of any school or other educational establishment attended by him,

(d)   the identity of any place of work, and

(e)   any still or moving picture of him.

(7)   Any appropriate criminal court may by order dispense, to any extent specified in the order, with the restrictions imposed by subsection (2) in relation to a person if it is satisfied that it is necessary in the interests of justice to do so.

(8)   However, when deciding whether to make such an order dispensing (to any extent) with the restrictions imposed by subsection (2) in relation to a person, the court shall have regard to the welfare of that person.

(9)   In subsection (7) 'appropriate criminal court' means—

(a)   in a case where this section applies by virtue of subsection (1)(a)(i) or (ii), any court in England and Wales or (as the case may be) in Northern Ireland which has any jurisdiction in, or in relation to, any criminal proceedings (but not a service court unless the offence is alleged to have been committed by a person subject to service law);

(b)   in a case where this section applies by virtue of subsection (1)(b), any court falling within paragraph (a) or a service court.

(10)   The power under subsection (7) of a magistrates' court in England and Wales may be exercised by a single justice.

(11)   In the case of a decision of a magistrates' court in England and Wales, or a court of summary jurisdiction in Northern Ireland, to make or refuse to make an order under subsection (7), the following persons, namely—

(a)   any person who was a party to the proceedings on the application for the order, and

(b)   with the leave of the Crown Court, any other person,

may, in accordance with rules of court, appeal to the Crown Court against that decision or appear or be represented at the hearing of such an appeal.

(12)   On such an appeal the Crown Court—

(a)   may make such order as is necessary to give effect to its determination of the appeal; and

(b)   may also make such incidental or consequential orders as appear to it to be just.

(13)   In this section—

(a)   'civil offence' means an act or omission which, if committed in England and Wales, would be an offence against the law of England and Wales;

(b)   any reference to a criminal investigation, in relation to an alleged offence, is to an investigation conducted by police officers, or other persons charged with the duty of investigating offences, with a view to it being ascertained whether a person should be charged with the offence;

(c)   any reference to a person subject to service law is to—

(i)   a person subject to military law, air-force law or the Naval Discipline Act 1957, or

(ii)   any other person to whom provisions of Part II of the Army Act 1955, Part II of the Air Force Act 1955 or Parts I and II of the Naval Discipline Act 1957 apply (whether with or without any modifications).

45. Power to restrict reporting of criminal proceedings involving persons under 18

(1)   This section applies (subject to subsection (2)) in relation to—

(a)   any criminal proceedings in any court (other than a service court) in England and Wales or Northern Ireland; and

(b)   any proceedings (whether in the United Kingdom or elsewhere) in any service court.

(2)   This section does not apply in relation to any proceedings to which section 49 of the Children and Young Persons Act 1933 applies.

(3)   The court may direct that no matter relating to any person concerned in the proceedings shall while he is under the age of 18 be included in any publication if it is likely to lead members of the public to identify him as a person concerned in the proceedings.

(4)   The court or an appellate court may by direction ('an excepting direction') dispense, to any extent specified in the excepting direction, with the restrictions imposed by a direction under subsection (3) if it is satisfied that it is necessary in the interests of justice to do so.

(5)   The court or an appellate court may also by direction ('an excepting direction') dispense, to any extent specified in the excepting direction, with the restrictions imposed by a direction under subsection (3) if it is satisfied—

(a)   that their effect is to impose a substantial and unreasonable restriction on the reporting of the proceedings, and

(b)   that it is in the public interest to remove or relax that restriction;

but no excepting direction shall be given under this subsection by reason only of the fact that the proceedings have been determined in any way or have been abandoned.

(6)   When deciding whether to make—

(a)   a direction under subsection (3) in relation to a person, or

(b)   an excepting direction under subsection (4) or (5) by virtue of which the restrictions imposed by a direction under subsection (3) would be dispensed with (to any extent) in relation to a person,

the court or (as the case may be) the appellate court shall have regard to the welfare of that person.

(7)   For the purposes of subsection (3) any reference to a person concerned in the proceedings is to a person—

(a)   against or in respect of whom the proceedings are taken, or

(b)   who is a witness in the proceedings.

(8)   The matters relating to a person in relation to which the restrictions imposed by a direction under subsection (3) apply (if their inclusion in any publication is likely to have the result mentioned in that subsection) include in particular—

(a)   his name,

(b)   his address,

(c)   the identity of any school or other educational establishment attended by him,

(d)   the identity of any place of work, and

(e)   any still or moving picture of him.

(9)   A direction under subsection (3) may be revoked by the court or an appellate court.

(10)   An excepting direction—

(a)   may be given at the time the direction under subsection (3) is given or subsequently; and

(b)   may be varied or revoked by the court or an appellate court.

(11)   In this section 'appellate court', in relation to any proceedings in a court, means a court dealing with an appeal (including an appeal by way of case stated) arising out of the proceedings or with any further appeal.

Reports relating to adult witnesses

46.   Power to restrict reports about certain adult witnesses in criminal proceedings

(1)   This section applies where—

(a)   in any criminal proceedings in any court (other than a service court) in England and Wales or Northern Ireland, or

(b)   in any proceedings (whether in the United Kingdom or elsewhere) in any service court, a party to the proceedings makes an application for the court to give a reporting direction in relation to a witness in the proceedings (other than the accused) who has attained the age of 18.

In this section 'reporting direction' has the meaning given by subsection (6).

(2)   If the court determines—

(a)   that the witness is eligible for protection, and

(b)   that giving a reporting direction in relation to the witness is likely to improve—

(i)   the quality of evidence given by the witness, or

(ii)   the level of co-operation given by the witness to any party to the proceedings in connection with that party's preparation of its case,

the court may give a reporting direction in relation to the witness.

(3)   For the purposes of this section a witness is eligible for protection if the court is satisfied—

(a)   that the quality of evidence given by the witness, or

(b)   the level of co-operation given by the witness to any party to the proceedings in connection with that party's preparation of its case,

is likely to be diminished by reason of fear or distress on the part of the witness in connection with being identified by members of the public as a witness in the proceedings.

(4)   In determining whether a witness is eligible for protection the court must take into account, in particular—

(a)   the nature and alleged circumstances of the offence to which the proceedings relate;

(b)   the age of the witness;

(c)   such of the following matters as appear to the court to be relevant, namely—

(i)   the social and cultural background and ethnic origins of the witness,

(ii)   the domestic and employment circumstances of the witness, and

(iii)   any religious beliefs or political opinions of the witness;

(d)   any behaviour towards the witness on the part of—

(i)   the accused,

(ii)   members of the family or associates of the accused, or

(iii)   any other person who is likely to be an accused or a witness in the proceedings.

(5)   In determining that question the court must in addition consider any views expressed by the witness.

(6)   For the purposes of this section a reporting direction in relation to a witness is a direction that no matter relating to the witness shall during the witness's lifetime be included in any publication if it is likely to lead members of the public to identify him as being a witness in the proceedings.

(7)   The matters relating to a witness in relation to which the restrictions imposed by a reporting direction apply (if their inclusion in any publication is likely to have the result mentioned in subsection (6)) include in particular—

    (a)   the witness's name,

    (b)   the witness's address,

    (c)   the identity of any educational establishment attended by the witness,

    (d)   the identity of any place of work, and

    (e)   any still or moving picture of the witness.

   (8)   In determining whether to give a reporting direction the court shall consider—

    (a)   whether it would be in the interests of justice to do so, and

    (b)   the public interest in avoiding the imposition of a substantial and unreasonable restriction on the reporting of the proceedings.

   (9)   The court or an appellate court may by direction ('an excepting direction') dispense, to any extent specified in the excepting direction, with the restrictions imposed by a reporting direction if—

    (a)   it is satisfied that it is necessary in the interests of justice to do so, or

    (b)   it is satisfied—

       (i)   that the effect of those restrictions is to impose a substantial and unreasonable restriction on the reporting of the proceedings, and

       (ii)   that it is in the public interest to remove or relax that restriction;

but no excepting direction shall be given under paragraph (b) by reason only of the fact that the proceedings have been determined in any way or have been abandoned.

   (10)   A reporting direction may be revoked by the court or an appellate court.

   (11)   An excepting direction—

    (a)   may be given at the time the reporting direction is given or subsequently; and

    (b)   may be varied or revoked by the court or an appellate court.

   (12)   In this section—

    (a)   'appellate court', in relation to any proceedings in a court, means a court dealing with an appeal (including an appeal by way of case stated) arising out of the proceedings or with any further appeal;

    (b)   references to the quality of a witness's evidence are to its quality in terms of completeness, coherence and accuracy (and for this purpose 'coherence' refers to a witness's ability in giving evidence to give answers which address the questions put to the witness and can be understood both individually and collectively);

    (c)   references to the preparation of the case of a party to any proceedings include, where the party is the prosecution, the carrying out of investigations into any offence at any time charged in the proceedings.

Reports relating to directions under Chapter I or II

47.   Restrictions on reporting directions under Chapter I or II

   (1)   Except as provided by this section, no publication shall include a report of a matter falling within subsection (2).

   (2)   The matters falling within this subsection are—

    (a)   a direction under section 19 or 36 or an order discharging, or (in the case of a direction under section 19) varying, such a direction;

    (b)   proceedings—

(i)   on an application for such a direction or order, or

(ii)   where the court acts of its own motion to determine whether to give or make any such direction or order.

(3)   The court dealing with a matter falling within subsection (2) may order that subsection (1) is not to apply, or is not to apply to a specified extent, to a report of that matter.

(4)   Where—

(a)   there is only one accused in the relevant proceedings, and

(b)   he objects to the making of an order under subsection (3),

the court shall make the order if (and only if) satisfied after hearing the representations of the accused that it is in the interests of justice to do so; and if the order is made it shall not apply to the extent that a report deals with any such objections or representations.

(5)   Where—

(a)   there are two or more accused in the relevant proceedings, and

(b)   one or more of them object to the making of an order under subsection (3),

the court shall make the order if (and only if) satisfied after hearing the representations of each of the accused that it is in the interests of justice to do so; and if the order is made it shall not apply to the extent that a report deals with any such objections or representations.

(6)   Subsection (1) does not apply to the inclusion in a publication of a report of matters after the relevant proceedings are either—

(a)   determined (by acquittal, conviction or otherwise), or

(b)   abandoned,

in relation to the accused or (if there is more than one) in relation to each of the accused.

(7)   In this section 'the relevant proceedings' means the proceedings to which any such direction as is mentioned in subsection (2) relates or would relate.

(8)   Nothing in this section affects any prohibition or restriction by virtue of any other enactment on the inclusion of matter in a publication.

Other restrictions

48.   Amendments relating to other reporting restrictions

Schedule 2, which contains amendments relating to reporting restrictions under—

(a)   the Children and Young Persons Act 1933,

(b)   the Sexual Offences (Amendment) Act 1976,

(c)   the Sexual Offences (Northern Ireland) Order 1978,

(d)   the Sexual Offences (Amendment) Act 1992, and

(e)   the Criminal Justice (Northern Ireland) Order 1994,

shall have effect.

Offences

49.   Offences under Chapter IV

(1)   This section applies if a publication—

(a)   includes any matter in contravention of section 44(2) or of a direction under section 45(3) or 46(2); or

(b)   includes a report in contravention of section 47.

(2)   Where the publication is a newspaper or periodical, any proprietor, any editor and any publisher of the newspaper or periodical is guilty of an offence.

(3)   Where the publication is a relevant programme—

(a)   any body corporate or Scottish partnership engaged in providing the programme service in which the programme is included, and

(b)   any person having functions in relation to the programme corresponding to those of an editor of a newspaper,

is guilty of an offence.

(4)   In the case of any other publication, any person publishing it is guilty of an offence.

(5)   A person guilty of an offence under this section is liable on summary conviction to a fine not exceeding level 5 on the standard scale.

(6)   Proceedings for an offence under this section in respect of a publication falling within subsection (1)(b) may not be instituted—

(a)   in England and Wales otherwise than by or with the consent of the Attorney General, or

(b)   in Northern Ireland otherwise than by or with the consent of the Attorney General for Northern Ireland.

50. Defences

(1)   Where a person is charged with an offence under section 49 it shall be a defence to prove that at the time of the alleged offence he was not aware, and neither suspected nor had reason to suspect, that the publication included the matter or report in question.

(2)   Where—

(a)   a person is charged with an offence under section 49, and

(b)   the offence relates to the inclusion of any matter in a publication in contravention of section 44(2),

it shall be a defence to prove that at the time of the alleged offence he was not aware, and neither suspected nor had reason to suspect, that the criminal investigation in question had begun.

(3)   Where—

(a)   paragraphs (a) and (b) of subsection (2) apply, and

(b)   the contravention of section 44(2) does not relate to either—

(i)   the person by whom the offence mentioned in that provision is alleged to have been committed, or

(ii)   (where that offence is one in relation to which section 1 of the Sexual Offences (Amendment) Act 1992 applies) a person who is alleged to be a witness to the commission of the offence,

it shall be a defence to show to the satisfaction of the court that the inclusion in the publication of the matter in question was in the public interest on the ground that, to the extent that they operated to prevent that matter from being so included, the effect of the restrictions imposed by section 44(2) was to impose a substantial and unreasonable restriction on the reporting of matters connected with that offence.

(4)   Subsection (5) applies where—

    (a)   paragraphs (a) and (b) of subsection (2) apply, and

    (b)   the contravention of section 44(2) relates to a person ('the protected person') who is neither—

       (i)   the person mentioned in subsection (3)(b)(i), nor

       (ii)   a person within subsection (3)(b)(ii) who is under the age of 16.

(5)   In such a case it shall be a defence, subject to subsection (6), to prove that written consent to the inclusion of the matter in question in the publication had been given—

    (a)   by an appropriate person, if at the time when the consent was given the protected person was under the age of 16, or

    (b)   by the protected person, if that person was aged 16 or 17 at that time,

and (where the consent was given by an appropriate person) that written notice had been previously given to that person drawing to his attention the need to consider the welfare of the protected person when deciding whether to give consent.

(6)   The defence provided by subsection (5) is not available if—

    (a)   (where the consent was given by an appropriate person) it is proved that written or other notice withdrawing the consent—

       (i)   was given to the appropriate recipient by any other appropriate person or by the protected person, and

       (ii)   was so given in sufficient time to enable the inclusion in the publication of the matter in question to be prevented; or

    (b)   subsection (8) applies.

(7)   Where—

    (a)   a person is charged with an offence under section 49, and

    (b)   the offence relates to the inclusion of any matter in a publication in contravention of a direction under section 46(2),

it shall be a defence, unless subsection (8) applies, to prove that the person in relation to whom the direction was given had given written consent to the inclusion of that matter in the publication.

(8)   Written consent is not a defence if it is proved that any person interfered—

    (a)   with the peace or comfort of the person giving the consent, or

    (b)   (where the consent was given by an appropriate person) with the peace or comfort of either that person or the protected person,

with intent to obtain the consent.

(9)   In this section—

    'an appropriate person' means (subject to subsections (10) to (12))—

       (a)   in England and Wales or Northern Ireland, a person who is a parent or guardian of the protected person, or

       (b)   in Scotland, a person who has parental responsibilities (within the meaning of section 1(3) of the Children (Scotland) Act 1995) in relation to the protected person;

'guardian', in relation to the protected person, means any person who is not a parent of the protected person but who has parental responsibility for the protected person within the meaning of—

    (a)   (in England and Wales) the Children Act 1989, or

    (b)   (in Northern Ireland) the Children (Northern Ireland) Order 1995.

(10)   Where the protected person is (within the meaning of the Children Act 1989) a child who is looked after by a local authority, 'an appropriate person' means a person who is—

    (a)   a representative of that authority, or

    (b)   a parent or guardian of the protected person with whom the protected person is allowed to live.

(11)   Where the protected person is (within the meaning of the Children (Northern Ireland) Order 1995) a child who is looked after by an authority, 'an appropriate person' means a person who is—

    (a)   an officer of that authority, or

    (b)   a parent or guardian of the protected person with whom the protected person is allowed to live.

(12)   Where the protected person is (within the meaning of section 17(6) of the Children (Scotland) Act 1995) a child who is looked after by a local authority, 'an appropriate person' means a person who is—

    (a)   a representative of that authority, or

    (b)   a person who has parental responsibilities (within the meaning of section 1(3) of that Act) in relation to the protected person and with whom the protected person is allowed to live.

(13)   However, no person by whom the offence mentioned in section 44(2) is alleged to have been committed is, by virtue of subsections (9) to (12), an appropriate person for the purposes of this section.

(14)   In this section 'the appropriate recipient', in relation to a notice under subsection (6)(a), means—

    (a)   the person to whom the notice giving consent was given,

    (b)   (if different) the person by whom the matter in question was published, or

    (c)   any other person exercising, on behalf of the person mentioned in paragraph (b), any responsibility in relation to the publication of that matter;

and for this purpose 'person' includes a body of persons and a partnership.

51.   Offences committed by bodies corporate or Scottish partnerships

(1)   If an offence under section 49 committed by a body corporate is proved—

    (a)   to have been committed with the consent or connivance of, or

    (b)   to be attributable to any neglect on the part of,

an officer, the officer as well as the body corporate is guilty of the offence and liable to be proceeded against and punished accordingly.

(2)   In subsection (1) 'officer' means a director, manager, secretary or other similar officer of the body, or a person purporting to act in any such capacity.

(3)   If the affairs of a body corporate are managed by its members, 'director' in subsection (2) means a member of that body.

(4)   Where an offence under section 49 is committed by a Scottish partnership and is proved to have been committed with the consent or connivance of a partner, he as well as the partnership shall be guilty of the offence and shall be liable to be proceeded against and punished accordingly.

Supplementary

52.   Decisions as to public interest for purposes of Chapter IV

(1)   Where for the purposes of any provision of this Chapter it falls to a court to determine whether anything is (or, as the case may be, was) in the public interest, the court must have regard, in particular, to the matters referred to in subsection (2) (so far as relevant).

(2)   Those matters are—

   (a)   the interest in each of the following—

      (i)   the open reporting of crime,

      (ii)   the open reporting of matters relating to human health or safety, and

      (iii)   the prevention and exposure of miscarriages of justice;

   (b)   the welfare of any person in relation to whom the relevant restrictions imposed by or under this Chapter apply or would apply (or, as the case may be, applied); and

   (c)   any views expressed—

      (i)   by an appropriate person on behalf of a person within paragraph (b) who is under the age of 16 ('the protected person'), or

      (ii)   by a person within that paragraph who has attained that age.

(3)   In subsection (2) 'an appropriate person', in relation to the protected person, has the same meaning as it has for the purposes of section 50.

CHAPTER V
COMPETENCE OF WITNESSES AND CAPACITY TO BE SWORN

Competence of witnesses

53.   Competence of witnesses to give evidence

(1)   At every stage in criminal proceedings all persons are (whatever their age) competent to give evidence.

(2)   Subsection (1) has effect subject to subsections (3) and (4).

(3)   A person is not competent to give evidence in criminal proceedings if it appears to the court that he is not a person who is able to—

   (a)   understand questions put to him as a witness, and

   (b)   give answers to them which can be understood.

(4)   A person charged in criminal proceedings is not competent to give evidence in the proceedings for the prosecution (whether he is the only person, or is one of two or more persons, charged in the proceedings).

(5)   In subsection (4) the reference to a person charged in criminal proceedings does not include a person who is not, or is no longer, liable to be convicted of any

offence in the proceedings (whether as a result of pleading guilty or for any other reason).

54. Determining competence of witnesses

(1)   Any question whether a witness in criminal proceedings is competent to give evidence in the proceedings, whether raised—

    (a)   by a party to the proceedings, or

    (b)   by the court of its own motion,

shall be determined by the court in accordance with this section.

(2)   It is for the party calling the witness to satisfy the court that, on a balance of probabilities, the witness is competent to give evidence in the proceedings.

(3)   In determining the question mentioned in subsection (1) the court shall treat the witness as having the benefit of any directions under section 19 which the court has given, or proposes to give, in relation to the witness.

(4)   Any proceedings held for the determination of the question shall take place in the absence of the jury (if there is one).

(5)   Expert evidence may be received on the question.

(6)   Any questioning of the witness (where the court considers that necessary) shall be conducted by the court in the presence of the parties.

Giving of sworn or unsworn evidence

55. Determining whether witness to be sworn

(1)   Any question whether a witness in criminal proceedings may be sworn for the purpose of giving evidence on oath, whether raised—

    (a)   by a party to the proceedings, or

    (b)   by the court of its own motion,

shall be determined by the court in accordance with this section.

(2)   The witness may not be sworn for that purpose unless—

    (a)   he has attained the age of 14, and

    (b)   he has a sufficient appreciation of the solemnity of the occasion and of the particular responsibility to tell the truth which is involved in taking an oath.

(3)   The witness shall, if he is able to give intelligible testimony, be presumed to have a sufficient appreciation of those matters if no evidence tending to show the contrary is adduced (by any party).

(4)   If any such evidence is adduced, it is for the party seeking to have the witness sworn to satisfy the court that, on a balance of probabilities, the witness has attained the age of 14 and has a sufficient appreciation of the matters mentioned in subsection (2)(b).

(5)   Any proceedings held for the determination of the question mentioned in subsection (1) shall take place in the absence of the jury (if there is one).

(6)   Expert evidence may be received on the question.

(7)   Any questioning of the witness (where the court considers that necessary) shall be conducted by the court in the presence of the parties.

(8)   For the purposes of this section a person is able to give intelligible testimony if he is able to—

(a) understand questions put to him as a witness, and

(b) give answers to them which can be understood.

56. Reception of unsworn evidence

(1) Subsections (2) and (3) apply to a person (of any age) who—

(a) is competent to give evidence in criminal proceedings, but

(b) (by virtue of section 55(2)) is not permitted to be sworn for the purpose of giving evidence on oath in such proceedings.

(2) The evidence in criminal proceedings of a person to whom this subsection applies shall be given unsworn.

(3) A deposition of unsworn evidence given by a person to whom this subsection applies may be taken for the purposes of criminal proceedings as if that evidence had been given on oath.

(4) A court in criminal proceedings shall accordingly receive in evidence any evidence given unsworn in pursuance of subsection (2) or (3).

(5) Where a person ('the witness') who is competent to give evidence in criminal proceedings gives evidence in such proceedings unsworn, no conviction, verdict or finding in those proceedings shall be taken to be unsafe for the purposes of any of sections 2(1), 13(1) and 16(1) of the Criminal Appeal Act 1968 (grounds for allowing appeals) by reason only that it appears to the Court of Appeal that the witness was a person falling within section 55(2) (and should accordingly have given his evidence on oath).

57. Penalty for giving false unsworn evidence

(1) This section applies where a person gives unsworn evidence in criminal proceedings in pursuance of section 56(2) or (3).

(2) If such a person wilfully gives false evidence in such circumstances that, had the evidence been given on oath, he would have been guilty of perjury, he shall be guilty of an offence and liable on summary conviction to—

(a) imprisonment for a term not exceeding 6 months, or

(b) a fine not exceeding £1,000,

or both.

(3) In relation to a person under the age of 14, subsection (2) shall have effect as if for the words following 'on summary conviction' there were substituted 'to a fine not exceeding £250'.

CHAPTER VI
RESTRICTIONS ON USE OF EVIDENCE

Additional restrictions

58. Inferences from silence not permissible where no prior access to legal advice

(1) Sections 34 and 36 to 38 of the Criminal Justice and Public Order Act 1994 (inferences from accused's silence) shall be amended as follows.

(2) In section 34 (effect of accused's failure to mention facts when questioned or charged), after subsection (2) there shall be inserted—

'(2A) Where the accused was at an authorised place of detention at the time of the failure, subsections (1) and (2) above do not apply if he had not been allowed an opportunity to consult a solicitor prior to being questioned, charged or informed as mentioned in subsection (1) above.'

(3) In section 36 (effect of accused's failure or refusal to account for objects, substances or marks), after subsection (4) there shall be inserted—

'(4A) Where the accused was at an authorised place of detention at the time of the failure or refusal, subsections (1) and (2) above do not apply if he had not been allowed an opportunity to consult a solicitor prior to the request being made.'

(4) In section 37 (effect of accused's failure or refusal to account for presence at a particular place), after subsection (3) there shall be inserted—

'(3A) Where the accused was at an authorised place of detention at the time of the failure or refusal, subsections (1) and (2) do not apply if he had not been allowed an opportunity to consult a solicitor prior to the request being made.'

(5) In section 38 (interpretation), after subsection (2) there shall be inserted—

'(2A) In each of sections 34(2A), 36(4A) and 37(3A) 'authorised place of detention' means—

 (a) a police station; or

 (b) any other place prescribed for the purposes of that provision by order made by the Secretary of State;

and the power to make an order under this subsection shall be exercisable by statutory instrument which shall be subject to annulment in pursuance of a resolution of either House of Parliament.'

59. Restriction on use of answers etc. obtained under compulsion

Schedule 3, which amends enactments providing for the use of answers and statements given under compulsion so as to restrict in criminal proceedings their use in evidence against the persons giving them, shall have effect.

Removal of restriction

60. Removal of restriction on use of evidence from computer records

Section 69 of the Police and Criminal Evidence Act 1984 (evidence from computer records inadmissible unless conditions relating to proper use and operation of computer shown to be satisfied) shall cease to have effect.

CHAPTER VII

GENERAL

61. Application of Part II to service courts

(1) The Secretary of State may by order direct that any provision of—

 (a) Chapters I to III and V, or

 (b) sections 62, 63 and 65 so far as having effect for the purposes of any of those Chapters,

shall apply, subject to such modifications as he may specify, to any proceedings before a service court.

(2)   Chapter IV (and sections 62, 63 and 65 so far as having effect for the purposes of that Chapter) shall have effect for the purposes of proceedings before a service court subject to any modifications which the Secretary of State may by order specify.

(3)   The power to make an order under section 39 of the Criminal Justice and Public Order Act 1994 (power to apply sections 34 to 38 to the armed forces) in relation to any provision of sections 34 to 38 of that Act shall be exercisable in relation to any provision of those sections as amended by section 58 above.

62.   Meaning of 'sexual offence' and other references to offences

(1)   In this Part 'sexual offence' means—

(a)   rape or burglary with intent to rape;

(b)   an offence under any of sections 2 to 12 and 14 to 17 of the Sexual Offences Act 1956 (unlawful intercourse, indecent assault, forcible abduction etc.);

(c)   an offence under section 128 of the Mental Health Act 1959 (unlawful intercourse with person receiving treatment for mental disorder by member of hospital staff etc.);

(d)   an offence under section 1 of the Indecency with Children Act 1960 (indecent conduct towards child under 14);

(e)   an offence under section 54 of the Criminal Law Act 1977 (incitement of child under 16 to commit incest).

(2)   In this Part any reference (including a reference having effect by virtue of this subsection) to an offence of any description ('the substantive offence') is to be taken to include a reference to an offence which consists of attempting or conspiring to commit, or of aiding, abetting, counselling, procuring or inciting the commission of, the substantive offence.

63.   General interpretation etc. of Part II

(1)   In this Part (except where the context otherwise requires)—

'accused', in relation to any criminal proceedings, means any person charged with an offence to which the proceedings relate (whether or not he has been convicted);

'the complainant', in relation to any offence (or alleged offence), means a person against or in relation to whom the offence was (or is alleged to have been) committed;

'court' (except in Chapter IV or V or subsection (2)) means a magistrates' court, the Crown Court or the criminal division of the Court of Appeal;

'legal representative' means any authorised advocate or authorised litigator (as defined by section 119(1) of the Courts and Legal Services Act 1990);

'picture' includes a likeness however produced;

'the prosecutor' means any person acting as prosecutor, whether an individual or body;

'publication' includes any speech, writing, relevant programme or other communication in whatever form, which is addressed to the public at large or any section of the public (and for this purpose every relevant programme shall be taken to be so addressed), but does not include an indictment or other document prepared for use in particular legal proceedings;

'relevant programme' means a programme included in a programme service, within the meaning of the Broadcasting Act 1990;

'service court' means—

    (a)   a court-martial constituted under the Army Act 1955, the Air Force Act 1955 or the Naval Discipline Act 1957 or a disciplinary court constituted under section 52G of the Naval Discipline Act 1957,

    (b)   the Courts-Martial Appeal Court, or

    (c)   a Standing Civilian Court;

'video recording' means any recording, on any medium, from which a moving image may by any means be produced, and includes the accompanying sound-track;

'witness', in relation to any criminal proceedings, means any person called, or proposed to be called, to give evidence in the proceedings.

(2)   Nothing in this Part shall affect any power of a court to exclude evidence at its discretion (whether by preventing questions being put or otherwise) which is exercisable apart from this Part.

PART III

FINAL PROVISIONS

64. Regulations and orders

(1)   Any power of the Secretary of State to make any regulations or order under this Act shall be exercised by statutory instrument.

(2)   A statutory instrument containing any regulations or order under section 6(4) or 61(1) or (2) shall be subject to annulment in pursuance of a resolution of either House of Parliament.

(3)   No regulations or order shall be made under—

    (a)   section 2(3), 18(5), 42(2) or 44(5), or

    (b)   paragraph 13(8) of Schedule 1,

unless a draft of the regulations or order has been laid before, and approved by a resolution of, each House of Parliament.

(4)   Any regulations or order made by the Secretary of State under this Act may make different provision for different cases, circumstances or areas and may contain such incidental, supplemental, saving or transitional provisions as the Secretary of State thinks fit.

65. General supplementary provisions

(1)   Rules of court may make such provision as appears to the authority making them to be necessary or expedient for the purposes of this Act (and nothing in this Act shall be taken to affect the generality of any enactment conferring power to make such rules).

(2)   In this Act 'rules of court' means—

    (a)   Magistrates' Courts Rules;

    (b)   Crown Court Rules;

    (c)   Criminal Appeal Rules.

(3)   For the purposes of this Act the age of a person shall be taken to be that which it appears to the court to be after considering any available evidence.

66.   Corresponding provisions for Northern Ireland

(1)   An Order in Council under section 85 of the Northern Ireland Act 1998 (provision dealing with certain reserved matters) which contains a statement that it is made only for purposes corresponding to the purposes of any of the relevant provisions of this Act—

(a)   shall not be subject to the procedures set out in subsections (3) to (8) of that section; but

(b)   shall be subject to annulment in pursuance of a resolution of either House of Parliament.

(2)   In subsection (1) 'the relevant provisions of this Act' means—

(a)   Chapters I to III of Part II;

(b)   section 47;

(c)   sections 49 to 51 so far as having effect for the purposes of section 47;

(d)   Chapters V to VII of Part II (other than section 59); and

(e)   this Part.

(3)   Until the day appointed under section 3 of the Northern Ireland Act 1998 for the commencement of Parts II and III of that Act, this section shall have effect with the substitution for subsection (1) of the following—

'(1)   An Order in Council under paragraph 1(1)(b) of Schedule 1 to the Northern Ireland Act 1974 (legislation for Northern Ireland in the interim period) which contains a statement that it is made only for purposes corresponding to the purposes of any of the relevant provisions of this Act—

(a)   shall not be subject to paragraph 1(4) and (5) of that Schedule (affirmative resolution of both Houses of Parliament), but

(b)   shall be subject to annulment in pursuance of a resolution of either House of Parliament.'

67.   Minor, consequential and pre-consolidation amendments, repeals and transitional provisions

(1)   The minor and consequential amendments specified in Schedule 4 shall have effect.

(2)   Schedule 5 (which contains pre-consolidation amendments relating to youth justice) shall have effect.

(3)   The enactments specified in Schedule 6 (which include certain spent enactments) are repealed or revoked to the extent specified.

(4)   The transitional provisions and savings in Schedule 7 shall have effect.

68.   Short title, commencement and extent

(1)   This Act may be cited as the Youth Justice and Criminal Evidence Act 1999.

(2)   For the purposes of the Scotland Act 1998, any provision of this Act which extends to Scotland shall be taken to be a pre-commencement enactment within the meaning of that Act.

(3)   Subject to subsection (4), this Act shall not come into force until such day as the Secretary of State may by order appoint; and different days may be appointed for different purposes or different areas.

(4)   The following provisions come into force on the day on which this Act is passed—

(a)   section 6(4);

(b)   the provisions of Chapters I to IV of Part II for the purpose only of the exercise of any power to make rules of court;

(c)   section 40(1);

(d)   sections 58(5) and 61(2) for the purpose only of the exercise of any power to make an order;

(e)   section 61(1) and (3), sections 62 to 66 and this section.

(5)   Subject to subsections (6) to (9) this Act extends to England and Wales only.

(6)   Subject to subsection (9), the following provisions extend also to Scotland and Northern Ireland—

(a)   the provisions of Chapter IV of Part II and section 63 so far as having effect for the purposes of those provisions;

(b)   the provisions of paragraph 6 of Schedule 7 and paragraph 1 of that Schedule so far as having effect for the purposes of those provisions; and

(c)   sections 59, 61 and 64 and this section.

(7)   Paragraph 3(4) of Schedule 1 extends also to Scotland.

(8)   Section 66 extends to Northern Ireland only.

(9)   The extent of any amendment, repeal or revocation made by this Act is the same as that of the enactment amended, repealed or revoked, except that—

(a)   the amendments made by Schedule 2 in section 49 of the Children and Young Persons Act 1933 and in the Sexual Offences (Amendment) Act 1992 extend to England and Wales, Scotland and Northern Ireland;

(b)   the repeal by Schedule 6 of section 62 of the Criminal Procedure and Investigations Act 1996 does not extend to Northern Ireland.

(10)   The following provisions, namely—

(a)   Chapter IV of Part II, so far as it relates to proceedings before a service court (within the meaning of Part II), and

(b)   section 61,

apply to such proceedings wherever they may take place (whether in the United Kingdom or elsewhere).

SCHEDULES

Section 13   SCHEDULE 1
YOUTH OFFENDER PANELS: FURTHER COURT PROCEEDINGS

PART I
REFERRAL BACK TO APPROPRIATE COURT

Introductory

1.—(1)   This Part of this Schedule applies where a youth offender panel refers an offender back to the appropriate court under section 7(2), 10(2) or (3), 11(5), (8) or (10) or 12(4).

(2)   For the purposes of this Part of this Schedule and the provisions mentioned in sub-paragraph (1) the appropriate court is—

(a)   in the case of an offender under the age of 18 at the time when (in pursuance of the referral back) he first appears before the court, a youth court acting for the petty sessions area in which it appears to the youth offender panel that the offender resides or will reside; and

(b)   otherwise, a magistrates' court (other than a youth court) acting for that area.

Mode of referral back to court

2.   The panel shall make the referral by sending a report to the appropriate court explaining why the offender is being referred back to it.

Bringing the offender before the court

3.—(1)   Where the appropriate court receives such a report, the court shall cause the offender to appear before it.

(2)   For the purpose of securing the attendance of the offender before the court, a justice acting for the petty sessions area for which the court acts may—

(a)   issue a summons requiring the offender to appear at the place and time specified in it, or

(b)   if the report is substantiated on oath, issue a warrant for the offender's arrest.

(3)   Any summons or warrant issued under sub-paragraph (2) shall direct the offender to appear or be brought before the appropriate court.

(4)   Section 4 of the Summary Jurisdiction (Process) Act 1881 (execution of process of English courts in Scotland) shall apply to any process issued under sub-paragraph (2) as it applies to process issued under the Magistrates' Courts Act 1980.

Detention and remand of arrested offender

4.—(1)   Where the offender is arrested in pursuance of a warrant under paragraph 3(2) and cannot be brought immediately before the appropriate court—

(a)   the person in whose custody he is may make arrangements for his detention in a place of safety (within the meaning given by section 107(1) of the Children and Young Persons Act 1933) for a period of not more than 72 hours from the time of the arrest (and it shall be lawful for him to be detained in pursuance of the arrangements); and

(b)   that person shall within that period bring him before a court which—

(i)   if he is under the age of 18 when he is brought before the court, shall be a youth court, and

(ii)   if he has then attained that age, shall be a magistrates' court other than a youth court.

(2)   Sub-paragraphs (3) to (5) apply where the court before which the offender is brought under sub-paragraph (1)(b) ('the alternative court') is not the appropriate court.

(3)   The alternative court may direct that he is to be released forthwith or remand him.

(4)   Section 128 of the Magistrates' Courts Act 1980 (remand in custody or on bail) shall have effect where the alternative court has power under sub-paragraph (3) to remand the offender as if the court referred to in subsections (1)(a), (3), (4)(a) and (5) were the appropriate court.

(5)   That section shall have effect where the alternative court has power to so remand him, or the appropriate court has (by virtue of sub-paragraph (4)) power to further remand him, as if in subsection (1) there were inserted after paragraph (c) 'or

(d)   if he is under the age of 18, remand him to accommodation provided by or on behalf of a local authority (within the meaning of the Children Act 1989) and, if it does so, shall designate as the authority who are to receive him the local authority for the area in which it appears to the court that he resides or will reside;'.

Power of court where it upholds panel's decision

5.—(1)   If it is proved to the satisfaction of the appropriate court as regards any decision of the panel which resulted in the offender being referred back to the court—

(a)   that, so far as the decision relied on any finding of fact by the panel, the panel was entitled to make that finding in the circumstances, and

(b)   that, so far as the decision involved any exercise of discretion by the panel, the panel reasonably exercised that discretion in the circumstances,
the court may exercise the power conferred by sub-paragraph (2).

(2)   That power is a power to revoke the referral order (or each of the referral orders).

(3)   The revocation under sub-paragraph (2) of a referral order has the effect of revoking any related order under paragraph 11 or 12.

(4)   Where any order is revoked under sub-paragraph (2) or by virtue of sub-paragraph (3), the appropriate court may deal with the offender in accordance with sub-paragraph (5) for the offence in respect of which the revoked order was made.

(5)   In so dealing with the offender for such an offence, the appropriate court—

(a)   may deal with him in any manner in which (assuming section 1 had not applied) he could have been dealt with for that offence by the court which made the order; and

(b)   shall have regard to—

(i)   the circumstances of his referral back to the court; and

(ii)   where a contract has taken effect under Section 8 between the offender and the panel, the extent of his compliance with the terms of the contract.

(6)   The appropriate court may not exercise the powers conferred by sub-paragraph (2) or (4) unless the offender is present before it; but those powers are exercisable even if, in a case where a contract has taken effect under section 8, the period for which the contract has effect has expired (whether before or after the referral of the offender back to the court).

(7)   Where, in exercise of the powers conferred by sub-paragraph (4), the appropriate court deals with the offender for an offence by committing him to the Crown Court for sentence, sub-paragraph (5) applies in relation to his being dealt with by the Crown Court, but as if—
    (a)   the reference to the appropriate court were to the Crown Court; and
    (b)   the reference in paragraph (b)(i) to the court were to the appropriate court.

Appeal

6.   Where the court in exercise of the power conferred by paragraph 5(4) deals with the offender for an offence, the offender may appeal to the Crown Court against the sentence.

Court not revoking referral order or orders

7.—(1)   This paragraph applies—
    (a)   where the appropriate court decides that the matters mentioned in paragraphs (a) and (b) of paragraph 5(1) have not been proved to its satisfaction; or
    (b)   where, although by virtue of paragraph 5(1) the appropriate court—
      (i)   is able to exercise the power conferred by paragraph 5(2), or
      (ii)   would be able to do so if the offender were present before it,
the court (for any reason) decides not to exercise that power.

(2)   If either—
    (a)   no contract has taken effect under section 8 between the offender and the panel, or
    (b)   a contract has taken effect under that section but the period for which it has effect has not expired,
the offender shall continue to remain subject to the referral order (or orders) in all respects as if he had not been referred back to the court.

(3)   If—
    (a)   a contract had taken effect under section 8, but
    (b)   the period for which it has effect has expired (otherwise than by virtue of section 9(6)),
the court shall make an order declaring that the referral order (or each of the referral orders) is discharged.

Exception where court satisfied as to completion of contract

8.   If, in a case where the offender is referred back to the court under section 12(4), the court decides (contrary to the decision of the panel) that the offender's compliance with the terms of the contract has, or will have, been such as to justify the conclusion that he has satisfactorily completed the contract, the court shall make an order declaring that the referral order (or each of the referral orders) is discharged.

Discharge of extension orders

9.   The discharge under paragraph 7(3) or 8 of a referral order has the effect of discharging any related order under paragraph 11 or 12.

PART II
FURTHER CONVICTIONS DURING REFERRAL

Extension of referral for further offences

10.—(1) Paragraphs 11 and 12 apply where, at a time when an offender under the age of 18 is subject to referral, a youth court or other magistrates' court ('the relevant court') is dealing with him for an offence in relation to which paragraphs (a) to (c) of section 1(1) are applicable.

(2) But paragraphs 11 and 12 do not apply unless the offender's compliance period is less than 12 months.

Extension where further offences committed pre-referral

11. If—

(a) the occasion on which the offender was referred to the panel is the only other occasion on which it has fallen to a court in the United Kingdom to deal with the offender for any offence or offences, and

(b) the offender committed the offence mentioned in paragraph 10, and any associated offence, before he was referred to the panel,

the relevant court may sentence the offender for the offence by making an order extending his compliance period.

Extension where further offence committed after referral

12.—(1) If—

(a) paragraph 11(a) applies, but

(b) the offender committed the offence mentioned in paragraph 10, or any associated offence, after he was referred to the panel,

the relevant court may sentence the offender for the offence by making an order extending his compliance period, but only if the requirements of sub-paragraph (2) are complied with.

(2) Those requirements are that the court must—

(a) be satisfied, on the basis of a report made to it by the relevant body, that there are exceptional circumstances which indicate that, even though the offender has re-offended since being referred to the panel, extending his compliance period is likely to help prevent further re-offending by him; and

(b) state in open court that it is so satisfied and why it is.

(3) In sub-paragraph (2) 'the relevant body' means the panel to which the offender has been referred or, if no contract has yet taken effect between the offender and the panel under section 8, the specified team.

Provisions supplementary to paragraphs 11 and 12

13.—(1) An order under paragraph 11 or 12, or two or more orders under one or other of those paragraphs made in respect of associated offences, must not so extend the offender's compliance period as to cause it to exceed twelve months.

(2)   Sub-paragraphs (3) to (5) apply where the relevant court makes an order under paragraph 11 or 12 in respect of the offence mentioned in paragraph 10; but sub-paragraphs (3) to (5) do not affect the exercise of any power to deal with the offender conferred by paragraph 5 or 14.

(3)   The relevant court may not deal with the offender for that offence in any of the prohibited ways specified in section 4(4).

(4)   The relevant court—
  (a)   shall, in respect of any associated offence, either—
      (i)   sentence the offender by making an order under the same paragraph, or
      (ii)   make an order discharging him absolutely; and
  (b)   may not deal with the offender for any associated offence in any of those prohibited ways.

(5)   The relevant court may not, in connection with the conviction of the offender for the offence or any associated offence, make any such order as is mentioned in section 4(5).

(6)   For the purposes of paragraphs 11 and 12 any occasion on which the offender was discharged absolutely in respect of the offence, or each of the offences, for which he was being dealt with shall be disregarded.

(7)   Any occasion on which, in criminal proceedings in England and Wales or Northern Ireland, the offender was bound over to keep the peace or to be of good behaviour shall be regarded for those purposes as an occasion on which it fell to a court in the United Kingdom to deal with the offender for an offence.

(8)   The Secretary of State may by regulations make such amendments of paragraphs 10 to 12 and this paragraph as he considers appropriate for altering in any way the descriptions of offenders in the case of which an order extending the compliance period may be made; and subsection (4) of section 2 shall apply in relation to regulations under this sub-paragraph as it applies in relation to regulations under subsection (3) of that section.

Further convictions which lead to revocation of referral

14.—(1)   This paragraph applies where, at a time when an offender is subject to referral, a court in England and Wales deals with him for an offence (whether committed before or after he was referred to the panel) by making an order other than—
  (a)   an order under paragraph 11 or 12, or
  (b)   an order discharging him absolutely.

(2)   In such a case the order of the court shall have the effect of revoking—
  (a)   the referral order (or orders), and
  (b)   any related order or orders under paragraph 11 or 12.

(3)   Where any order is revoked by virtue of sub-paragraph (2), the court may, if it appears to the court that it would be in the interests of justice to do so, deal with the offender for the offence in respect of which the revoked order was made in any manner in which (assuming section 1 had not applied) he could have been dealt with for that offence by the court which made the order.

(4)   When dealing with the offender under sub-paragraph (3) the court shall, where a contract has taken effect between the offender and the panel under section 8, have regard to the extent of his compliance with the terms of the contract.

(5)   Where, in exercise of the powers conferred by sub-paragraph (3), a magistrates' court deals with the offender for an offence by committing him to the Crown Court for sentence, the Crown Court—

(a)   may deal with him for the offence in any manner in which (assuming section 1 had not applied) he could have been dealt with for that offence by the court which made the revoked order; and

(b)   shall, where a contract has taken effect as mentioned in sub-paragraph (4), have regard to the extent of his compliance with the terms of the contract.

Interpretation

15.—(1)   For the purposes of this Part of this Schedule an offender is for the time being subject to referral if—

(a)   a referral order has been made in respect of him and that order has not, or

(b)   two or more referral orders have been made in respect of him and any of those orders has not,

been discharged (whether by virtue of section 12(3) or under paragraph 7(3) or 8) or revoked (whether under paragraph 5(2) or by virtue of paragraph 14(2)).

(2)   In this Part of this Schedule 'compliance period', in relation to an offender who is for the time being subject to referral, means the period for which (in accordance with section 9) any youth offender contract taking effect in his case under section 8 has (or would have) effect.

Section 48   SCHEDULE 2
REPORTING RESTRICTIONS: MISCELLANEOUS AMENDMENTS

Children and Young Persons Act 1933 (c. 12)

1.   The Children and Young Persons Act 1933 has effect subject to the following amendments.

2.—(1)   In section 39 (power of court in any proceedings to restrict reporting about children and young persons concerned in the proceedings), after subsection (2) insert—

'(3)   In this section "proceedings" means proceedings other than criminal proceedings.'

(2)   Sub-paragraph (1) shall not affect the continued operation of section 39 in relation to any criminal proceedings instituted (within the meaning given by paragraph 1(2) of Schedule 7 to this Act) before the day on which sub-paragraph (1) comes into force.

3.—(1)   Section 49 (restrictions on reports of proceedings in which children or young persons concerned) is amended as follows.

(2)   For subsection (1) substitute—

'(1)   No matter relating to any child or young person concerned in proceedings to which this section applies shall while he is under the age of 18 be included in any publication if it is likely to lead members of the public to identify him as someone concerned in the proceedings.'

(3)   For subsection (3) substitute—

'(3)   In this section "publication" includes any speech, writing, relevant programme or other communication in whatever form, which is addressed to the public at large or any section of the public (and for this purpose every relevant programme shall be taken to be so addressed), but does not include an indictment or other document prepared for use in particular legal proceedings.

(3A)   The matters relating to a person in relation to which the restrictions imposed by subsection (1) above apply (if their inclusion in any publication is likely to have the result mentioned in that subsection) include in particular—

    (a)   his name,

    (b)   his address,

    (c)   the identity of any school or other educational establishment attended by him,

    (d)   the identity of any place of work, and

    (e)   any still or moving picture of him.'

(4)   In subsection (4), for the words from 'whether as being' onwards substitute 'if he is—

    (a)   a person against or in respect of whom the proceedings are taken, or

    (b)   a person called, or proposed to be called, to give evidence in the proceedings.'

(5)   In subsection (4A), for 'requirements of this section' substitute 'restrictions imposed by subsection (1) above'.

(6)   In subsection (8), after 'subsection' insert '(4A) or'.

(7)   For subsection (9) substitute—

'(9)   If a publication includes any matter in contravention of subsection (1) above, the following persons shall be guilty of an offence and liable on summary conviction to a fine not exceeding level 5 on the standard scale—

    (a)   where the publication is a newspaper or periodical, any proprietor, any editor and any publisher of the newspaper or periodical;

    (b)   where the publication is a relevant programme—

        (i)   any body corporate or Scottish partnership engaged in providing the programme service in which the programme is included; and

        (ii)   any person having functions in relation to the programme corresponding to those of an editor of a newspaper;

    (c)   in the case of any other publication, any person publishing it.

(9A)   Where a person is charged with an offence under subsection (9) above it shall be a defence to prove that at the time of the alleged offence he was not aware, and neither suspected nor had reason to suspect, that the publication included the matter in question.

(9B)   If an offence under subsection (9) above committed by a body corporate is proved—

(a)   to have been committed with the consent or connivance of, or

(b)   to be attributable to any neglect on the part of,

an officer, the officer as well as the body corporate is guilty of the offence and liable to be proceeded against and punished accordingly.

(9C)   In subsection (9B) above ''officer'' means a director, manager, secretary or other similar officer of the body, or a person purporting to act in any such capacity.

(9D)   If the affairs of a body corporate are managed by its members, ''director'' in subsection (9C) above means a member of that body.

(9E)   Where an offence under subsection (9) above is committed by a Scottish partnership and is proved to have been committed with the consent or connivance of a partner, he as well as the partnership shall be guilty of the offence and shall be liable to be proceeded against and punished accordingly.'

(8)   In subsection (11), for the definition of 'programme' and 'programme service' substitute—

''picture'' includes a likeness however produced;

''relevant programme'' means a programme included in a programme service, within the meaning of the Broadcasting Act 1990;'.

(9)   After subsection (11) insert—

'(12)   This section extends to England and Wales, Scotland and Northern Ireland, but no reference in this section to any court includes a court in Scotland.

(13)   In its application to Northern Ireland, this section has effect as if—

(a)   in subsection (1) for the reference to the age of 18 there were substituted a reference to the age of 17;

(b)   subsection (2)(c) and (d) were omitted;

(c)   in subsection (4A)—

(i)   in paragraph (d) for the reference to section 16(3) of the Criminal Justice Act 1982 there were substituted a reference to Article 50(3) of the Criminal Justice (Children) (Northern Ireland) Order 1998; and

(ii)   in paragraph (e) for the references to a detention and training order and to section 76(6)(b) of the Crime and Disorder Act 1998 there were substituted references to a juvenile justice centre order and to Article 40(2) of the Criminal Justice (Children) (Northern Ireland) Order 1998;

(d)   in subsection (5) for references to a court (other than the reference in paragraph (b)) there were substituted references to a court or the Secretary of State;

(e)   in subsection (7)—

(i)   for the references to the Director of Public Prosecutions there were substituted references to the Director of Public Prosecutions for Northern Ireland; and

(ii)   in paragraph (b) for the reference to any legal representative of the child or young person there were substituted a reference to any barrister or solicitor acting for the child or young person;

(f)   subsections (8) and (10) were omitted; and

(g)   in subsection (11)—

    (i)   the definition of 'legal representative' were omitted; and

    (ii)   for the references to section 31(1) of the Criminal Justice Act 1991 there were substituted references to Article 2(2) of the Criminal Justice (Northern Ireland) Order 1996.

(14)   References in this section to a young person concerned in proceedings are, where the proceedings are in a court in Northern Ireland, to a person who has attained the age of 14 but is under the age of 17.'

(10)   The amendments made by this paragraph do not apply to the inclusion of matter in a publication if—

(a)   where the publication is a relevant programme, it is transmitted, or

(b)   in the case of any other publication, it is published,

before the coming into force of this paragraph.

Sexual Offences (Amendment) Act 1976 (c. 82)

4.—(1)   The Sexual Offences (Amendment) Act 1976 has effect subject to the following amendments.

(2)   Omit sections 4 and 5 (which provide for the anonymity of complainants in rape etc. cases and are superseded by the amendments made by this Schedule to the Sexual Offences (Amendment) Act 1992).

(3)   In section 7(6) (extent), for the words after 'Scotland' substitute 'or Northern Ireland.'

Sexual Offences (Northern Ireland) Order 1978 (NI 15)

5.   In the Sexual Offences (Northern Ireland) Order 1978, omit Articles 6 and 7 (which provide for the anonymity of complainants in rape offence cases and are superseded by the amendments made by this Schedule to the Sexual Offences (Amendment) Act 1992).

Sexual Offences (Amendment) Act 1992 (c. 34)

6.   The Sexual Offences (Amendment) Act 1992 has effect subject to the following amendments.

7.—(1)   Section 1 (anonymity of victims of certain sexual offences) is amended as follows.

(2)   In subsection (1), for the words from 'neither the name' to the end of paragraph (b) substitute 'no matter relating to that person shall during that person's lifetime be included in any publication'.

(3)   In subsection (2), for the words after 'complainant's lifetime' substitute 'be included in any publication.'

(4)   For subsection (3) substitute—

'(3)   This section—

(a)   does not apply in relation to a person by virtue of subsection (1) at any time after a person has been accused of the offence, and

(b) in its application in relation to a person by virtue of subsection (2), has effect subject to any direction given under section 3.

(3A) The matters relating to a person in relation to which the restrictions imposed by subsection (1) or (2) apply (if their inclusion in any publication is likely to have the result mentioned in that subsection) include in particular—

(a) the person's name,

(b) the person's address,

(c) the identity of any school or other educational establishment attended by the person,

(d) the identity of any place of work, and

(e) any still or moving picture of the person.'

(5) In subsection (4), for 'publication or inclusion in a relevant programme' substitute 'inclusion in a publication'.

8.—(1) Section 2 (offences to which Act applies) is amended as follows.

(2) In subsection (1), after 'This Act applies to the following offences' insert 'against the law of England and Wales—

(aa) rape;

(ab) burglary with intent to rape;'.

(3) In subsection (1)(e), for '(a)' substitute '(aa)'.

(4) In subsection (1), after paragraph (g) insert—

'(h) aiding, abetting, counselling or procuring the commission of any of the offences mentioned in paragraphs (aa) to (e) and (g);'.

(5) In subsection (2), after paragraph (m) insert—

'(n) section 17 (abduction of woman by force).'

(6) After subsection (2) insert—

'(3) This Act applies to the following offences against the law of Northern Ireland—

(a) rape;

(b) burglary with intent to rape;

(c) any offence under any of the following provisions of the Offences against the Person Act 1861—

(i) section 52 (indecent assault on a female);

(ii) section 53 so far as it relates to abduction of a woman against her will;

(iii) section 61 (buggery);

(iv) section 62 (attempt to commit buggery, assault with intent to commit buggery or indecent assault on a male);

(d) any offence under any of the following provisions of the Criminal Law Amendment Act 1885—

(i) section 3 (procuring unlawful carnal knowledge of woman by threats, false pretences or administering drugs);

(ii) section 4 (unlawful carnal knowledge, or attempted unlawful carnal knowledge, of a girl under 14);

(iii)   section 5 (unlawful carnal knowledge of a girl under 17);

(e)   any offence under any of the following provisions of the Punishment of Incest Act 1908—

(i)   section 1 (incest, attempted incest by males);

(ii)   section 2 (incest by females over 16);

(f)   any offence under section 22 of the Children and Young Persons Act (Northern Ireland) 1968 (indecent conduct towards child);

(g)   any offence under Article 9 of the Criminal Justice (Northern Ireland) Order 1980 (inciting girl under 16 to have incestuous sexual intercourse);

(h)   any offence under any of the following provisions of the Mental Health (Northern Ireland) Order 1986—

(i)   Article 122(1)(a) (unlawful sexual intercourse with a woman suffering from severe mental handicap);

(ii)   Article 122(1)(b) (procuring a woman suffering from severe mental handicap to have unlawful sexual intercourse);

(iii)   Article 123 (unlawful sexual intercourse by hospital staff, etc. with a person receiving treatment for mental disorder);

(i)   any attempt to commit any of the offences mentioned in paragraphs (a) to (h);

(j)   any conspiracy to commit any of those offences;

(k)   any incitement of another to commit any of those offences;

(l)   aiding, abetting, counselling or procuring the commission of any of the offences mentioned in paragraphs (a) to (i) and (k).'

9.—(1)   Section 3 (power to displace reporting restrictions under section 1) is amended as follows.

(2)   In subsection (6)(b) (meaning of 'judge'), after 'Crown Court' insert 'in England and Wales.'

(3)   After subsection (6) insert—

'(6A)   In its application to Northern Ireland, this section has effect as if—

(a)   in subsections (1) and (2) for any reference to the judge there were substituted a reference to the court; and

(b)   subsection (6) were omitted.'

10.   In section 4 (special rules for cases of incest or buggery), after subsection (7) insert—

'(8)   In its application to Northern Ireland, this section has effect as if—

(a)   subsection (1) were omitted;

(b)   for references to a section 10 offence there were substituted references to an offence under section 1 of the Punishment of Incest Act 1908 (incest by a man) or an attempt to commit that offence;

(c)   for references to a section 11 offence there were substituted references to an offence under section 2 of that Act (incest by a woman) or an attempt to commit that offence; and

(d)   for references to a section 12 offence there were substituted references to an offence under section 61 of the Offences against the Person Act 1861 (buggery) or an attempt to commit that offence.'

11.—(1)   Section 5 (offences) is amended as follows.

(2)   For subsection (1) substitute—

'(1)   If any matter is included in a publication in contravention of section 1, the following persons shall be guilty of an offence and liable on summary conviction to a fine not exceeding level 5 on the standard scale—

(a)   where the publication is a newspaper or periodical, any proprietor, any editor and any publisher of the newspaper or periodical;

(b)   where the publication is a relevant programme—

(i)   any body corporate or Scottish partnership engaged in providing the programme service in which the programme is included; and

(ii)   any person having functions in relation to the programme corresponding to those of an editor of a newspaper;

(c)   in the case of any other publication, any person publishing it.'

(3)   In subsection (2) (defence where victim consented to publication)—

(a)   for 'publication of any matter or the inclusion of any matter in a relevant programme' substitute 'inclusion of any matter in a publication', and

(b)   omit 'or programme'.

(4)   In subsection (3) (cases where written consent not a defence), at the end insert ', or that person was under the age of 16 at the time when it was given.'

(5)   In subsection (4) (Attorney General's consent to prosecution), at the end insert 'if the offence is alleged to have been committed in England and Wales or of the Attorney General for Northern Ireland if the offence is alleged to have been committed in Northern Ireland'.

(6)   In subsection (5) (defence for person unaware of inclusion of prohibited matter), for the words from 'or programme' onwards substitute 'included the matter in question'.

(7)   After subsection (5) insert—

'(5A)   Where—

(a)   a person is charged with an offence under this section, and

(b)   the offence relates to the inclusion of any matter in a publication in contravention of section 1(1),

it shall be a defence to prove that at the time of the alleged offence he was not aware, and neither suspected nor had reason to suspect, that the allegation in question had been made.'

(8)   After subsection (7) insert—

'(8)   Where an offence under this section is committed by a Scottish partnership and is proved to have been committed with the consent or connivance of a partner, he as well as the partnership shall be guilty of the offence and shall be liable to be proceeded against and punished accordingly.'

12.—(1)   Section 6 (interpretation) is amended as follows.

(2)   In subsection (1), omit the definition of 'written publication' (and the word 'and' preceding it) and after the definition of 'picture' insert—

'"publication" includes any speech, writing, relevant programme or other communication in whatever form, which is addressed to the public at large or any section of the public (and for this purpose every relevant programme shall be taken to be so addressed), but does not include an indictment or other document prepared for use in particular legal proceedings;'.

(3)   In subsection (2A) (victims of conspiracy etc.), for the words from 'accusation that' to 'committed, the' substitute 'accusation—

(a)   that an offence of conspiracy or incitement of another to commit an offence mentioned in section 2(1)(aa) to (d) or (3)(a) to (h) has been committed, or

(b)   that an offence of aiding, abetting, counselling or procuring the commission of an offence of incitement of another to commit an offence mentioned in section 2(1)(aa) to (d) or (3)(a) to (h) has been committed, the'.

(4)   In subsection (3) (time when person is accused of an offence), in paragraph (a) after 'is laid' insert ', or (in Northern Ireland) a complaint is made,'.

13.—(1)   Section 7 (application of Act to courts-martial) is amended as follows.

(2)   In subsection (1) (Act to apply with modifications where in pursuance of armed forces law a person is charged with an offence to which the Act applies), after 'applies' insert 'by virtue of section 2(1)'.

(3)   In subsection (2) (modifications with which Act applies to courts-martial)—

(a)   omit paragraph (b);

(b)   for paragraph (c) substitute—

'(c)   in section 3(1) any reference to a judge, in relation to the person charged with the offence, shall be read as a reference to the judge advocate appointed to conduct proceedings under section 3(1) relating to the offence (whether or not also appointed to conduct other preliminary proceedings relating to the offence);';

(c)   in paragraph (d), for 'court' substitute 'judge advocate appointed to be a member of the court-martial'; and

(d)   omit paragraph (e) except for the word 'and' at the end.

14.   For section 8(6) and (7) (application of Act to Scotland and to Northern Ireland) substitute—

'(6)   This Act extends to England and Wales, Scotland and Northern Ireland.

(7)   This Act, so far as it relates to proceedings before a court-martial or the Courts-Martial Appeal Court, applies to such proceedings wherever they may take place (whether in the United Kingdom or elsewhere).'

Criminal Justice (Northern Ireland) Order 1994 (NI 15)

15.   In the Criminal Justice (Northern Ireland) Order 1994, omit Articles 19 to 24 (which provide for the anonymity of victims of certain sexual offences and are

superseded by the amendments made by this Schedule to the Sexual Offences (Amendment) Act 1992).

Section 59   SCHEDULE 3
RESTRICTION ON USE OF ANSWERS ETC. OBTAINED
UNDER COMPULSION

Insurance Companies Act 1982 (c. 50)

1.   The Insurance Companies Act 1982 is amended as follows.

2.   In section 43A (general investigations into insurance companies), after subsection (5) (use of statements made under the section) add—

'(6)   However, in criminal proceedings in which that person is charged with an offence to which this subsection applies—

(a)   no evidence relating to the statement may be adduced, and

(b)   no question relating to it may be asked,

by or on behalf of the prosecution, unless evidence relating to it is adduced, or a question relating to it is asked, in the proceedings by or on behalf of that person.

(7)   Subsection (6) above applies to any offence other than—

(a)   an offence under section 71(1)(b) or (3) below;

(b)   an offence under section 5 of the Perjury Act 1911 (false statements made otherwise than on oath);

(c)   an offence under section 44(2) of the Criminal Law (Consolidation) (Scotland) Act 1995 (false statements made otherwise than on oath); or

(d)   an offence under Article 10 of the Perjury (Northern Ireland) Order 1979 (false statements made otherwise than on oath).'

3.   In section 44 (obtaining information and documents from companies), after subsection (5) (use of statements made under the section) insert—

'(5A)   However, in criminal proceedings in which that person is charged with an offence to which this subsection applies—

(a)   no evidence relating to the statement may be adduced, and

(b)   no question relating to it may be asked,

by or on behalf of the prosecution, unless evidence relating to it is adduced, or a question relating to it is asked, in the proceedings by or on behalf of that person.

(5B)   Subsection (5A) above applies to any offence other than—

(a)   an offence under section 71(1)(b), (3) or (4) below;

(b)   an offence under section 5 of the Perjury Act 1911 (false statements made otherwise than on oath);

(c)   an offence under section 44(2) of the Criminal Law (Consolidation) (Scotland) Act 1995 (false statements made otherwise than on oath); or

(d)   an offence under Article 10 of the Perjury (Northern Ireland) Order 1979 (false statements made otherwise than on oath).'

Companies Act 1985 (c. 6)

4.   The Companies Act 1985 is amended as follows.

5.   In section 434 (production of documents and evidence to inspectors conducting investigations into companies), after subsection (5) (use of answers given to inspectors) insert—

'(5A)   However, in criminal proceedings in which that person is charged with an offence to which this subsection applies—

(a)   no evidence relating to the answer may be adduced, and

(b)   no question relating to it may be asked,

by or on behalf of the prosecution, unless evidence relating to it is adduced, or a question relating to it is asked, in the proceedings by or on behalf of that person.

(5B)   Subsection (5A) applies to any offence other than—

(a)   an offence under section 2 or 5 of the Perjury Act 1911 (false statements made on oath otherwise than in judicial proceedings or made otherwise than on oath); or

(b)   an offence under section 44(1) or (2) of the Criminal Law (Consolidation) (Scotland) Act 1995 (false statements made on oath or otherwise than on oath).'

6.   In section 447 (production of company documents to Secretary of State), after subsection (8) (use of statements made under the section) insert—

'(8A)   However, in criminal proceedings in which that person is charged with an offence to which this subsection applies—

(a)   no evidence relating to the statement may be adduced, and

(b)   no question relating to it may be asked,

by or on behalf of the prosecution, unless evidence relating to it is adduced, or a question relating to it is asked, in the proceedings by or on behalf of that person.

(8B)   Subsection (8A) applies to any offence other than—

(a)   an offence under subsection (6) or section 451;

(b)   an offence under section 5 of the Perjury Act 1911 (false statements made otherwise than on oath); or

(c)   an offence under section 44(2) of the Criminal Law (Consolidation) (Scotland) Act 1995 (false statements made otherwise than on oath).'

Insolvency Act 1986 (c. 45)

7.—(1)   Section 433 of the Insolvency Act 1986 (admissibility in evidence of statements of affairs etc.) is amended as follows.

(2)   That section is renumbered as subsection (1) of that section.

(3)   After that subsection insert—

'(2)   However, in criminal proceedings in which any such person is charged with an offence to which this subsection applies—

(a)   no evidence relating to the statement may be adduced, and

(b)   no question relating to it may be asked,

by or on behalf of the prosecution, unless evidence relating to it is adduced, or a question relating to it is asked, in the proceedings by or on behalf of that person.

(3)   Subsection (2) applies to any offence other than—

(a) an offence under section 22(6), 47(6), 48(8), 66(6), 67(8), 95(8), 98(6), 99(3)(a), 131(7), 192(2), 208(1)(a) or (d) or (2), 210, 235(5), 353(1), 354(1)(b) or (3) or 356(1) or (2)(a) or (b) or paragraph 4(3)(a) of Schedule 7;

(b) an offence which is—

(i) created by rules made under this Act, and

(ii) designated for the purposes of this subsection by such rules or by regulations made by the Secretary of State;

(c) an offence which is—

(i) created by regulations made under any such rules, and

(ii) designated for the purposes of this subsection by such regulations;

(d) an offence under section 1, 2 or 5 of the Perjury Act 1911 (false statements made on oath or made otherwise than on oath); or

(e) an offence under section 44(1) or (2) of the Criminal Law (Consolidation) (Scotland) Act 1995 (false statements made on oath or otherwise than on oath).

(4) Regulations under subsection (3)(b)(ii) shall be made by statutory instrument and, after being made, shall be laid before each House of Parliament.'

Company Directors Disqualification Act 1986 (c. 46)

8.—(1) Section 20 of the Company Directors Disqualification Act 1986 (admissibility in evidence of statements) is amended as follows.

(2) That section is renumbered as subsection (1) of that section.

(3) After that subsection insert—

'(2) However, in criminal proceedings in which any such person is charged with an offence to which this subsection applies—

(a) no evidence relating to the statement may be adduced, and

(b) no question relating to it may be asked,

by or on behalf of the prosecution, unless evidence relating to it is adduced, or a question relating to it is asked, in the proceedings by or on behalf of that person.

(3) Subsection (2) applies to any offence other than—

(a) an offence which is—

(i) created by rules made for the purposes of this Act under the Insolvency Act, and

(ii) designated for the purposes of this subsection by such rules or by regulations made by the Secretary of State;

(b) an offence which is—

(i) created by regulations made under any such rules, and

(ii) designated for the purposes of this subsection by such regulations;

(c) an offence under section 5 of the Perjury Act 1911 (false statements made otherwise than on oath); or

(d) an offence under section 44(2) of the Criminal Law (Consolidation) (Scotland) Act 1995 (false statements made otherwise than on oath).

(4) Regulations under subsection (3)(a)(ii) shall be made by statutory instrument and, after being made, shall be laid before each House of Parliament.'

Building Societies Act 1986 (c. 53)

9.   In section 57 of the Building Societies Act 1986 (use of answers given to inspectors conducting investigations into building societies), after subsection (5) (use of answers given to inspectors) insert—

'(5A)   However, in criminal proceedings in which that person is charged with an offence to which this subsection applies—

(a)   no evidence relating to the answer may be adduced, and

(b)   no question relating to it may be asked,

by or on behalf of the prosecution, unless evidence relating to it is adduced, or a question relating to it is asked, in the proceedings by or on behalf of that person.

(5B)   Subsection (5A) above applies to any offence other than—

(a)   an offence under section 2 or 5 of the Perjury Act 1911 (false statements made on oath otherwise than in judicial proceedings or made otherwise than on oath);

(b)   an offence under section 44(1) or (2) of the Criminal Law (Consolidation) (Scotland) Act 1995 (false statements made on oath or otherwise than on oath); or

(c)   an offence under Article 7 or 10 of the Perjury (Northern Ireland) Order 1979 (false statements made on oath otherwise than in judicial proceedings or made otherwise than on oath).'

Financial Services Act 1986 (c. 60)

10.   The Financial Services Act 1986 is amended as follows.

11.   In section 105 (powers of Secretary of State to investigate affairs of person carrying on investment business), after subsection (5) (use of statements made under the section) insert—

'(5A)   However, in criminal proceedings in which that person is charged with an offence to which this subsection applies—

(a)   no evidence relating to the statement may be adduced, and

(b)   no question relating to it may be asked.

by or on behalf of the prosecution, unless evidence relating to it is adduced, or a question relating to it is asked, in the proceedings by or on behalf of that person.

(5B)   Subsection (5A) above applies to any offence other than—

(a)   an offence under subsection (10) or section 200(1) below;

(b)   an offence under section 5 of the Perjury Act 1911 (false statements made otherwise than on oath);

(c)   an offence under section 44(2) of the Criminal Law (Consolidation) (Scotland) Act 1995 (false statements made otherwise than on oath); or

(d)   an offence under Article 10 of the Perjury (Northern Ireland) Order 1979 (false statements made otherwise than on oath).'

12.   In section 177 (investigations into insider dealing), after subsection (6) (use of statements made under the section) insert—

'(6A)   However, in criminal proceedings in which that person is charged with an offence to which this subsection applies—

(a)   no evidence relating to the statement may be adduced, and

(b)   no question relating to it may be asked,

by or on behalf of the prosecution, unless evidence relating to it is adduced, or a question relating to it is asked, in the proceedings by or on behalf of that person.

(6B)   Subsection (6A) above applies to any offence other than—

(a)   an offence under section 200(1) below;

(b)   an offence under section 2 or 5 of the Perjury Act 1911 (false statements made on oath otherwise than in judicial proceedings or made otherwise than on oath);

(c)   an offence under section 44(1) or (2) of the Criminal Law (Consolidation) (Scotland) Act 1995 (false statements made on oath or otherwise than on oath); or

(d)   an offence under Article 7 or 10 of the Perjury (Northern Ireland) Order 1979 (false statements made on oath otherwise than in judicial proceedings or made otherwise than on oath).'

Companies (Northern Ireland) Order 1986 (NI 6)

13.   The Companies (Northern Ireland) Order 1986 is amended as follows.

14.   In Article 427 (production of documents and evidence to inspectors conducting investigations into companies), after paragraph (5) (use of answers given to inspectors) insert—

'(5A)   However, in criminal proceedings in which that person is charged with an offence to which this paragraph applies—

(a)   no evidence relating to the answer may be adduced, and

(b)   no question relating to it may be asked,

by or on behalf of the prosecution, unless evidence relating to it is adduced, or a question relating to it is asked, in the proceedings by or on behalf of that person.

(5B)   Paragraph (5A) applies to any offence other than an offence under Article 7 or 10 of the Perjury (Northern Ireland) Order 1979 (false statements made on oath otherwise than in judicial proceedings or made otherwise than on oath).'

15.   In Article 440 (production of company documents to Department), after paragraph (8) (use of statements made under the Article) insert—

'(8A)   However, in criminal proceedings in which that person is charged with an offence to which this paragraph applies—

(a)   no evidence relating to the statement may be adduced, and

(b)   no question relating to it may be asked,

by or on behalf of the prosecution, unless evidence relating to it is adduced, or a question relating to it is asked, in the proceedings by or on behalf of that person.

(8B)   Paragraph (8A) applies to any offence other than—

(a)   an offence under paragraph (6) or Article 444; or

(b)   an offence under Article 10 of the Perjury (Northern Ireland) Order 1979 (false statements made otherwise than on oath).'

Banking Act 1987 (c. 22)

16.   The Banking Act 1987 is amended as follows.

17.   In section 39 (power of Financial Services Authority to obtain information etc. from authorised institutions), after subsection (12) (use of statements made under the section) insert—

'(12A)   However, in criminal proceedings in which that person is charged with an offence to which this subsection applies—

   (a)   no evidence relating to the statement may be adduced, and

   (b)   no question relating to it may be asked,

by or on behalf of the prosecution, unless evidence relating to it is adduced, or a question relating to it is asked, in the proceedings by or on behalf of that person.

   (12B)   Subsection (12A) above applies to any offence other than—

   (a)   an offence under subsection (11) above or section 94(1)(a) below;

   (b)   an offence under section 5 of the Perjury Act 1911 (false statements made otherwise than on oath);

   (c)   an offence under section 44(2) of the Criminal Law (Consolidation) (Scotland) Act 1995 (false statements made otherwise than on oath); or

   (d)   an offence under Article 10 of the Perjury (Northern Ireland) Order 1979 (false statements made otherwise than on oath).'

18.   In section 41 (investigations into authorised institutions by Financial Services Authority), after subsection (10) (use of statements made under the section) insert—

'(10A)   However, in criminal proceedings in which that person is charged with an offence to which this subsection applies—

   (a)   no evidence relating to the statement may be adduced, and

   (b)   no question relating to it may be asked,

by or on behalf of the prosecution, unless evidence relating to it is adduced, or a question relating to it is asked, in the proceedings by or on behalf of that person.

   (10B)   Subsection (10A) above applies to any offence other than—

   (a)   an offence under subsection (9)(c) above or section 94(4) below;

   (b)   an offence under section 5 of the Perjury Act 1911 (false statements made otherwise than on oath);

   (c)   an offence under section 44(2) of the Criminal Law (Consolidation) (Scotland) Act 1995 (false statements made otherwise than on oath); or

   (d)   an offence under Article 10 of the Perjury (Northern Ireland) Order 1979 (false statements made otherwise than on oath).'

19.   In section 42 (investigations by Financial Services Authority into suspected contraventions of sections 3 and 35), after subsection (5) (use of statements made under the section) insert—

'(5A)   However, in criminal proceedings in which that person is charged with an offence to which this subsection applies—

   (a)   no evidence relating to the statement may be adduced, and

(b)   no question relating to it may be asked,
by or on behalf of the prosecution, unless evidence relating to it is adduced, or a
question relating to it is asked, in the proceedings by or on behalf of that person.
(5B)   Subsection (5A) above applies to any offence other than—
(a)   an offence under subsection (4) above or section 94(1)(a) below;
(b)   an offence under section 5 of the Perjury Act 1911 (false statements
made otherwise than on oath);
(c)   an offence under section 44(2) of the Criminal Law (Consolidation)
(Scotland) Act 1995 (false statements made otherwise than on oath); or
(d)   an offence under Article 10 of the Perjury (Northern Ireland) Order 1979
(false statements made otherwise than on oath).'

Criminal Justice Act 1987 (c. 38)

20.   After subsection (8) of section 2 of the Criminal Justice Act 1987 (use of
statements made in response to requirements imposed by the Director of the Serious
Fraud Office) insert—
'(8AA)   However, the statement may not be used against that person by virtue
of paragraph (b) of subsection (8) unless evidence relating to it is adduced, or a
question relating to it is asked, by or on behalf of that person in the proceedings
arising out of the prosecution.'

Companies Act 1989 (c. 40)

21.   In section 83 (powers exercisable for purposes of assisting an overseas
regulatory authority), after subsection (6) (use of statements made under the section)
insert—
'(6A)   However, in criminal proceedings in which that person is charged with
an offence to which this subsection applies—
(a)   no evidence relating to the statement may be adduced, and
(b)   no question relating to it may be asked,
by or on behalf of the prosecution, unless evidence relating to it is adduced, or a
question relating to it is asked, in the proceedings by or on behalf of that person.
(6B)   Subsection (6A) applies to any offence other than—
(a)   an offence under section 85;
(b)   an offence under section 2 or 5 of the Perjury Act 1911 (false statements
made on oath otherwise than in judicial proceedings or made otherwise than on
oath);
(c)   an offence under section 44(1) or (2) of the Criminal Law (Consolidation) (Scotland) Act 1995 (false statements made on oath or otherwise than on
oath); or
(d)   an offence under Article 7 or 10 of the Perjury (Northern Ireland) Order
1979 (false statements made on oath otherwise than in judicial proceedings or
made otherwise than on oath).'

Companies (Northern Ireland) Order 1989 (NI 18)

22.—(1)   Article 23 of the Companies (Northern Ireland) Order 1989 (admissibility in evidence of statements) is amended as follows.

(2)   That Article is renumbered as paragraph (1) of that Article.

(3)   After that paragraph insert—

'(2)   However, in criminal proceedings in which any such person is charged with an offence to which this paragraph applies—

(a)   no evidence relating to the statement may be adduced, and

(b)   no question relating to it may be asked,

by or on behalf of the prosecution, unless evidence relating to it is adduced, or a question relating to it is asked, in the proceedings by or on behalf of that person.

(3)   Paragraph (2) applies to any offence other than—

(a)   an offence which is—

(i)   created by rules made for the purposes of this Order under the Insolvency Order, and

(ii)   designated for the purposes of this paragraph by such rules or by regulations;

(b)   an offence which is—

(i)   created by regulations made under any such rules, and

(ii)   designated for the purposes of this paragraph by such regulations; or

(c)   an offence under Article 10 of the Perjury (Northern Ireland) Order 1979 (false statements made otherwise than on oath).

(4)   Regulations under paragraph (3)(a)(ii) shall after being made be laid before the Assembly.'

Insolvency (Northern Ireland) Order 1989 (NI 19)

23.—(1)   Article 375 of the Insolvency (Northern Ireland) Order 1989 (admissibility in evidence of statements of affairs etc.) is amended as follows.

(2)   That Article is renumbered as paragraph (1) of that Article.

(3)   After that paragraph insert—

'(2)   However, in criminal proceedings in which any such person is charged with an offence to which this paragraph applies—

(a)   no evidence relating to the statement may be adduced, and

(b)   no question relating to it may be asked,

by or on behalf of the prosecution, unless evidence relating to it is adduced, or a question relating to it is asked, in the proceedings by or on behalf of that person.

(3)   Paragraph (2) applies to any offence other than—

(a)   an offence under Article 34(6), 57(6), 58(8), 81(7), 84(5), 85(3)(a), 111(7), 162(2), 172(1)(a) or (d) or (2), 174, 199(5), 324(1), 325(1)(b) or (5) or 327(1) or (3)(a) or (b);

(b)   an offence which is—

(i)   created by rules made under this Order, and

(ii)   designated for the purposes of this paragraph by such rules or by regulations;
   (c)   an offence which is—
      (i)   created by regulations made under any such rules, and
      (ii)   designated for the purposes of this paragraph by such regulations; or
   (d)   an offence under Article 3, 7 or 10 of the Perjury (Northern Ireland) Order 1979 (false statements made on oath or made otherwise than on oath).
   (4)   Regulations under paragraph (3)(b)(ii) shall after being made be laid before the Assembly.'

Friendly Societies Act 1992 (c. 40)

24.   In section 67 of the Friendly Societies Act 1992 (supplementary provisions about inspections carried out at the behest of the Friendly Societies Commission), after subsection (5) (use of statements made under the section) insert—
   '(5A)   However, in criminal proceedings in which that person is charged with an offence to which this subsection applies—
   (a)   no evidence relating to the statement may be adduced, and
   (b)   no question relating to it may be asked,
by or on behalf of the prosecution, unless evidence relating to it is adduced, or a question relating to it is asked, in the proceedings by or on behalf of that person.
   (5B)   Subsection (5A) above applies to any offence other than—
   (a)   an offence under section 2 or 5 of the Perjury Act 1911 (false statements made on oath otherwise than in judicial proceedings or made otherwise than on oath);
   (b)   an offence under section 44(1) or (2) of the Criminal Law (Consolidation) (Scotland) Act 1995 (false statements made on oath or otherwise than on oath); or
   (c)   an offence under Article 7 or 10 of the Perjury (Northern Ireland) Order 1979 (false statements made on oath otherwise than in judicial proceedings or made otherwise than on oath).'

Criminal Law (Consolidation) (Scotland) Act 1995 (c. 39)

25.   After subsection (5) of section 28 of the Criminal Law (Consolidation) (Scotland) Act 1995 (use of statements made in response to requirements imposed by a nominated officer) insert—
   '(5A)   However, the statement may not be used against that person by virtue of paragraph (b) of subsection (5) unless evidence relating to it is adduced, or a question relating to it is asked, by or on behalf of that person in the proceedings arising out of the prosecution.'

Proceeds of Crime (Northern Ireland) Order 1996 (NI 9)

26.   In paragraph 6 of Schedule 2 to the Proceeds of Crime (Northern Ireland) Order 1996 (admissibility of evidence), for sub-paragraph (b) substitute—

'(b)   on his prosecution for some other offence where evidence relating to any such answer or information is adduced, or a question relating to it is asked, by or on behalf of that person; or'.

Section 67   SCHEDULE 4
                  MINOR AND CONSEQUENTIAL AMENDMENTS

Criminal Evidence Act 1898 (c. 36)

1.—(1)   Section 1 of the Criminal Evidence Act 1898 (competence of accused as witness for the defence) is amended as follows.

(2)   Omit the words from the beginning to 'Provided as follows:—'.

(3)   In paragraph (a) of the proviso—

(a)   for 'so charged' substitute 'charged in criminal proceedings'; and

(b)   for 'in pursuance of this Act' substitute 'in the proceedings'.

(4)   In paragraph (e) of the proviso—

(a)   for 'and being a witness in pursuance of this Act' substitute 'in criminal proceedings who is called as a witness in the proceedings'; and

(b)   for 'the offence charged' substitute 'any offence with which he is charged in the proceedings'.

(5)   In paragraph (f) of the proviso—

(a)   for 'and called as a witness in pursuance of this Act' substitute 'in criminal proceedings who is called as a witness in the proceedings';

(b)   for 'that wherewith' substitute 'one with which'; and

(c)   in sub-paragraph (i), for 'the offence wherewith' substitute 'an offence with which'.

(6)   In paragraph (g) of the proviso, for 'called as a witness in pursuance of this Act' substitute 'charged in criminal proceedings who is called as a witness in the proceedings'.

(7)   Paragraphs (a), (e), (f) and (g) of the proviso shall be respectively numbered as subsections (1), (2), (3) and (4) of the section.

Children and Young Persons Act 1933 (c. 12)

2.—(1)   The Children and Young Persons Act 1933 has effect subject to the following amendments.

(2)   In section 37(1) (power to clear court, where child or young person giving evidence, of persons other than bona fide representatives of newspapers or news agencies), for 'newspaper or news agency' substitute 'news gathering or reporting organisation'.

(3)   In section 47(2)(c) (bona fide representatives of newspapers or news agencies entitled to be present at sitting of youth court), for 'newspapers or news agencies' substitute 'news gathering or reporting organisations'.

Children and Young Persons Act 1963 (c. 37)

3.   In section 57(3) of the Children and Young Persons Act 1963 (which provides for sections 39 and 49 of the Children and Young Persons Act 1933 to extend to Scotland), for 'sections 39 and 49', in both places, substitute 'section 39'.

Criminal Appeal Act 1968 (c. 19)

4.—(1)   The Criminal Appeal Act 1968 has effect subject to the following amendments.

(2)   In section 10(2)(b) (appeal by offender who is further dealt with by the Crown Court), after 'conditional discharge' insert ', a referral order within the meaning of Part I of the Youth Justice and Criminal Evidence Act 1999 (referral to youth offender panel)'.

(3)   In section 31(1)(b) (power to give directions exercisable by single judge), for 'section 4(4) of the Sexual Offences (Amendment) Act 1976' substitute 'section 3(4) of the Sexual Offences (Amendment) Act 1992'.

Children and Young Persons Act 1969 (c. 54)

5.   In section 7(8) of the Children and Young Persons Act 1969 (remission to youth court for sentence), for the words 'unless the court' substitute 'unless the case falls within subsection (8A) or (8B) of this section.

(8A)   The case falls within this subsection if the court would, were it not to so remit the case, be required by section 1(2) of the Youth Justice and Criminal Evidence Act 1999 to refer him to a youth offender panel (in which event the court may, but need not, so remit the case).

(8B)   The case falls within this subsection if the court would not be so required to refer him to such a panel in the event of its not so remitting the case and'.

Rehabilitation of Offenders Act 1974 (c. 53)

6.—(1)   Section 5 of the Rehabilitation of Offenders Act 1974 is amended as follows.

(2)   In Table A in subsection (2), in the entry relating to fines or other sentences subject to rehabilitation under that Act, for ', (4A) to (8)' substitute 'to (8)'.

(3)   After subsection (4A) insert—

'(4B)   Where in respect of a conviction a referral order (within the meaning of Part I of the Youth Justice and Criminal Evidence Act 1999) is made in respect of the person convicted, the rehabilitation period applicable to the sentence shall be—

(a)   if a youth offender contract takes effect under section 8 of that Act between him and a youth offender panel, the period beginning with the date of conviction and ending on the date when (in accordance with section 9 of that Act) the contract ceases to have effect;

(b)   if no such contract so takes effect, the period beginning with the date of conviction and having the same length as the period for which such a contract would (ignoring any order under paragraph 11 or 12 of Schedule 1 to that Act) have had effect had one so taken effect.

(4C)   Where in respect of a conviction an order is made in respect of the person convicted under paragraph 11 or 12 of Schedule 1 to the Youth Justice and Criminal Evidence Act 1999 (extension of period for which youth offender contract has effect), the rehabilitation period applicable to the sentence shall be—

(a)   if a youth offender contract takes effect under section 8 of that Act between the offender and a youth offender panel, the period beginning with the date of conviction and ending on the date when (in accordance with section 9 of that Act) the contract ceases to have effect;

(b)   if no such contract so takes effect, the period beginning with the date of conviction and having the same length as the period for which, in accordance with the order, such a contract would have had effect had one so taken effect.'

Magistrates' Courts Act 1980 (c. 43)

7.   The Magistrates' Courts Act 1980 has effect subject to the following amendments.

8.   In section 125(4)(c) (warrants which constable may execute when not in his possession), after sub-paragraph (iv) insert 'and

(v)   paragraph 3(2) of Schedule 1 to the Youth Justice and Criminal Evidence Act 1999 (offender referred to court by youth offender panel).'

9.   In section 126 (execution of warrants in Channel Islands and Isle of Man under section 13 of the Indictable Offences Act 1848), after paragraph (e) insert 'and

(f)   warrants of arrest issued under paragraph 3(2) of Schedule 1 to the Youth Justice and Criminal Evidence Act 1999 (offender referred to court by youth offender panel).'

Criminal Justice Act 1982 (c. 48)

10.   In section 72(1) of the Criminal Justice Act 1982 (accused to give evidence on oath), after 'if he gives evidence, he shall do so' insert '(subject to sections 55 and 56 of the Youth Justice and Criminal Evidence Act 1999)'.

Mental Health Act 1983 (c. 20)

11.   In section 37(8) of the Mental Health Act 1983 (combining hospital and guardianship orders with other orders), for the words from 'shall not' to 'which the court' substitute 'shall not—

(a)   pass sentence of imprisonment or impose a fine or make a probation order in respect of the offence,

(b)   if the order under this section is a hospital order, make a referral order (within the meaning of Part I of the Youth Justice and Criminal Evidence Act 1999) in respect of the offence, or

(c)   make in respect of the offender any such order as is mentioned in section 7(7)(b) of the Children and Young Persons Act 1969 or section 58 of the Criminal Justice Act 1991,

but the court may make any other order which it'.

Police and Criminal Evidence Act 1984 (c. 33)

12. The Police and Criminal Evidence Act 1984 has effect subject to the following amendments.

13.—(1) Section 80 (competence and compellability of accused's spouse) is amended as follows.

(2) Omit subsections (1) and (8).

(3) For subsections (2) to (4) substitute—

'(2) In any proceedings the wife or husband of a person charged in the proceedings shall, subject to subsection (4) below, be compellable to give evidence on behalf of that person.

(2A) In any proceedings the wife or husband of a person charged in the proceedings shall, subject to subsection (4) below, be compellable—

(a) to give evidence on behalf of any other person charged in the proceedings but only in respect of any specified offence with which that other person is charged; or

(b) to give evidence for the prosecution but only in respect of any specified offence with which any person is charged in the proceedings.

(3) In relation to the wife or husband of a person charged in any proceedings, an offence is a specified offence for the purposes of subsection (2A) above if—

(a) it involves an assault on, or injury or a threat of injury to, the wife or husband or a person who was at the material time under the age of 16;

(b) it is a sexual offence alleged to have been committed in respect of a person who was at the material time under that age; or

(c) it consists of attempting or conspiring to commit, or of aiding, abetting, counselling, procuring or inciting the commission of, an offence falling within paragraph (a) or (b) above.

(4) No person who is charged in any proceedings shall be compellable by virtue of subsection (2) or (2A) above to give evidence in the proceedings.

(4A) References in this section to a person charged in any proceedings do not include a person who is not, or is no longer, liable to be convicted of any offence in the proceedings (whether as a result of pleading guilty or for any other reason).'

(4) In subsection (5), omit 'competent and' and, in the side-note, omit 'Competence and'.

14. After section 80 insert—

'80A. Rule where accused's spouse not compellable
The failure of the wife or husband of a person charged in any proceedings to give evidence in the proceedings shall not be made the subject of any comment by the prosecution.'

Criminal Justice Act 1988 (c. 33)

15. The Criminal Justice Act 1988 has effect subject to the following amendments.

16. In subsection (1) of each of sections 23 and 24 (first-hand hearsay; business etc. documents), at the end of paragraph (a) insert 'and'.

17. In section 34(3) (unsworn evidence may corroborate other evidence), for 'section 52 of the Criminal Justice Act 1991' substitute 'section 56 of the Youth Justice and Criminal Evidence Act 1999'.

Companies (Northern Ireland) Order 1989 (NI 18)

18. In Article 3(1) of the Companies (Northern Ireland) Order 1989 (interpretation), in the definition of 'regulations' after 'subject' insert '(except in Article 23(3)(a)(ii))'.

Insolvency (Northern Ireland) Order 1989 (NI 19)

19. In Article 2(2) of the Insolvency (Northern Ireland) Order 1989 (interpretation), in the definition of 'regulations' for 'Article 359(5)' substitute 'Articles 359(5) and 375(3)(b)(ii)'.

Criminal Justice Act 1991 (c. 53)

20. In section 58 of the Criminal Justice Act 1991 (binding over of parent or guardian), after subsection (1) insert—

'(1A) Subsection (1) has effect subject to section 4(5) of, and paragraph 13(5) of Schedule 1 to, the Youth Justice and Criminal Evidence Act 1999.'

Criminal Justice and Public Order Act 1994 (c. 33)

21. The Criminal Justice and Public Order Act 1994 has effect subject to the following amendments.

22.—(1) Section 51 (intimidation etc. of witnesses, jurors and others) is amended as follows.

(2) For subsections (1) to (3) (offences of intimidating, and of doing or threatening harm to, witnesses etc.) substitute—

'(1) A person commits an offence if—

(a) he does an act which intimidates, and is intended to intimidate, another person (''the victim''),

(b) he does the act knowing or believing that the victim is assisting in the investigation of an offence or is a witness or potential witness or a juror or potential juror in proceedings for an offence, and

(c) he does it intending thereby to cause the investigation or the course of justice to be obstructed, perverted or interfered with.

(2) A person commits an offence if—

(a) he does an act which harms, and is intended to harm, another person or, intending to cause another person to fear harm, he threatens to do an act which would harm that other person,

(b) he does or threatens to do the act knowing or believing that the person harmed or threatened to be harmed (''the victim''), or some other person, has assisted in an investigation into an offence or has given evidence or particular evidence in proceedings for an offence, or has acted as a juror or concurred in a particular verdict in proceedings for an offence, and

  (c) he does or threatens to do it because of that knowledge or belief.

 (3) For the purposes of subsections (1) and (2) it is immaterial that the act is or would be done, or that the threat is made—

  (a) otherwise than in the presence of the victim, or

  (b) to a person other than the victim.'

 (3) In subsection (8) (presumption in proceedings for offence under subsection (2))—

  (a) for 'he did or threatened to do an act falling within paragraph (a) within the relevant period' substitute 'within the relevant period—

  (a) he did an act which harmed, and was intended to harm, another person, or

  (b) intending to cause another person fear of harm, he threatened to do an act which would harm that other person,

and that he did the act, or (as the case may be) threatened to do the act,'; and

  (b) after 'to have done the act' insert 'or (as the case may be) threatened to do the act'.

 23. In section 136 (cross-border execution of arrest warrants), after subsection (7) insert—

  '(7A) This section applies as respects a warrant issued under paragraph 3(2) of Schedule 1 to the Youth Justice and Criminal Evidence Act 1999 (warrant for arrest of offender referred back to court by youth offender panel) as it applies to a warrant issued in England or Wales for the arrest of a person charged with an offence.'

 24. In Schedule 11 (repeals), the entry relating to section 57(4) of the Children and Young Persons Act 1969 shall be treated as, and as always having been, an entry relating to section 57(4) of the Children and Young Persons Act 1963.

Crime and Disorder Act 1998 (c. 37)

 25. The Crime and Disorder Act 1998 has effect subject to the following amendments.

 26. In section 8(2) (power to make parenting orders), after 'Subject to subsection (3) and section 9(1) below' insert 'and to section 4(5) of, and paragraph 13(5) of Schedule 1 to, the Youth Justice and Criminal Evidence Act 1999'.

 27. In section 9, after subsection (1) (duty to make parenting order where person under 16 convicted of offence) insert—

  '(1A) Subsection (1) above has effect subject to section 4(5) of, and paragraph 13(5) of Schedule 1 to, the Youth Justice and Criminal Evidence Act 1999.'

 28. In section 38(4) (definition of 'youth justice services'), after paragraph (j) there shall be inserted—

'(k)   the implementation of referral orders within the meaning of Part I of the Youth Justice and Criminal Evidence Act 1999.'

29.   In section 67(4)(b) (court may not make reparation order where it proposes to make certain other orders), for 'or an action plan order' substitute ', an action plan order or a referral order under Part I of the Youth Justice and Criminal Evidence Act 1999'.

30.   In section 69(4)(b) (court may not make action plan order where it proposes to make certain other orders), for 'or an attendance centre order' substitute ', an attendance centre order or a referral order under Part I of the Youth Justice and Criminal Evidence Act 1999'.

Section 67   SCHEDULE 5
YOUTH JUSTICE: PRE-CONSOLIDATION AMENDMENTS

Children and Young Persons Act 1969 (c. 54)

1.   The Children and Young Persons Act 1969 has effect subject to the following amendments.

2.   In section 12A (requirements that may be included in supervision orders), at the end add—
    '(14)   In this section ''make reparation'' means make reparation for the offence otherwise than by the payment of compensation.'

3.—(1)   Section 15 (variation and discharge of supervision orders) is amended as follows.
    (2)   In subsection (3)(b) (magistrates' powers of re-sentence on breach of supervision order), for 'relevant court' substitute 'magistrates' court'.
    (3)   After subsection (8) insert—
    '(8A)   Where a supervision order has been made on appeal, for the purposes of subsection (3) above it shall be deemed—
        (a)   if it was made on an appeal brought from a magistrates' court, to have been made by that magistrates' court;
        (b)   if it was made on an appeal brought from the Crown Court or from the criminal division of the Court of Appeal, to have been made by the Crown Court;
    and, in relation to a supervision order made on appeal, subsection (3)(b) above shall have effect as if the words ''if the order had not been made'' were omitted and subsection (5) above shall have effect as if the words ''if it had not made the order'' were omitted.'

4.—(1)   Section 16 (provisions supplementary to section 15) is amended as follows.
    (2)   In subsection (3A), for '(3C)' substitute '(4A)'.
    (3)   Omit subsections (3B) and (3C).

(4)   In subsection (4), at the beginning insert 'Subject to subsection (4A) of this section,'.

(5)   After subsection (4) insert—

'(4A)   Where a supervised person has attained the age of eighteen at the time when he is brought before a justice under subsection (3) of this section, or has attained that age at a time when (apart from this subsection) a youth court could exercise its powers under subsection (4) of this section in respect of him, he shall not be remanded to local authority accommodation but may instead be remanded—

(a)   to a remand centre, if the justice or youth court has been notified that such a centre is available for the reception of persons under this subsection; or

(b)   to a prison, if the justice or youth court has not been so notified.

(4B)   A court or justice remanding a person to local authority accommodation under this section shall designate, as the authority who are to receive him, the authority named in the supervision order.'

Crime and Disorder Act 1998 (c. 37)

5.   The Crime and Disorder Act 1998 has effect subject to the following amendments.

6.—(1)   Section 74 (duties and powers of court in relation to detention and training orders) is amended as follows.

(2)   For subsection (2) substitute—

'(2)   Subject to subsections (3) and (4A) below, a court making a detention and training order may order that its term shall commence on the expiration of the term of any other detention and training order made by that or any other court.'

(3)   After subsection (4) insert—

'(4A)   A court making a detention and training order shall not order that its term shall commence on the expiration of the term of a detention and training order under which the period of supervision has already begun (under section 76(1) below).

(4B)   Where a detention and training order ("the new order") is made in respect of an offender who is subject to a detention and training order under which the period of supervision has begun ("the old order"), the old order shall be disregarded in determining—

(a)   for the purposes of subsection (3) above whether the effect of the new order would be that the offender would be subject to detention and training orders for a term which exceeds 24 months; and

(b)   for the purposes of subsection (4) above whether the term of the detention and training orders to which the offender would (apart from that subsection) be subject exceeds 24 months.'

(4)   After subsection (5) insert—

'(5A)   Where a court proposes to make detention and training orders in respect of an offender for two or more offences—

(a)   subsection (5) above shall not apply, but

(b)   in determining the total term of the detention and training orders it proposes to make in respect of the offender, the court shall take account of the total period for which he has been remanded in custody in connection with any of those offences, or any other offence the charge for which was founded on the same facts or evidence.

(5B)   Once a period of remand has, under subsection (5) or (5A) above, been taken account of in relation to a detention and training order made in respect of an offender for any offence or offences, it shall not subsequently be taken account of (under either of those subsections) in relation to such an order made in respect of the offender for any other offence or offences.'

(5)   In subsection (6), for 'The reference in subsection (5) above' substitute 'Any reference in subsection (5) or (5A) above'.

(6)   In subsection (8), omit 'this section or'.

7.   In section 75(5) (alteration of release of offender subject to detention and training order), for 'the youth court' substitute 'a youth court'.

8.   In section 77 (detention and training orders: breach of supervision requirements), after subsection (4) insert—

'(5)   An offender may appeal to the Crown Court against any order made under subsection (3)(a) or (b) above.'

9.   In section 79 (interaction of detention and training order with sentences of detention), after subsection (2) insert—

'(2A)   Subsection (1)(a) above has effect subject to section 78(3)(a) above and subsection (2)(a) above has effect subject to section 40(4)(b) of the 1991 Act.'

10.—(1)   Paragraph 3 of Schedule 5 (failure to comply with reparation and action plan orders) is amended as follows.

(2)   In sub-paragraph (2)(b), for 'youth court' substitute 'magistrates' court'.

(3)   Omit sub-paragraph (3).

(4)   After sub-paragraph (8) insert—

'(9)   Where a reparation order or action plan order has been made on appeal, for the purposes of this paragraph it shall be deemed—

(a)   if it was made on an appeal brought from a magistrates' court, to have been made by that magistrates' court;

(b)   if it was made on an appeal brought from the Crown Court or from the criminal division of the Court of Appeal, to have been made by the Crown Court;

and, in relation to a reparation order or action plan order made on appeal, sub-paragraph (2)(b) above shall have effect as if the words "if the order had not been made" were omitted and sub-paragraph (5) above shall have effect as if the words "if it had not made the order" were omitted.'

11.—(1)   Paragraph 4 of that Schedule (presence of offender in court, remands, etc.) is amended as follows.

(2)   In sub-paragraph (5)(b), for '(6)' substitute '(7A)'.

(3) Omit sub-paragraph (6).

(4) In sub-paragraph (7), at the beginning insert 'Subject to sub-paragraph (7A) below,'.

(5) After sub-paragraph (7) insert—

'(7A) Where the offender is aged 18 or over at the time when he is brought before a youth court other than the appropriate court under sub-paragraph (4) above, or is aged 18 or over at a time when (apart from this sub-paragraph) the appropriate court could exercise its powers under sub-paragraph (7) above in respect of him, he shall not be remanded to local authority accommodation but may instead be remanded—

(a) to a remand centre, if the court has been notified that such a centre is available for the reception of persons under this sub-paragraph; or

(b) to a prison, if it has not been so notified.'

12. Omit paragraph 5(6) of that Schedule.

Section 67   SCHEDULE 6
REPEALS

Reference	Short title or title	Extent of repeal or revocation
61 & 62 Vict. c. 36.	Criminal Evidence Act 1898.	In section 1, the words from the beginning to 'Provided as follows:—'.
23 & 24 Geo. 5 c. 12.	Children and Young Persons Act 1933.	Section 38.
12, 13 & 14 Geo. 6 c. 88.	Registered Designs Act 1949.	Section 17(11).
1955 c. 18.	Army Act 1955.	Section 93(1B) and (2).
1955 c. 19.	Air Force Act 1955.	Section 93(1B) and (2).
1957 c. 53.	Naval Discipline Act 1957.	Section 60(2) and (3).
1963 c. 37.	Children and Young Persons Act 1963.	Section 57(2) and (4).
1968 c. 19.	Criminal Appeal Act 1968.	In section 10(2)(b), the words ', a referral order within the meaning of Part I of the Youth Justice and Criminal Evidence Act 1999 (referral to youth offender panel)'.
1968 c. 20.	Courts-Martial (Appeals) Act 1968.	In section 36(1), the words 'section 4(4) of the Sexual Offences (Amendment) Act 1976 as adapted by section 5(1)(d) of that Act or'.
1968 c. 60.	Theft Act 1968.	In section 30(2), the words from 'and a person bringing' onwards.
1969 c. 54.	Children and Young Persons Act 1969.	Section 16(3B) and (3C).
1976 c. 52.	Armed Forces Act 1976.	In Schedule 3, in paragraph 3(2), the words from 'or direct that' onwards.

Reference	Short title or title	Extent of repeal or revocation
1976 c. 82.	Sexual Offences (Amendment) Act 1976.	Sections 2 to 5. In section 7(4), the words from 'except that' onwards. Section 7(5).
1977 c. 37.	Patents Act 1977.	Section 32(12).
SI 1978/460 (NI 5).	Sexual Offences (Northern Ireland) Order 1978.	In Article 1(2), the words from 'and Articles 6 and 8' onwards. Articles 6 and 7.
1978 c. 23.	Judicature (Northern Ireland) Act 1978.	In Part II of Schedule 5, the amendment of the Sexual Offences (Northern Ireland) Order 1978.
1979 c. 2.	Customs and Excise Management Act 1979.	Section 75A(6)(b). In section 118A(6)(b), the words 'sections 69 and 70 of the Police and Criminal Evidence Act 1984 and'.
1980 c. 43.	Magistrates' Courts Act 1980.	In section 125(4)(c)(iii), the 'and' at the end. In section 126(d), the 'and' at the end. In Schedule 7, paragraph 148.
1981 c. 55.	Armed Forces Act 1981.	In Schedule 2, paragraph 9.
1984 c. 60.	Police and Criminal Evidence Act 1984.	Sections 69 and 70. Section 80(1). In section 80(5), the words 'competent and'. Section 80(8). In section 82(1), in the definition of 'proceedings', in paragraph (a) the words after 'court-martial' and, in paragraph (b)(i), the words 'so constituted'. Schedule 3.
1985 c. 9.	Companies Act 1985.	In section 709(3), the words from 'In England and Wales' onwards.
1988 c.33.	Criminal Justice Act 1988.	In section 23(1), paragraph (c) and the 'and' preceding it. In section 24(1), paragraph (c) and the 'and' preceding it. In section 32(1), paragraph (b) and the 'or' preceding it. Section 32(2), (3A) to (3E) and (6). Section 32A. Section 33A. Section 34A. Section 158(2) to (4). In Schedule 13, in paragraph 8, sub-paragraph (2)(b) and the 'and' preceding it and, in sub-paragraph (3), ', (2)'. In Schedule 15, paragraph 53.

Reference	Short title or title	Extent of repeal or revocation
1990 c. 42.	Broadcasting Act 1990.	In Schedule 20, paragraphs 26 and 27.
1991 c. 53.	Criminal Justice Act 1991.	Section 52. Section 54. Section 55(2)(b), (4), (6) and (7). In Schedule 9, paragraphs 3 and 7. In Schedule 11, paragraph 1 and, in paragraph 37, the words from 'and, in subsection (3)' onwards.
1992 c. 34.	Sexual Offences (Amendment) Act 1992.	In section 5(2), the words 'or programme'. In section 6(1), the definition of 'written publication' and the 'and' preceding it. In section 7(2), paragraph (b) and paragraph (e) except for the 'and' at the end. Section 7(3).
1994 c. 9.	Finance Act 1994.	In section 22(2)(b), the words 'sections 69 and 70 of the Police and Criminal Evidence Act 1984 and'. In Schedule 7, in paragraph 1(6)(b), the words 'sections 69 and 70 of the Police and Criminal Evidence Act 1984 and'.
1994 c. 23.	Value Added Tax Act 1994.	In Schedule 11, in paragraph 6(6)(b), the words 'sections 69 and 70 of the Police and Criminal Evidence Act 1984 and'.
1994 c. 33.	Criminal Justice and Public Order Act 1994.	Section 50. In Schedule 9, paragraphs 11(1)(a), 13 and 33. In Schedule 10, paragraphs 32, 35(3) and 36.
SI 1994/2795 (NI 15).	Criminal Justice (Northern Ireland) Order 1994.	Article 2(3). Article 18(3). Articles 19 to 24.
1995 c. 35.	Criminal Appeal Act 1995.	In Schedule 2, paragraph 16(2)(b) and (3).
1995 c. 38.	Civil Evidence Act 1995.	In Schedule 1, paragraph 10.
1996 c. 8.	Finance Act 1996.	In Schedule 5, in paragraph 2(6)(a), the words 'sections 69 and 70 of the Police and Criminal Evidence Act 1984 and'.
1996 c. 25.	Criminal Procedure and Investigations Act 1996.	Section 62. In Schedule 1, paragraphs 23, 27 and 33.
1996 c. 46.	Armed Forces Act 1996.	In Schedule 1, paragraph 107(a).

Reference	Short title or title	Extent of repeal or revocation
1998 c. 37.	Crime and Disorder Act 1998.	In section 74(8), the words 'this section or'. In Schedule 5, paragraphs 3(3), 4(6) and 5(6).
SI 1998/1504 (NI 9).	Criminal Justice (Children) (Northern Ireland) Order 1998.	Article 22.
1999 c. 23.	Youth Justice and Criminal Evidence Act 1999.	Section 4(7)(d) except for the 'or' at the end. In section 15(1), in the definition of 'custodial sentence', the words from 'a sentence of detention in' to '1994,'. In Schedule 1, paragraphs 5(7) and 14(5). In Schedule 4, paragraph 4(2).

Section 67

SCHEDULE 7

TRANSITIONAL PROVISIONS AND SAVINGS

Interpretation

1.—(1)   In this Schedule—

'the 1988 Act' means the Criminal Justice Act 1988;

'commencement date', in relation to any provisions of this Act and proceedings of any description, means the date on which those provisions come into force in relation to such proceedings;

'continuing proceedings' (except in paragraph 3) means proceedings instituted before the commencement date;

'existing special measures power' means any power of the court to make an order or give leave, in the exercise of its inherent jurisdiction, for the taking of measures in relation to a witness which are similar to those which could be provided for by a special measures direction.

(2)   For the purposes of this Schedule—

(a)   proceedings other than proceedings on appeal are to be taken to be instituted at the time when they would be taken to be instituted for the purposes of Part I of the Prosecution of Offences Act 1985 in accordance with section 15(2) of that Act; and

(b)   proceedings on appeal are to be taken to be instituted at the time when the notice of appeal is given or (as the case may be) the reference under section 9 or 11 of the Criminal Appeal Act 1995 is made.

(3)   Expressions used in this Schedule which are also used in Part II of this Act have the same meaning in this Schedule as in that Part.

Referral orders under Part I

2.   No referral order (within the meaning of Part I) may be made in respect of any offence committed before the commencement date for section 1.

Special measures under Chapter I of Part II

3.—(1)   A special measures direction may be given in relation to a witness in continuing proceedings unless the court has before the specified date—

(a)   given leave in relation to the witness in connection with those proceedings under section 32 (evidence through television links) or section 32A (video recordings of testimony of child witnesses) of the 1988 Act, or

(b)   exercised any existing special measures power in relation to the witness in connection with those proceedings.

(2)   The repeals made by this Act shall not affect the continued operation in relation to a witness in continuing proceedings of section 32 or 32A of the 1988 Act where before the specified date leave was given in relation to the witness in connection with those proceedings by virtue of section 32(1)(b) or section 32A, as the case may be.

(3)   Nothing in this Act affects the continued operation in relation to a witness in continuing proceedings of any order made or leave given under any existing special measures power exercised by the court before the specified date in relation to the witness in connection with those proceedings.

(4)   In this paragraph—

(a)   'continuing proceedings' means proceedings instituted before the specified date;

(b)   'the specified date', in relation to a witness in any proceedings, means such date as may be specified by the Secretary of State in a notice given to the court in question under section 18(2), where the date is expressed to apply—

(i)   for the purposes of this paragraph, and

(ii)   in relation to any description of witnesses and proceedings within which the witness and the proceedings fall.

Protection of witnesses from cross-examination by accused in person

4.   Nothing in Chapter II of Part II applies in relation to proceedings instituted before the commencement date for that Chapter.

Protection of complainants in proceedings for sexual offences

5.—(1)   Nothing in Chapter III of Part II applies in relation to continuing proceedings in which leave has been given before the commencement date for that Chapter—

(a)   under section 2 of the Sexual Offences (Amendment) Act 1976, or

(b)   (in the case of proceedings to which section 2 does not apply) in the exercise of any similar power of the court exercisable by virtue of its inherent jurisdiction.

(2)   Nothing in this Act affects the continued operation of any leave so given in relation to any such proceedings.

Reporting restrictions

6.—(1)   Section 44 applies in relation to an alleged offence whether the criminal investigation into it is begun before or after the coming into force of that section.

(2)   The restrictions imposed by subsection (2) of section 44 do not apply to the inclusion of matter in a publication if—
   (a)   where the publication is a relevant programme, it is transmitted, or
   (b)   in the case of any other publication, it is published,
before the coming into force of that section.
(3)   Nothing in section 45 or 46 applies in relation to proceedings instituted before the commencement date for that section.
(4)   In sub-paragraph (3) the reference to the institution of proceedings shall be construed—
   (a)   in the case of proceedings in England in Wales (other than proceedings before a service court), in accordance with paragraph 1(2);
   (b)   in the case of proceedings in Northern Ireland (other than proceedings before a service court), in accordance with sub-paragraph (5);
   (c)   in the case of proceedings before a service court (wherever held) in accordance with sub-paragraph (6).
(5)   In the case of proceedings falling within sub-paragraph (4)(b)—
   (a)   proceedings other than proceedings on appeal are to be taken to be instituted—
      (i)   where a justice of the peace issues a summons under Article 20 of the Magistrates' Courts (Northern Ireland) Order 1981, when the complaint for the offence is made;
      (ii)   where a justice of the peace issues a warrant for the arrest of any person under that Article, when the complaint for the offence is made;
      (iii)   where a person is charged with the offence after being taken into custody without a warrant, when he is informed of the particulars of the charge;
      (iv)   where an indictment is presented under the authority of section 2(2)(c), (d), (e) or (f) of the Grand Jury (Abolition) Act (Northern Ireland) 1969, when the indictment is presented to the court;
and where the application of this paragraph would result in there being more than one time for the institution of the proceedings, they shall be taken to have been instituted at the earliest of those times; and
   (b)   proceedings on appeal are to be taken to be instituted at the time when the notice of appeal is given or (as the case may be) the reference under section 10 or 12 of the Criminal Appeal Act 1995 is made.
(6)   In the case of proceedings falling within sub-paragraph (4)(c)—
   (a)   proceedings other than proceedings on appeal are to be taken to be instituted when the prosecuting authority prefers a charge in respect of the offence under section 83B(4) of the Army Act 1955, section 83B(4) of the Air Force Act 1955 or section 521(4) of the Naval Discipline Act 1957; and
   (b)   proceedings on appeal are to be taken to be instituted when the application for leave to appeal is lodged in accordance with section 9 of the Courts-Martial (Appeals) Act 1968 or (as the case may be) the reference under section 34 of that Act is made.

Competence of witnesses and capacity to be sworn

7.   Nothing in Chapter V of Part II applies in relation to proceedings instituted before the commencement date for that Chapter.

Inferences from silence

8.   The amendments made by section 58—

(a)   apply only to proceedings instituted on or after the commencement date for that section; but

(b)   so apply whether the relevant failure or refusal on the part of the accused took place before or after that date.

Appendix 2
Text of Part III and schedule 1 of the Powers of the Criminal Courts (Sentencing) Act 2000, which replace Part I and schedule 1 of the Youth Justice and Criminal Evidence Act 1999

PART III
MANDATORY AND DISCRETIONARY REFERRAL OF YOUNG OFFENDERS
Referral orders

16. Duty and power to refer certain young offenders to youth offender panels

(1) This section applies where a youth court or other magistrates' court is dealing with a person aged under 18 for an offence and—

(a) neither the offence nor any connected offence is one for which the sentence is fixed by law;

(b) the court is not, in respect of the offence or any connected offence, proposing to impose a custodial sentence on the offender or make a hospital order (within the meaning of the Mental Health Act 1983) in his case; and

(c) the court is not proposing to discharge him absolutely in respect of the offence.

(2) If—

(a) the compulsory referral conditions are satisfied in accordance with section 17 below, and

(b) referral is available to the court,

the court shall sentence the offender for the offence by ordering him to be referred to a youth offender panel.

(3) If—

(a) the discretionary referral conditions are satisfied in accordance with section 17 below, and

(b) referral is available to the court,

the court may sentence the offender for the offence by ordering him to be referred to a youth offender panel.

(4) For the purposes of this Part an offence is connected with another if the offender falls to be dealt with for it at the same time as he is dealt with for the other

offence (whether or not he is convicted of the offences at the same time or by or before the same court).

(5)   For the purposes of this section referral is available to a court if—

(a)   the court has been notified by the Secretary of State that arrangements for the implementation of referral orders are available in the area in which it appears to the court that the offender resides or will reside; and

(b)   the notice has not been withdrawn.

(6)   An order under subsection (2) or (3) above is in this Act referred to as a 'referral order'.

(7)   No referral order may be made in respect of any offence committed before the commencement of section 1 of the Youth Justice and Criminal Evidence Act 1999.

17.   The referral conditions

(1)   For the purposes of section 16(2) above the compulsory referral conditions are satisfied in relation to an offence if the offender—

(a)   pleaded guilty to the offence and to any connected offence;

(b)   has never been convicted by or before a court in the United Kingdom of any offence other than the offence and any connected offence; and

(c)   has never been bound over in criminal proceedings in England and Wales or Northern Ireland to keep the peace or to be of good behaviour.

(2)   For the purposes of section 16(3) above the discretionary referral conditions are satisfied in relation to an offence if—

(a)   the offender is being dealt with by the court for the offence and one or more connected offences;

(b)   although he pleaded guilty to at least one of the offences mentioned in paragraph (a) above, he also pleaded not guilty to at least one of them;

(c)   he has never been convicted by or before a court in the United Kingdom of any offence other than the offences mentioned in paragraph (a) above; and

(d)   he has never been bound over in criminal proceedings in England and Wales or Northern Ireland to keep the peace or to be of good behaviour.

(3)   The Secretary of State may by regulations make such amendments of this section as he considers appropriate for altering in any way the descriptions of offenders in the case of which the compulsory referral conditions or the discretionary referral conditions fall to be satisfied for the purposes of section 16(2) or (3) above (as the case may be).

(4)   Any description of offender having effect for those purposes by virtue of such regulations may be framed by reference to such matters as the Secretary of State considers appropriate, including (in particular) one or more of the following—

(a)   the offender's age;

(b)   how the offender has pleaded;

(c)   the offence (or offences) of which the offender has been convicted;

(d)   the offender's previous convictions (if any);

(e)   how (if at all) the offender has been previously punished or otherwise dealt with by any court; and

(f)   any characteristics or behaviour of, or circumstances relating to, any person who has at any time been charged in the same proceedings as the offender (whether or not in respect of the same offence).

(5)   For the purposes of this section an offender who has been convicted of an offence in respect of which he was conditionally discharged (whether by a court in England and Wales or in Northern Ireland) shall be treated, despite—

(a)   section 14(1) above (conviction of offence for which offender so discharged deemed not a conviction), or

(b)   Article 6(1) of the Criminal Justice (Northern Ireland) Order 1996 (corresponding provision for Northern Ireland),

as having been convicted of that offence.

18.   Making of referral orders: general

(1)   A referral order shall—

(a)   specify the youth offending team responsible for implementing the order;

(b)   require the offender to attend each of the meetings of a youth offender panel to be established by the team for the offender; and

(c)   specify the period for which any youth offender contract taking effect between the offender and the panel under section 23 below is to have effect (which must not be less than three nor more than twelve months).

(2)   The youth offending team specified under subsection (1)(a) above shall be the team having the function of implementing referral orders in the area in which it appears to the court that the offender resides or will reside.

(3)   On making a referral order the court shall explain to the offender in ordinary language—

(a)   the effect of the order; and

(b)   the consequences which may follow—

(i)   if no youth offender contract takes effect between the offender and the panel under section 23 below; or

(ii)   if the offender breaches any of the terms of any such contract.

(4)   Subsections (5) to (7) below apply where, in dealing with an offender for two or more connected offences, a court makes a referral order in respect of each, or each of two or more, of the offences.

(5)   The orders shall have the effect of referring the offender to a single youth offender panel; and the provision made by them under subsection (1) above shall accordingly be the same in each case, except that the periods specified under subsection (1)(c) may be different.

(6)   The court may direct that the period so specified in either or any of the orders is to run concurrently with or be additional to that specified in the other or any of the others; but in exercising its power under this subsection the court must ensure that the total period for which such a contract as is mentioned in subsection (1)(c) above is to have effect does not exceed twelve months.

(7)   Each of the orders mentioned in subsection (4) above shall, for the purposes of this Part, be treated as associated with the other or each of the others.

19. Making of referral orders: effect on court's other sentencing powers

(1)   Subsections (2) to (5) below apply where a court makes a referral order in respect of an offence.

(2)   The court may not deal with the offender for the offence in any of the prohibited ways.

(3)   The court—

(a)   shall, in respect of any connected offence, either sentence the offender by making a referral order or make an order discharging him absolutely; and

(b)   may not deal with the offender for any such offence in any of the prohibited ways.

(4)   For the purposes of subsections (2) and (3) above the prohibited ways are—

(a)   imposing a community sentence on the offender;

(b)   ordering him to pay a fine;

(c)   making a reparation order in respect of him; and

(d)   making an order discharging him conditionally.

(5)   The court may not make, in connection with the conviction of the offender for the offence or any connected offence—

(a)   an order binding him over to keep the peace or to be of good behaviour;

(b)   an order under section 150 below (binding over of parent or guardian); or

(c)   a parenting order under section 8 of the Crime and Disorder Act 1998.

(6)   Subsections (2), (3) and (5) above do not affect the exercise of any power to deal with the offender conferred by paragraph 5 (offender referred back to court by panel) or paragraph 14 (powers of a court where offender convicted while subject to referral) of Schedule 1 to this Act.

(7)   Where section 16(2) above requires a court to make a referral order, the court may not under section 1 above defer passing sentence on him, but section 16(2) and subsection (3)(a) above do not affect any power or duty of a magistrates' court under—

(a)   section 8 above (remission to youth court, or another such court, for sentence);

(b)   section 10(3) of the Magistrates' Courts Act 1980 (adjournment for inquiries); or

(c)   section 35, 38, 43 or 44 of the Mental Health Act 1983 (remand for reports, interim hospital orders and committal to Crown Court for restriction order).

20. Making of referral orders: attendance of parents etc.

(1)   A court making a referral order may make an order requiring—

(a)   the appropriate person, or

(b)   in a case where there are two or more appropriate persons, any one or more of them,

to attend the meetings of the youth offender panel.

(2)   Where an offender is aged under 16 when a court makes a referral order in his case—

(a)   the court shall exercise its power under subsection (1) above so as to require at least one appropriate person to attend meetings of the youth offender panel; and

(b)   if the offender falls within subsection (6) below, the person or persons so required to attend those meetings shall be or include a representative of the local authority mentioned in that subsection.

(3)   The court shall not under this section make an order requiring a person to attend meetings of the youth offender panel—

(a)   if the court is satisfied that it would be unreasonable to do so; or

(b)   to an extent which the court is satisfied would be unreasonable.

(4)   Except where the offender falls within subsection (6) below, each person who is a parent or guardian of the offender is an 'appropriate person' for the purposes of this section.

(5)   Where the offender falls within subsection (6) below, each of the following is an 'appropriate person' for the purposes of this section—

(a)   a representative of the local authority mentioned in that subsection; and

(b)   each person who is a parent or guardian of the offender with whom the offender is allowed to live.

(6)   An offender falls within this subsection if he is (within the meaning of the Children Act 1989) a child who is looked after by a local authority.

(7)   If, at the time when a court makes an order under this section—

(a)   a person who is required by the order to attend meetings of a youth offender panel is not present in court, or

(b)   a local authority whose representative is so required to attend such meetings is not represented in court,

the court must send him or (as the case may be) the authority a copy of the order forthwith.

Youth offender panels

21.   Establishment of panels

(1)   Where a referral order has been made in respect of an offender (or two or more associated referral orders have been so made), it is the duty of the youth offending team specified in the order (or orders)—

(a)   to establish a youth offender panel for the offender;

(b)   to arrange for the first meeting of the panel to be held for the purposes of section 23 below; and

(c)   subsequently to arrange for the holding of any further meetings of the panel required by virtue of section 25 below (in addition to those required by virtue of any other provision of this Part).

(2)   A youth offender panel shall—

(a)   be constituted,

(b)   conduct its proceedings, and

254 of the PCC(S)A 2000

(c)   discharge its functions under this Part (and in particular those arising under section 23 below),

in accordance with guidance given from time to time by the Secretary of State.

(3)   At each of its meetings a panel shall, however, consist of at least—

(a)   one member appointed by the youth offending team from among its members; and

(b)   two members so appointed who are not members of the team.

(4)   The Secretary of State may by regulations make provision requiring persons appointed as members of a youth offender panel to have such qualifications, or satisfy such other criteria, as are specified in the regulations.

(5)   Where it appears to the court which made a referral order that, by reason of either a change or a prospective change in the offender's place or intended place of residence, the youth offending team for the time being specified in the order ('the current team') either does not or will not have the function of implementing referral orders in the area in which the offender resides or will reside, the court may amend the order so that it instead specifies the team which has the function of implementing such orders in that area ('the new team').

(6)   Where a court so amends a referral order—

(a)   subsection (1)(a) above shall apply to the new team in any event;

(b)   subsection (1)(b) above shall apply to the new team if no youth offender contract has (or has under paragraph (c) below been treated as having) taken effect under section 23 below between the offender and a youth offender panel established by the current team;

(c)   if such a contract has (or has previously under this paragraph been treated as having) so taken effect, it shall (after the amendment) be treated as if it were a contract which had taken effect under section 23 below between the offender and the panel being established for the offender by the new team.

(7)   References in this Part to the meetings of a youth offender panel (or any such meeting) are to the following meetings of the panel (or any of them)—

(a)   the first meeting held in pursuance of subsection (1)(b) above;

(b)   any further meetings held in pursuance of section 25 below;

(c)   any progress meeting held under section 26 below; and

(d)   the final meeting held under section 27 below.

22.   Attendance at panel meetings

(1)   The specified team shall, in the case of each meeting of the panel established for the offender, notify—

(a)   the offender, and

(b)   any person to whom an order under section 20 above applies, of the time and place at which he is required to attend that meeting.

(2)   If the offender fails to attend any part of such a meeting the panel may—

(a)   adjourn the meeting to such time and place as it may specify; or

(b)   end the meeting and refer the offender back to the appropriate court;

and subsection (1) above shall apply in relation to any such adjourned meeting.

(3)   One person aged 18 or over chosen by the offender, with the agreement of the panel, shall be entitled to accompany the offender to any meeting of the panel (and it need not be the same person who accompanies him to every meeting).

(4)   The panel may allow to attend any such meeting—

(a)   any person who appears to the panel to be a victim of, or otherwise affected by, the offence, or any of the offences, in respect of which the offender was referred to the panel;

(b)   any person who appears to the panel to be someone capable of having a good influence on the offender.

(5)   Where the panel allows any such person as is mentioned in subsection (4)(a) above ('the victim') to attend a meeting of the panel, the panel may allow the victim to be accompanied to the meeting by one person chosen by the victim with the agreement of the panel.

Youth offender contracts

23.   First meeting: agreement of contract with offender

(1)   At the first meeting of the youth offender panel established for an offender the panel shall seek to reach agreement with the offender on a programme of behaviour the aim (or principal aim) of which is the prevention of re-offending by the offender.

(2)   The terms of the programme may, in particular, include provision for any of the following—

(a)   the offender to make financial or other reparation to any person who appears to the panel to be a victim of, or otherwise affected by, the offence, or any of the offences, for which the offender was referred to the panel;

(b)   the offender to attend mediation sessions with any such victim or other person;

(c)   the offender to carry out unpaid work or service in or for the community;

(d)   the offender to be at home at times specified in or determined under the programme;

(e)   attendance by the offender at a school or other educational establishment or at a place of work;

(f)   the offender to participate in specified activities (such as those designed to address offending behaviour, those offering education or training or those assisting with the rehabilitation of persons dependent on, or having a propensity to misuse, alcohol or drugs);

(g)   the offender to present himself to specified persons at times and places specified in or determined under the programme;

(h)   the offender to stay away from specified places or persons (or both);

(i)   enabling the offender's compliance with the programme to be supervised and recorded.

(3)   The programme may not, however, provide—

(a)   for the electronic monitoring of the offender's whereabouts; or

(b)   for the offender to have imposed on him any physical restriction on his movements.

(4)   No term which provides for anything to be done to or with any such victim or other affected person as is mentioned in subsection (2)(a) above may be included in the programme without the consent of that person.

(5)   Where a programme is agreed between the offender and the panel, the panel shall cause a written record of the programme to be produced forthwith—

(a)   in language capable of being readily understood by, or explained to, the offender; and

(b)   for signature by him.

(6)   Once the record has been signed—

(a)   by the offender, and

(b)   by a member of the panel on behalf of the panel,

the terms of the programme, as set out in the record, take effect as the terms of a 'youth offender contract' between the offender and the panel; and the panel shall cause a copy of the record to be given or sent to the offender.

24.   First meeting: duration of contract

(1)   This section applies where a youth offender contract has taken effect under section 23 above between an offender and a youth offender panel.

(2)   The day on which the contract so takes effect shall be the first day of the period for which it has effect.

(3)   Where the panel was established in pursuance of a single referral order, the length of the period for which the contract has effect shall be that of the period specified under section 18(1)(c) above in the referral order.

(4)   Where the panel was established in pursuance of two or more associated referral orders, the length of the period for which the contract has effect shall be that resulting from the court's directions under section 18(6) above.

(5)   Subsections (3) and (4) above have effect subject to—

(a)   any order under paragraph 11 or 12 of Schedule 1 to this Act extending the length of the period for which the contract has effect; and

(b)   subsection (6) below.

(6)   If the referral order, or each of the associated referral orders, is revoked (whether under paragraph 5(2) of Schedule 1 to this Act or by virtue of paragraph 14(2) of that Schedule), the period for which the contract has effect expires at the time when the order or orders is or are revoked unless it has already expired.

25.   First meeting: failure to agree contract

(1)   Where it appears to a youth offender panel to be appropriate to do so, the panel may—

(a)   end the first meeting (or any further meeting held in pursuance of paragraph (b) below) without having reached agreement with the offender on a programme of behaviour of the kind mentioned in section 23(1) above; and

(b)   resume consideration of the offender's case at a further meeting of the panel.

(2)   If, however, it appears to the panel at the first meeting or any such further meeting that there is no prospect of agreement being reached with the offender within a reasonable period after the making of the referral order (or orders)—

(a)   subsection (1)(b) above shall not apply; and

(b)   instead the panel shall refer the offender back to the appropriate court.

(3)   If at a meeting of the panel—

(a)   agreement is reached with the offender but he does not sign the record produced in pursuance of section 23(5) above, and

(b)   his failure to do so appears to the panel to be unreasonable,

the panel shall end the meeting and refer the offender back to the appropriate court.

26.   Progress meetings

(1)   At any time—

(a)   after a youth offender contract has taken effect under section 23 above, but

(b)   before the end of the period for which the contract has effect,

the specified team shall, if so requested by the panel, arrange for the holding of a meeting of the panel under this section ('a progress meeting').

(2)   The panel may make a request under subsection (1) above if it appears to the panel to be expedient to review—

(a)   the offender's progress in implementing the programme of behaviour contained in the contract; or

(b)   any other matter arising in connection with the contract.

(3)   The panel shall make such a request if—

(a)   the offender has notified the panel that—

(i)   he wishes to seek the panel's agreement to a variation in the terms of the contract; or

(ii)   he wishes the panel to refer him back to the appropriate court with a view to the referral order (or orders) being revoked on account of a significant change in his circumstances (such as his being taken to live abroad) making compliance with any youth offender contract impractical; or

(b)   it appears to the panel that the offender is in breach of any of the terms of the contract.

(4)   At a progress meeting the panel shall do such one or more of the following things as it considers appropriate in the circumstances, namely—

(a)   review the offender's progress or any such other matter as is mentioned in subsection (2) above;

(b)   discuss with the offender any breach of the terms of the contract which it appears to the panel that he has committed;

(c)   consider any variation in the terms of the contract sought by the offender or which it appears to the panel to be expedient to make in the light of any such review or discussion;

(d)   consider whether to accede to any request by the offender that he be referred back to the appropriate court.

(5)   Where the panel has discussed with the offender such a breach as is mentioned in subsection (4)(b) above—

(a)   the panel and the offender may agree that the offender is to continue to be required to comply with the contract (either in its original form or with any agreed variation in its terms) without being referred back to the appropriate court; or

(b)   the panel may decide to end the meeting and refer the offender back to that court.

(6)   Where a variation in the terms of the contract is agreed between the offender and the panel, the panel shall cause a written record of the variation to be produced forthwith—

(a)   in language capable of being readily understood by, or explained to, the offender; and

(b)   for signature by him.

(7)   Any such variation shall take effect once the record has been signed—

(a)   by the offender; and

(b)   by a member of the panel on behalf of the panel;

and the panel shall cause a copy of the record to be given or sent to the offender.

(8)   If at a progress meeting—

(a)   any such variation is agreed but the offender does not sign the record produced in pursuance of subsection (6) above, and

(b)   his failure to do so appears to the panel to be unreasonable,

the panel may end the meeting and refer the offender back to the appropriate court.

(9)   Section 23(2) to (4) above shall apply in connection with what may be provided for by the terms of the contract as varied under this section as they apply in connection with what may be provided for by the terms of a programme of behaviour of the kind mentioned in section 23(1).

(10)   Where the panel has discussed with the offender such a request as is mentioned in subsection (4)(d) above, the panel may, if it is satisfied that there is (or is soon to be) such a change in circumstances as is mentioned in subsection (3)(a)(ii) above, decide to end the meeting and refer the offender back to the appropriate court.

27.   Final meeting

(1)   Where the compliance period in the case of a youth offender contract is due to expire, the specified team shall arrange for the holding, before the end of that period, of a meeting of the panel under this section ('the final meeting').

(2)   At the final meeting the panel shall—

(a)   review the extent of the offender's compliance to date with the terms of the contract; and

(b)   decide, in the light of that review, whether his compliance with those terms has been such as to justify the conclusion that, by the time the compliance period expires, he will have satisfactorily completed the contract;

and the panel shall give the offender written confirmation of its decision.

(3)   Where the panel decides that the offender's compliance with the terms of the contract has been such as to justify that conclusion, the panel's decision shall have

the effect of discharging the referral order (or orders) as from the end of the compliance period.

(4) Otherwise the panel shall refer the offender back to the appropriate court.

(5) Nothing in section 22(2) above prevents the panel from making the decision mentioned in subsection (3) above in the offender's absence if it appears to the panel to be appropriate to do that instead of exercising either of its powers under section 22(2).

(6) Section 22(2)(a) above does not permit the final meeting to be adjourned (or re-adjourned) to a time falling after the end of the compliance period.

(7) In this section 'the compliance period', in relation to a youth offender contract, means the period for which the contract has effect in accordance with section 24 above.

Further court proceedings

28. Offender referred back to court or convicted while subject to referral order
Schedule 1 to this Act, which—

(a) in Part I makes provision for what is to happen when a youth offender panel refers an offender back to the appropriate court, and

(b) in Part II makes provision for what is to happen when an offender is convicted of further offences while for the time being subject to a referral order,

shall have effect.

Supplementary

29. Functions of youth offending teams

(1) The functions of a youth offending team responsible for implementing a referral order include, in particular, arranging for the provision of such administrative staff, accommodation or other facilities as are required by the youth offender panel established in pursuance of the order.

(2) During the period for which a youth offender contract between a youth offender panel and an offender has effect—

(a) the specified team shall make arrangements for supervising the offender's compliance with the terms of the contract; and

(b) the person who is the member of the panel referred to in section 21(3)(a) above shall ensure that records are kept of the offender's compliance (or non-compliance) with those terms.

(3) In implementing referral orders a youth offending team shall have regard to any guidance given from time to time by the Secretary of State.

30. Regulations under Part III

(1) Any power of the Secretary of State to make regulations under section 17(3) or 21(4) above or paragraph 13(8) of Schedule 1 to this Act shall be exercisable by statutory instrument.

(2) A statutory instrument containing any regulations under section 21(4) shall be subject to annulment in pursuance of a resolution of either House of Parliament.

(3)   No regulations shall be made under—
   (a)   section 17(3), or
   (b)   paragraph 13(8) of Schedule 1,
unless a draft of the regulations has been laid before, and approved by a resolution of, each House of Parliament.

(4)   Any regulations made by the Secretary of State under section 17(3) or 21(4) or paragraph 13(8) of Schedule 1 may make different provision for different cases, circumstances or areas and may contain such incidental, supplemental, saving or transitional provisions as the Secretary of State thinks fit.

31.   Rules of court

(1)   Rules of court may make such provision as appears to the authority making them to be necessary or expedient for the purposes of this Part (and nothing in this section shall be taken to affect the generality of any enactment conferring power to make such rules).

(2)   In this section 'rules of court' means—
   (a)   Magistrates' Courts Rules;
   (b)   Crown Court Rules;
   (c)   Criminal Appeal Rules.

32.   Definitions for purposes of Part III

In this Part—
   'the appropriate court' shall be construed in accordance with paragraph 1(2) of Schedule 1 to this Act;
   'associated', in relation to referral orders, shall be construed in accordance with section 18(7) above;
   'connected', in relation to offences, shall be construed in accordance with section 16(4) above;
   'meeting', in relation to a youth offender panel, shall be construed in accordance with section 21(7) above;
   'the specified team', in relation to an offender to whom a referral order applies (or two or more associated referral orders apply), means the youth offending team for the time being specified in the order (or orders).

SCHEDULES

Section 28   SCHEDULE 1

YOUTH OFFENDER PANELS: FURTHER COURT PROCEEDINGS

PART I
REFERRAL BACK TO APPROPRIATE COURT

Introductory

1.—(1)   This Part of this Schedule applies where a youth offender panel refers an offender back to the appropriate court under section 22(2), 25(2) or (3), 26(5), (8) or (10) or 27(4) of this Act.

(2)   For the purposes of this Part of this Schedule and the provisions mentioned in sub-paragraph (1) above the appropriate court is—

(a)   in the case of an offender aged under 18 at the time when (in pursuance of the referral back) he first appears before the court, a youth court acting for the petty sessions area in which it appears to the youth offender panel that the offender resides or will reside; and

(b)   otherwise, a magistrates' court (other than a youth court) acting for that area.

Mode of referral back to court

2.   The panel shall make the referral by sending a report to the appropriate court explaining why the offender is being referred back to it.

Bringing the offender before the court

3.—(1)   Where the appropriate court receives such a report, the court shall cause the offender to appear before it.

(2)   For the purpose of securing the attendance of the offender before the court, a justice acting for the petty sessions area for which the court acts may—

(a)   issue a summons requiring the offender to appear at the place and time specified in it; or

(b)   if the report is substantiated on oath, issue a warrant for the offender's arrest.

(3)   Any summons or warrant issued under sub-paragraph (2) above shall direct the offender to appear or be brought before the appropriate court.

Detention and remand of arrested offender

4.—(1)   Where the offender is arrested in pursuance of a warrant under paragraph 3(2) above and cannot be brought immediately before the appropriate court—

(a)   the person in whose custody he is may make arrangements for his detention in a place of safety (within the meaning given by section 107(1) of the Children and Young Persons Act 1933) for a period of not more than 72 hours from the tiine of the arrest (and it shall be lawful for him to be detained in pursuance of the arrangements); and

(b)   that person shall within that period bring him before a court which—

(i)   if he is under the age of 18 when he is brought before the court, shall be a youth court; and

(ii)   if he has then attained that age, shall be a magistrates' court other than a youth court.

(2)   Sub-paragraphs (3) to (5) below apply where the court before which the offender is brought under sub-paragraph (1)(b) above ('the alternative court') is not the appropriate court.

(3)   The alternative court may direct that he is to be released forthwith or remand him.

(4)   Section 128 of the Magistrates' Courts Act 1980 (remand in custody or on bail) shall have effect where the alternative court has power under sub-paragraph (3) above to remand the offender as if the court referred to in subsections (1)(a), (3), (4)(a) and (5) were the appropriate court.

(5)   That section shall have effect where the alternative court has power so to remand him, or the appropriate court has (by virtue of sub-paragraph (4) above) power to further remand him, as if in subsection (1) there were inserted after paragraph (c) 'or

(d)   if he is aged under 18, remand him to accommodation provided by or on behalf of a local authority (within the meaning of the Children Act 1989) and, if it does so, shall designate as the authority who are to receive him the local authority for the area in which it appears to the court that he resides or will reside;'.

Power of court where it upholds panel's decision

5.—(1)   If it is proved to the satisfaction of the appropriate court as regards any decision of the panel which resulted in the offender being referred back to the court—

(a)   that, so far as the decision relied on any finding of fact by the panel, the panel was entitled to make that finding in the circumstances, and

(b)   that, so far as the decision involved any exercise of discretion by the panel, the panel reasonably exercised that discretion in the circumstances,
the court may exercise the power conferred by sub-paragraph (2) below.

(2)   That power is a power to revoke the referral order (or each of the referral orders).

(3)   The revocation under sub-paragraph (2) above of a referral order has the effect of revoking any related order under paragraph 11 or 12 below.

(4)   Where any order is revoked under sub-paragraph (2) above or by virtue of sub-paragraph (3) above, the appropriate court may deal with the offender in accordance with sub-paragraph (5) below for the offence in respect of which the revoked order was made.

(5)   In so dealing with the offender for such an offence, the appropriate court—

(a)   may deal with him in any way in which (assuming section 16 of this Act had not applied) he could have been dealt with for that offence by the court which made the order; and

(b)   shall have regard to—

(i)   the circumstances of his referral back to the court; and

(ii)   where a contract has taken effect under section 23 of this Act between the offender and the panel, the extent of his compliance with the terms of the contract.

(6)   The appropriate court may not exercise the powers conferred by sub-paragraph (2) or (4) above unless the offender is present before it; but those powers are exercisable even if, in a case where a contract has taken effect under section 23, the period for which the contract has effect has expired (whether before or after the referral of the offender back to the court).

Appeal

6.   Where the court in exercise of the power conferred by paragraph 5(4) above deals with the offender for an offence, the offender may appeal to the Crown Court against the sentence.

Court not revoking referral order or orders

7.—(1)   This paragraph applies—

(a)   where the appropriate court decides that the matters mentioned in paragraphs (a) and (b) of paragraph 5(1) above have not been proved to its satisfaction; or

(b)   where, although by virtue of paragraph 5(1) above the appropriate court—

(i)   is able to exercise the power conferred by paragraph 5(2) above, or

(ii)   would be able to do so if the offender were present before it, the court (for any reason) decides not to exercise that power.

(2)   If either—

(a)   no contract has taken effect under section 23 of this Act between the offender and the panel, or

(b)   a contract has taken effect under that section but the period for which it has effect has not expired,

the offender shall continue to remain subject to the referral order (or orders) in all respects as if he had not been referred back to the court.

(3)   If—

(a)   a contract had taken effect under section 23 of this Act, but

(b)   the period for which it has effect has expired (otherwise than by virtue of section 24(6)),

the court shall make an order declaring that the referral order (or each of the referral orders) is discharged.

Exception where court satisfied as to completion of contract

8.   If, in a case where the offender is referred back to the court under section 27(4) of this Act, the court decides (contrary to the decision of the panel) that the offender's compliance with the terms of the contract has, or will have, been such as to justify the conclusion that he has satisfactorily completed the contract, the court shall make an order declaring that the referral order (or each of the referral orders) is discharged.

Discharge of extension orders

9.   The discharge under paragraph 7(3) or 8 above of a referral order has the effect of discharging any related order under paragraph 11 or 12 below.

PART II
FURTHER CONVICTIONS DURING REFERRAL

Extension of referral for further offences

10.—(1)   Paragraphs 11 and 12 below apply where, at a time when an offender aged under 18 is subject to referral, a youth court or other magistrates' court ('the relevant court') is dealing with him for an offence in relation to which paragraphs (a) to (c) of section 16(1) of this Act are applicable.

(2) But paragraphs 11 and 12 do not apply unless the offender's compliance period is less than twelve months.

Extension where further offences committed pre-referral

11. If—

(a) the occasion on which the offender was referred to the panel is the only other occasion on which it has fallen to a court in the United Kingdom to deal with the offender for any offence or offences, and

(b) the offender committed the offence mentioned in paragraph 10 above, and any connected offence, before he was referred to the panel,

the relevant court may sentence the offender for the offence by making an order extending his compliance period.

Extension where further offence committed after referral

12.—(1) If—

(a) paragraph 11(a) above applies, but

(b) the offender committed the offence mentioned in paragraph 10 above, or any connected offence, after he was referred to the panel,

the relevant court may sentence the offender for the offence by making an order extending his compliance period, but only if the requirements of sub-paragraph (2) below are complied with.

(2) Those requirements are that the court must—

(a) be satisfied, on the basis of a report made to it by the relevant body, that there are exceptional circumstances which indicate that, even though the offender has re-offended since being referred to the panel, extending his compliance period is likely to help prevent further re-offending by him; and

(b) state in open court that it is so satisfied and why it is.

(3) In sub-paragraph (2) above 'the relevant body' means the panel to which the offender has been referred or, if no contract has yet taken effect between the offender and the panel under section 23 of this Act, the specified team.

Provisions supplementary to paragraphs 11 and 12

13.—(1) An order under paragraph 11 or 12 above, or two or more orders under one or other of those paragraphs made in respect of connected offences, must not so extend the offender's compliance period as to cause it to exceed twelve months.

(2) Sub-paragraphs (3) to (5) below apply where the relevant court makes an order under paragraph 11 or 12 above in respect of the offence mentioned in paragraph 10 above; but sub-paragraphs (3) to (5) do not affect the exercise of any power to deal with the offender conferred by paragraph 5 or 14 of this Schedule.

(3) The relevant court may not deal with the offender for that offence in any of the prohibited ways specified in section 19(4) of this Act.

(4) The relevant court—

(a)   shall, in respect of any connected offence, either—
    (i)   sentence the offender by making an order under the same paragraph; or
    (ii)   make an order discharging him absolutely; and
(b)   may not deal with the offender for any connected offence in any of those prohibited ways.

(5)   The relevant court may not, in connection with the conviction of the offender for the offence or any connected offence, make any such order as is mentioned in section 19(5) of this Act.

(6)   For the purposes of paragraphs 11 and 12 above any occasion on which the offender was discharged absolutely in respect of the offence, or each of the offences, for which he was being dealt with shall be disregarded.

(7)   Any occasion on which, in criminal proceedings in England and Wales or Northern Ireland, the offender was bound over to keep the peace or to be of good behaviour shall be regarded for those purposes as an occasion on which it fell to a court in the United Kingdom to deal with the offender for an offence.

(8)   The Secretary of State may by regulations make such amendments of paragraphs 10 to 12 above and this paragraph as he considers appropriate for altering in any way the descriptions of offenders in the case of which an order extending the compliance period may be made; and subsection (4) of section 17 of this Act shall apply in relation to regulations under this sub-paragraph as it applies in relation to regulations under subsection (3) of that section.

Further convictions which lead to revocation of referral

14.—(1)   This paragraph applies where, at a time when an offender is subject to referral, a court in England and Wales deals with him for an offence (whether committed before or after he was referred to the panel) by making an order other than—
(a)   an order under paragraph 11 or 12 above; or
(b)   an order discharging him absolutely.

(2)   In such a case the order of the court shall have the effect of revoking—
(a)   the referral order (or orders); and
(b)   any related order or orders under paragraph 11 or 12 above.

(3)   Where any order is revoked by virtue of sub-paragraph (2) above, the court may, if it appears to the court that it would be in the interests of justice to do so, deal with the offender for the offence in respect of which the revoked order was made in any way in which (assuming section 16 of this Act had not applied) he could have been dealt with for that offence by the court which made the order.

(4)   When dealing with the offender under sub-paragraph (3) above the court shall, where a contract has taken effect between the offender and the panel under section 23 of this Act, have regard to the extent of his compliance with the terms of the contract.

Interpretation

15.—(1)   For the purposes of this Part of this Schedule an offender is for the time being subject to referral if—

(a) a referral order has been made in respect of him and that order has not, or

(b) two or more referral orders have been made in respect of him and any of those orders has not,

been discharged (whether by virtue of section 27(3) of this Act or under paragraph 7(3) or 8 above) or revoked (whether under paragraph 5(2) above or by virtue of paragraph 14(2) above).

(2) In this Part of this Schedule 'compliance period', in relation to an offender who is for the time being subject to referral, means the period for which (in accordance with section 24 of this Act) any youth offender contract taking effect in his case under section 23 of this Act has (or would have) effect.

Index